Rajasthan Judicial Services Examination

Previous Years Solved MCQs

RJS (Civil Judge) Exam
Previous Year Prelims Question Papers with Answer Key

WITH EXPLANATIONS

2011-2024

Fourth Edition

2026

Compiled by
Abhishek Choudhary
Advocate, Supreme Court of India
Gold Medalist, B.Sc. LL.B (Hons.), L.L.M.

A work of

LEGIS ORBIS

(A Micro Enterprise registered with Ministry of MSME, Government of India)

In case of any query, please write to us at
support@legisorbis.com

2026

This book is a publication of Legis Orbis

First Edition   2022
Second Edition   2024
Third Edition   2025
Fourt Edition (Reprint) 2026

© **Legis Orbis**

Legis Orbis
(A Micro Enterprise registered with Ministry of MSME, Government of India)
Website: www.legisorbis.in | E-mail: contact@legisorbis.in

MRP ₹ 399/-

ISBN: 9798885918367

Disclaimer

Printed by: Notion Press Media Private Limited
For: **Legis Orbis**

Table of Contents

Other available books by Legis Orbis

Multiple Choice Questions on **Bharatiya Sakshya Adhiniyam, 2023** by Abhishek Choudhary

Multiple Choice Questions on **Company Law** by Ritika Ritu & Abhishek Choudhary

Multiple Choice Questions on **Jurisprudence** by Abhishek Choudhary & Rajashree Kanungo

Multiple Choice Questions on **Law of Criminal Procedure** by Navonita Mallick

Multiple Choice Questions on **Law of Civil Procedure** by Rajashree Kanungo

Multiple Choice Questions on **Limitation & Specific Relief** by Abhishek Choudhary

Multiple Choice Questions on **Law of Crimes** by Navonita Mallick & Ritika Ritu

Multiple Choice Questions on **Law of Evidence** by Aditya Kumar

Multiple Choice Questions on **Law of Contract** by Ritika Ritu

Multiple Choice Questions on **Laws of Transfer of Property** by Dinesh Kumar Patra & Rajashree Kanungo

Previous Year Solved Papers of the **All-India Bar Examination** by Abhishek Choudhary

Multiple Choice Questions on the **Muslim Law** by Abhishek Choudhary

Multiple Choice Questions on the **Constitutional Law** by Ankita Prakash & Abhishek Choudhary

Multiple Choice Questions on the **Law of Torts** by Aditya Kumar

PREFACE

The Rajasthan Judicial Services (RJS) Examination is a prestigious and highly competitive examination conducted for the recruitment of Civil Judges in the State of Rajasthan. As aspirants prepare to face this rigorous examination, access to reliable and well-structured study material becomes essential for success. Clearing the RJS (Civil Judge) Prelims requires not only a strong foundation in law but also a focused and strategic approach to practice and revision.

This book, Rajasthan Judicial Services Examination: RJS (Civil Judge) Exam Previous Year Prelims Question Papers with Answer Key, is designed to serve as a comprehensive resource for candidates preparing for the Rajasthan Civil Judge Examination. Meticulously compiled from previous years' question papers spanning 2011 to 2024, this book enables aspirants to gain a clear understanding of the examination pattern, question trends, and frequently tested areas.

A key strength of this edition lies in the inclusion of the latest RJS Prelims Question Paper for the year 2024, complete with detailed answers and explanations. Each question is supported by clear, concise, and accurate explanations, helping candidates understand the underlying legal principles and reasoning behind the correct answers. This approach not only enhances conceptual clarity but also strengthens exam-oriented preparation.

By practicing previous years' question papers, candidates can simulate real examination conditions, improve their time-management skills, and build the confidence required to perform effectively in the actual examination. Additionally, this book is carefully updated in line with the latest syllabus and examination trends, ensuring its continued relevance for aspirants.

We hope that this book serves as a reliable companion in your journey toward success in the Rajasthan Judicial Services Examination and assists you in achieving your goal of becoming a Civil Judge in the State of Rajasthan.

Best of luck in your preparation!

Legis Orbis

FROM THE FOUNDER'S DESK

It is with great pride and a deep sense of responsibility that we present this comprehensive guide to your preparation for the Rajasthan Judicial Services (RJS) Examination. As educators and publishers, we fully understand the importance of reliable, accurate, and up-to-date resources when preparing for such a significant milestone in your legal career. At Legis Orbis, our mission has always been to provide aspirants with high-quality study material that not only supports effective preparation but also motivates them to achieve their fullest potential.

The Rajasthan Judicial Services Examination, being one of the most sought-after judicial exams for aspiring legal professionals in the State of Rajasthan, demands rigorous preparation and a thorough understanding of the examination pattern. With this book, we have endeavored to simplify your preparation journey by compiling an extensive collection of previous years' Prelims question papers from 2011 to 2024, including the latest 2024 question paper with detailed answers and explanations. Each question has been carefully analyzed to ensure that candidates not only arrive at the correct answer but also clearly understand the legal principles and reasoning involved.

This book distinguishes itself through its comprehensive coverage, lucid explanations, and emphasis on delivering current and relevant content in line with the evolving syllabus and examination trends. It is our sincere hope that this resource equips you with confidence, clarity, and a competitive edge as you prepare for the RJS (Pre.) Examination.

We firmly believe that with consistent effort, proper guidance, and unwavering dedication, your aspiration to become a Civil Judge can be transformed into reality. We wish you every success in your preparation and trust that this book will serve as a valuable companion throughout your journey.

Happy studying, and may your pursuit of judicial excellence be rewarding and successful!

Abhishek Choudhary
Founder, Legis Orbis

Legis Orbis

ABOUT EDITOR IN CHIEF

Abhishek Choudhary, recipient of the prestigious University Gold Medal for excellence in the five-year integrated B.Sc. LL.B (Hons) program, is a distinguished member of the Bar Council of Delhi.

With over nine years of legal practice, he has established himself as a proficient advocate at the Hon'ble Supreme Court of India, various High Courts, and National and State Commissions. Abhishek's expertise spans a broad range of legal fields, with a particular focus on dispute resolution and alternative dispute resolution mechanisms. As a member of the Supreme Court Bar Association (SCBA), he has consistently demonstrated his ability to lead and manage complex legal projects.

In addition to his professional accomplishments, Abhishek holds an LL.M. in Corporate and Commercial Laws, further enriching his knowledge and capabilities in these specialized areas. His academic and professional journey reflects a commitment to excellence and a dedication to advancing the practice of law.

ACKNOWLEDGEMENT

We would like to extend our sincere gratitude to all those who have contributed to the creation of this book, Rajasthan Judicial Services Examination: RJS (Civil Judge) Exam Previous Year Prelims Question Papers with Answer Key.

First and foremost, we are deeply grateful to the esteemed faculty members, legal experts, and subject matter specialists whose invaluable insights, knowledge, and guidance have shaped the content of this book. Their expertise has been instrumental in ensuring the accuracy, relevance, and clarity of the explanations provided in this compilation.

We also wish to express our heartfelt thanks to the candidates who have shared their experiences, feedback, and suggestions over the years. Your inputs have been a constant source of motivation for us to refine and improve this book to better serve your needs.

A special mention goes to our editorial team, designers, and production staff, who have worked tirelessly to ensure that this book is presented in the most effective, user-friendly manner. Their attention to detail, dedication, and commitment to excellence have played a pivotal role in bringing this resource to life.

We also acknowledge the support of our family and friends for their constant encouragement, understanding, and belief in our vision to provide top-quality study material for aspirants.

Lastly, we extend our gratitude to the Rajasthan High Court and the Rajasthan Public Service Commission (RPSC) for conducting the Rajasthan Judicial Services Examination and for providing an opportunity to aspiring legal professionals to serve the judiciary.

This book is dedicated to every aspirant striving to realize the dream of becoming a Civil Judge. We hope that it serves as a valuable aid in your preparation and contributes meaningfully to your success in the RJS (Civil Judge) Examination.

Thank you for trusting us as your guide on this important journey.

With humility and gratitude,

Legis Orbis Team

Preliminary Examination 2011

1. Ban on smoking in public place is a violation of which one of following articles of the constitution?

[A] Article 14

[B] Article 20

[C] Article 21

[D] Article 25

2. In which one of the following cases it was held that telephone tapping is an invasion of right to privacy?

[A] Peoples' Union for Civil Liberties vs. Union of India

[B] State of Maharashtra vs. Murali Deora

[C] Govind vs. State of Madhya Pradesh

[D] Mr. X vs. Hospital Z

3. Which one out of the following is not a Fundamental Right?

[A] Right to Strike

[B] Right against exploitation

[C] Right to equality

[D] Right to freedom of religion

4. The Jurisdiction of the Supreme Court may be enlarged by the ___.

[A] Parliament by law

[B] Parliament by resolution

[C] President of India

[D] President of India in consultation with the Chief Justice of India

5. When can a state law on a subject in the Concurrent List get precedence over a Central law on the same subject?

[A] In on circumstances

[B] If it was made before the Central law

[C] If it had got the President's assent before the enactment of the Central law

[D] If consent of the President was taken before its introduction as a bill in the State legislature.

6. Who out of the following nominates the Chairman of the Public Accounts Committee of the Parliament?

[A] Prime Minister of India

[B] President of India

[C] Speaker of the Lok Sabha

[D] Chairman of the Rajya Sabha

7. A legislation made by the State legislature is ___.

[A] Subordinate legislation

[B] Supreme legislation

[C] Autonomous legislation

[D] Delegated legislation

8. Under Section 9, Code of Civil Procedure, 1908, a Court during pendency of a suit before it ___.

[A] can entertain and try second suit

[B] cannot entertain and proceed to try second suit

[C] shall not proceed to try though may entertain second suit

[D] neither can entertain nor shall proceed for second suit

9. While executing a decree of other State on reciprocity, a Court ___.

[A] can execute the decree in the same manner as. if it it-self had passed it

[B] can decide all questions relating to execution

[C] can provide any incidental and consequential relief

[D] cannot execute a decree relating to fine, charges, penalty, taxes, or arbitration award of that State

10. A Court to which decree has been transferred for execution cannot, while executing?

[A] order attachment

[B] execute the decree against the legal representatives of the deceased judgment debtor

[C] send the decree for execution to another Court

[D] order execution at the instance of the transferee of the decree

11. The transferee of a decree ___.

[A] may enforce the decree against the legal representatives too

[B] may enforce the decree against the sureties available with the judgment debtor

[C] may enforce the decree against the securities available with the judgment debtor

[D] Shall hold the equities which the

judgment debtor might have enforced against the original decree holder.

12. When a commission has been issued under Section 75, Code of Civil Procedure, 1908, the commission, if not a Judge of civil Court?

[A] can call any witness relating to that matter

[B] can determine the legality of questions asked during the conduct of proceedings by the commission

[C] can extend time and grant exemption from personal appearance

[D] cannot impose penalties or fine and initiate contempt of Court proceedings

13. Under which of the following provisions of the Code of Civil Procedure, 1908 an ex-parte order and ex-parte decree may be set aside?

[A] Order 9, Rule 7 and Order 9, Rule 10

[B] Order 9, Rule 4 and Order 9, Rule 5

[C] Order 9, Rule 7 and Order 9, Rule 13

[D] Order 9, Rule 11 and Order 9, Rule 12

14. Interpleader suit cannot be instituted ___.

[A] for any property which relates to two persons but which is being held by a third person for the time being

[B] for determining the relationship between a property and the persons claiming it

[C] for getting himself absolved from the liability to keep the property which is not being held by him

[D] where a suit is pending in which the rights of all parties can properly be decided

15. Once revision is made before the Court under the Code of Civil Procedure, 1908, it ___.

[A] acts as a stay on the proceedings

[B] acts as a res-judicata on the issues

[C] acts as an injunction for immediate relief

[D] shall not operate as a stay of suit or other proceeding before the Court except where such suit or proceeding is stayed by the Court

16. A caveat under the Code of Civil Procedure, 1908 may be lodged when any ___.

[A] suit is instituted

[B] proceeding is initiated or instituted

[C] suit is about to be instituted

[D] suit or proceeding is instituted or about to be instituted

17. "A" and "B" two members of a three-member partnership firm, bring a suit for recovery of the debt due from "X" to the firm, but their firm is not registered on the date of the institution of the suit. The suit ___.

[A] is maintainable with leave of the Court

[B] is maintainable with the concurrence of "X"

[C] is liable to be rejected in view of Section 69, Partnership Act

[D] will become maintainable after the original defect is cured by subsequent registration

18. Which one of the following contracts is specifically enforceable?

[A] A, an author, contracts with B, a publisher, to complete a literary work

[B] A contracts to sell and "B" contracts to buy a residential building

[C] A contracts to marry "B"

[D] A context by a guardian to purchase immovable property on behalf of a minor

19. Crossword competition is ___.

[A] wagering agreement

[B] contingent contract

[C] illegal agreement

[D] valid agreement

20. An advertisement of auction is ___.

[A] Proposal

[B] mere statement

[C] invitation to offer

[D] standing offer

21. In which one of the following, consideration is not required?

[A] Contract of insurance

[B] Contract of bailment

[C] Contract of guarantee

[D] Contract of service

22. A agrees to pay B a sum of money

if B gets married to [C] C marries [D] In such a situation, which one of the following statements, is correct?

[A] The agreement will be effective when C will divorce D

[B] The performance of the agreement will be deemed impossible

[C] B is bound to get married to C under the agreement

[D] A is bound to pay B the agreed sum of money

23. A asked B: I want to purchase your bike. What will be the cost? B replied that the cost will not be less than Rs.20,000/. A was interested to purchase it for Rs.20,000/-. Which one of the following statements is correct?

[A] There was a proposal which was accepted

[B] There was neither a proposal nor an acceptance

[C] There was proposal but no acceptance

[D] There was a counter offer which was accepted

24. An easement which, not being an easement of absolute necessity, comes into existence by presumed grand or operation of law is called ___.

[A] easement by prescription

[B] easement by local custom

[C] easement by necessity

[D] quasi-easement

25. Neighbour principle was propounded by Lord Atkin in ___.

[A] Donoghue vs. Stevenson

[B] Polemis case

[C] Deny vs. Peek

[D] Rylands vs. Fletcher

26. "The rule of last opportunity" was laid down in ___.

[A] Thomas vs. Quartermaine

[B] Davies vs. Mann

[C] Smith vs. Baker

[D] Fardon vs. Harcourt Rivington

27. Which one of the following is defamatory?

[A] Publishing a false report in a newspaper for which the editor tendered an apology

[B] Publishing a report of parliamentary proceedings showing the misconduct of a member present there

[C] Publishing a report of judicial proceeding showing statement made by a witness

[D] Publishing a false report in newspaper that a minister was involved in a kidnapping case

28. Joint tort-feasors may be held liable ____.

[A] jointly and severally for the whole damage

[B] for damage caused by a person employed by any of them

[C] for damage caused independently of their plan

[D] for damage caused by stranger

29. As a result of a collision between two buses a passenger in one of the buses died. The accident occurred due to negligence of the drivers of both the buses. In a suit by the legal representative of the deceased against owners of both the buses, which one of the following statements is legally sustainable?

[A] Each owner of the buses is liable for the whole damage

[B] The owners of the buses are not joint tort-feasors

[C] Neither of the owners of the buses is liable as the defence of act of God applies

[D] Each owner of the buses was liable for one-half of the damage.

30. Which one of the following did not emerge from the case of Donoghue v. Stevenson?

[A] A manufacturer of products will be liable if he fails to take reasonable care to ensure that his products are reasonably safe.

[B] In order to successfully claim for negligence, the plaintiff does not need to have a contract with the defendant

[C] Manufacturers have to pay damages to consumers whenever damages caused by their products.

[D] The neighbour principle can be used to establish the existence of a duty of care in negligence.

31. Who cannot file an application for compensation under Section 166 of the Motor Vehicles Act, 1988?

[A] The injured person

[B] The owner of property

[C] The legal representative of the deceased

[D] A public interested person

32. If within thirty days the parties fail to appoint their arbitrators, or the arbitrators fail to appoint the third arbitrator, the arbitrator shall be appointed by the ___.

[A] National Arbitration Council, New Delhi

[B] District Judge of the Local Court

[C] State Legal Services Authority of the State concerned

[D] Chief Justice or a person/institution designated by him

33. If within thirty days the parties fail to appoint their arbitrators, or the arbitrators fail to appoint the third arbitrator, the arbitrator shall be appointed by the ___.

[A] National Arbitration Council, New Delhi

[B] 'District Judge of the Local Court

[C] State Legal Services Authority of the State Concerned

[D] Chief Justice or a person / institution designated by him

34. Specific performance of contract is allowed where ___.

[A] the plaintiff is not entitled to recover compensation

[B] the defendant is incompetent to perform the contract

[C] compensation is not the adequate relief

[D] the defendant has died

35. Under pious obligation a son is obliged to pay a debt contracted by his father ___.

[A] before partition

[B] after partition

[C] either before or after partition

[D] for immoral purpose before partition

36. A Hindu woman aged twenty years adopts a Hindu boy aged twenty years. The adoption is ___

[A] Void

[B] voidable at the instance of the boy

[C] immoral and unenforceable

[D] valid, if taken with leave of Court

37. Which one of following statements is not correct?

Hindu Marriage Act, 1955 applies to ___.

[A] Jains

[B] Buddhists

[C] Sikhs

[D] Persons belonging to Scheduled Tribe

38. If a Hindu boy marries a Hindu girl of the same gotra under the Hindu Marriage Act, 1955, the marriage is ___.

[A] Void

[B] Voidable

[C] Valid

[D] unenforceable under law

39. Under Hindu law a mother, in the absence of her son's father, sells her minor son's immovable property. The minor son, on attaining majority, can challenge this transaction ___.

[A] on the ground of not taking permission from the Court

[B] as the transaction was not done by his father

[C] as no such transaction can be done for minor son

[D] but he will be unsuccessful because the transaction is valid

40. Which one of the following is not correct? Under Hindu Law a person can be adopted if he is ___.

[A] Hindu

[B] Unmarried

[C] Above fifteen years of age

[D] Not already adopted

41. Maina Bibi vs. Choudhary Vakil Ahmed is related to ___.

[A] Mahar

[B] Guardianship

[C] Maintenance

[D] Wakf

42. Which one of the following is not a ground for dissolution of a Muslim marriage under the Dissolution of Muslim Marriage Act, 1939?

[A] Whereabouts of the husband is not known for four years

[B] Option of puberty

[C] Non-maintenance of the wife by the husband for two years

[D] Non-payment of Mahar

43. Which one of the following is not an actionable claim?

[A] Claim for arrears of rent

[B] Provident fund payable after retirement

[C] A share in partnership

[D] A secured debt

44. Which one of the following is an exception to the rule against perpetuity?

[A] Permanent transfer for gift

[B] Personal covenants

[C] Pre-emption

[D] All the above

45. Under the Transfer of Property Act, 1882 a charge may be created by ___.

[A] acts of the parties

[B] process of law

[C] presumption

[D] acts of parties and process of law

46. A borrowed a sum of money from B. The last date for filing the suit falls on a Sunday. On Monday, the next day, A gives a written acknowledgment to B. In this case ___.

[A] A should file the suit on Monday

[B] Section 18, Limitation Act, 1963 gives a fresh period of limitation

[C] The suit is barred by limitation under all circumstances

[D] The suit can be filed any time subject to the provisions of Section 12, Limitation Act, 1963

47. A permanent Lok Adalat shall take cognizance of any ___.

[A] matter relating to an offence not compoundable under any law

[B] matter relating to an offence compoundable under any law

[C] public utility service-related matter where the value of the property in dispute exceeds 10 lakh rupees

[D] matter referred to it by the District Judge

48. An application for residential order shall be made by a victim of domestic violence before a ___.

[A] Civil Judge (Senior Division)

[B] Magistrate of the First Class

[C] Family Court

[D] Mediation Centre established by the High Court

49. Code of Civil Procedure, 1908 is a ___.

[A] Substantive law

[B] Procedural law

[C] Combination of substantive law and procedural law

[D] Directory law

50. Which one of the following is not correct?

[A] High Courts should not pass interim orders which are likely to hamper investigation

[B] A Magistrate can under Section 156 (3), Code of Criminal Procedure, 1973 send a complaint of non-cognizable offence to the police

[C] The power of the Magistrate of the first class to take cognizance of cognizable offence may be impaired by territorial restrictions

[D] During the course of investigation by the police, the question of cross examination does not arise

51. An accused can make an application for plea bargaining if and when he is alleged to have committed the offence ___.

[A] Of Murder

[B] Affecting socio economic condition of the country

[C] Theft

[D] Affecting women or children below the age of 14 years

52. When at the stage of framing of charge the Sessions Court feels that the case is not exclusively triable by it, it may ___.

[A] Send the case to the Chief Judicial Magistrate for framing of the charge

[B] Frame the charge and transfer the case to the Chief Judicial Magistrate/Magistrate of the First Class.

[C] Frame the charge and transfer the case to a Magistrate of the Second

Class

[D] Send the case to Lok Adalat

53. The term 'bail' signifies the conditional release of an accused or arrested person by the ___.

[A] Police during investigation, but not by the Magistrate during enquiry.

[B] Magistrate during inquiry, but not by the Court during trial

[C] Court during trial, but not during revision

[D] Police, Magistrate or Court during investigation, enquiry or trial.

54. A memorandum of arrest of an arrested person is required to be signed and attested by one member of ___.

[A] his family and one of his relatives

[B] The locality and one of his relatives

[C] other locality and one member of his family

[D] his family and one member of the locality, and countersigned by the arrested person.

55. An Executive Magistrate may act even ex-parte under Section 144, Code of Criminal Procedure, 1973, if immediate prevention or speedy remedy is desirable ___.

[A] to prevent obstruction, annoyance or injury to any lawfully employed person

[B] to avoid danger to human life, health or safety

[C] To avoid disturbance to public peace and tranquility, riot or affray.

[D] on any one or all of the above grounds.

56. While exercising its inherent powers under Section 482, Code of Criminal Procedure, 1973 even the High Court cannot ___.

[A] Review its own Judgment.

[B] Do all these mentioned things.

[C] Convert itself Court of appeal when the legislature has not conferred a right to appeal to it.

[D] Grant police custody from Judicial Custody.

57. Habitual offender is one who ___.

[A] habitually commits offence

[B] habitually remains in company of

habitual offenders

[C] deals with and gives asylum to habitual offenders

[D] commits offences mentioned in Section 110 and against whom record of commission of more than two offences is available at the time of initiation of proceeding against him.

58. Who out of the following may investigate a cognizable case even without the order of the Magistrate?

[A] Superintendent of Police

[B] Deputy Inspector General of Police

[C] Deputy Superintendent of Police

[D] In charge Police Station

59. 'A' is tried for a riot and is proved to have marched as the head of a mo[B] The cries of the mob are relevant as ___.

[A] They are related to things said or done by the conspirators in reference to the common design.

[B] Explanation of the nature of the transaction

[C] Explanatory of motive or preparation

[D] Explanatory of occasion, cause or effects of facts

60. The expression 'Police custody' means and includes ___.

[A] Control by the police over the accused directly

[B] Control by the police directly as well as through third persons indirectly over the accused

[C] Control over the accused indirectly through third persons

[D] Some kind of surveillance and restrictions over the accused by Police or through third persons.

61. The evidentiary value of a retracted confession is that it ___.

[A] Still remains evidence

[B] Remains evidence but weak evidence

[C] Becomes corroborative evidence

[D] Becomes 'other evidence' from 'only evidence'

62. A prosecutes B for adultery with C who is A's wife B denies that C is A's wife, But the Court convicts B for adultery, Thereafter, C is prosecuted for

bigamy for marrying B during A's lifetime C says that she was never A's wife. The judgment against B is ___.

[A] Irrelevant against C

[B] Relevant against B

[C] Not relevant against B and C

[D] Relevant against C

63. Newspaper report about any matter is which one of the following kinds of evidence?

[A] Hearsay

[B] Circumstantial

[C] Primary

[D] Secondary

64. Hostile witness is one who ___.

[A] Does not tell the truth

[B] Gives statements against the opposite party

[C] Gives statement against the party who called him as a witness

[D] Is not desirous to tell the truth, and gives testimony against the party who called him as a witness in his favor.

65. A prostitute, suffering from communicable disease, has sexual intercourse with a man representing that she was free from any disease commits ___.

[A] Unnatural offence

[B] Hurt

[C] Cheating

[D] Mischief

66. A hangman who hangs a prisoner pursuant to an order of a Court is exempt from criminal liability under the Indian Penal Code under ___.

[A] Section 76

[B] Section 77

[C] Section 78

[D] Section 79

67. A knows that B is suffering from a heart disease and, also, that if a blow is given to B on his chest, it is likely to cause his death. Knowing this A gives blow on B's chest causing B's death. A is guilty of ___.

[A] Murder

[B] Culpable homicide not amounting to murder

[C] Grievous hurt

[D] Causing death by rash of negligent act

68. Which one of the following statements is correct?

[A] Every, culpable homicide is murder

[B] Death caused by negligent act is murder

[C] Every murder is culpable homicide

[D] Death caused in course of quarrel is murder.

69. Which one of the following statements is correct?

[A] The principal offender must have the same guilty mind as that of the abettor.

[B] Abettor's liability is dependent on the liability of the principal offender.

[C] Abettor and principal offender may be differently liable for different offences.

[D] If the abettor is innocent, the principal offender is also not liable.

70. Which one of the following correctly distinguishes theft from extortion?

[A] In theft movable property must be dishonestly taken whereas in extortion there is delivery of the thing extorted.

[B] In extortion there must be dishonest intention whereas in theft the same is not necessary.

[C] Theft requires dishonest intention whereas extortion requires fraudulent intention.

[D] Theft in an offence against movable property whereas extortion is an offence against immovable property.

71. A intentionally causes Z's death partly by illegally omitting to give Z food and partly by beating Z, A is liable for murder by virtue of which one of the following Section s of the Indian Penal Code?

[A] Section 36

[B] Section 37

[C] Section 34

[D] Section 35

72. A signs his own name to a bill of exchange, intending that it may be believed that the bill was drawn by another person of the same name. A has committed ___.

[A] Forgery

[B] Forgery for the purpose of cheating

[C] Cheating by personation

[D] Attempt to commit forgery

73. A Spanish citizen, who was residing in Paris, instigated the commission of an offence which in consequence was committed in India. He ___.

[A] is liable as the offence was committed in India

[B] is liable since the Indian Penal Code also extends to extra-territorial acts

[C] Can be held liable because the offence was to be committed in India,

[D] Cannot be held liable because instigation was not given on Indian Territory.

74. Offence under Chapter IV of the Narcotic Drugs and Psychotropic Substances Act, 1985 are cognizable ___.

[A] but bailable

[B] as well as non-cognizable

[C] and compoundable

[D] and non bailable

75. The establishment of a Sessions Court as a Special Court to try offences under the Scheduled Caste and Scheduled Tribe (Prevention of Atrocities) Act, 1989 requires concurrence of ___.

[A] State Government

[B] Chief Justice of the concerned High Court

[C] District Judge of the concerned area

[D] Advocate General of the State

76. Any Person aggrieved by the order made by the competent authority under the Juvenile Justice (Care and Protection of Children) Act, 2000 can appeal to ___.

[A] The Sessions Court

[B] The High Court

[C] Home Minister

[D] Chief Judicial Magistrate

77. Which one of the following is not a condition precedent to the release of an offender on probation under Section 4, Probation of Offenders Act, 1958?

[A] Circumstances of the case

[B] Nature of the offence

[C] Character of the offender

[D] Amount of damage caused by the offender

78. Which one of the following is not theft of electricity?

[A] Using electricity through a tampered meter

[B] Tapping of any connection with underground cables

[C] Using electricity for the purpose other than the authorised

[D] Using electricity as per the licence

79. Which one of the following is correct?

The Information Technology Act, 2000 applies also to an offence committed outside of India when the ___.

[A] accused is an Indian national only

[B] accused is of any nationality

[C] act or conduct constituting the offence involves, a computer, computer system or computer network irrespective of its location

[D] act or conduct constituting the offence involves a computer, computer system or computer network is located in India.

80. In a criminal case, documents are exhibited as which one of the following?

[A] Ex-1 by one party and Ex-A-1 by the other

[B] Ex-P-1 by one party and Ex-D-1 by the other

[C] Ex-X-1 by one party and Ex-Y-1 by the other

[D] Ex-M-1 by one party and Ex-N-1 by the other

81. Select the right option based on following Assertion-Reason:

Assertion (A): The principle of equality before law means that there should be equality of treatment under equal circumstances.

Reason (R): All persons are not equal by nature, attainment or circumstances.

[A] Both (A) and (R) are individually true and (R) is a correct explanation of (A)

[B] Both (A) and (R) are individually true but (R) is nor the correct explanation of (A)

[C] (A) is true but (R) is false

[D] (A) is false but (R) is true

82. Select the right option based on following Assertion-Reason:

Assertion (A): Non-inclusion of Rajasthan Language in the Eighth schedule of the Constitution does not violate Article 14.

Reason (R): Such policy matters have to be left to the State.

[A] Both (A) and (R) are individually true and (R) is a correct explanation of (A)

[B] Both (A) and (R) are individually true but (R) is a correct explanation of (A)

[C] (A) is true but (R) is false

[D] (A) is false but (R) is true

83. Select the right option based on following Assertion-Reason:

Assertion (A): The evidence of an accomplice requires to be accepted with a great degree of caution and scrutiny.

Reason (R): He hopes for pardon or has secured it and so favors the prosecution.

[A] Both (A) and (R) are individually true and (R) is a correct explanation of (A)

[B] Both (A) and (R) are individually true but (R) is a correct explanation of (A)

[C] (A) is true but (R) is false

[D] (A) is false but (R) is true

84. Select the right option based on following Assertion-Reason:

Assertion (A): The offence of dishonour of cheque excludes mens rea.

Reason (R): It creates strict liability.

[A] Both (A) and (R) are individually true and (R) is a correct explanation of (A)

[B] Both (A) and (R) are individually true but (R) is not the correct explanation of (A)

[C] (A) is true but (R) is false

[D] (A) is false but (R) is true

85. 'आच्छादन' शब्द में उपसर्ग है –

[A] आः

[B] आ

[C] आच्छ

[D] अ

86. 'ग्रामागत' शब्द का समास विच्छेद होगा –

[A] ग्राम को गया हुआ

[B] ग्राम को आया हुआ

[C] ग्राम से गया हुआ

[D] ग्राम में आया हुआ

87. 'रसोत्पत्ति' शब्द संधि से बना है जिसका निर्माण इन वर्णों के मिलने से हुआ है :

[A] उ+उ

[B] आ+उ

[C] ओ+उ

[D] अ+उ

88. इनमें से एक शब्द "रात" का पर्यायवाची नहीं है –

[A] निशा

[B] यामिनी

[C] उर्मि

[D] विभावरी

89. 'अपकर्ष' का विलोम शब्द है -

[A] उत्कर्ष

[B] विकर्ष

[C] निष्कर्ष

[D] दुर्धर्ष

90. इनमें विदेशज शब्द है -

[A] शिक्षा

[B] रज्जु

[C] सांस

[D] जलेबी

91. इनमें एक शब्द "सरस्वती" का पर्यायवाची शब्द है -

[A] गिरा

[B] इला

[C] सविता

[D] श्री

92. इनमें से कौन-सा वाक्य 'पूर्ण भूतकाल' का धोतक है -

[A] मैं अपना काम कर रहा था ।

[B] मैं तो कब का अपना काम कर चुका था ।

[C] मैंने अपना काम किया ।

[D] मैं आपके आने पर अपने काम् में लग गया

93. "भारी मुसीबत में भी कुछ अनिष्ट न होने" के लिए उपयुक्तः मुहावरा है -

[A] तीन तेरह होना

[B] बाल बाँका न होना

[C] दाँत खट्टे करना

[D] आसन डोलना

94. "तबेल की बला बंदर के सिर" लोकोक्ति का अर्थ -

[A] दोषि कोई, फँसे कोई

[B] दोषि को पहचान ना

[C] दोष स्वीकार

[D] दोषि को खोजक

95. साक्ष्य या गवाही के लिए अंग्रेजी का उपयुक्त शब्द है -

[A] Estimate

[B] Present

[C] Evidence

[D] Exempt

96. अंग्रेजी के 'SINE DINE' पद के लिए हिन्दी में उपयुक्त पद है -

[A] बंद करना

[B] स्थगित

[C] तिरस्त करना

[D] अनिश्चित काल के लिए

97. अंग्रेजी के Autonomus शब्द के लिए हिन्दी का सही पद है -

[A] स्वगत

[B] स्वायत

[C] स्वचालित

[D] स्ववित्तपाणी

98. "कानूनी प्रक्रिया" के लिए अंग्रेजी का उपयुक्त पद है -

[A] Legal process

[B] Legal notice

[C] Legal work

[D] Legal right

99. "कृपया आवश्यक कार्यवाही करें" टिप्पण के लिए अंग्रेजी में लिखा जाता है -

[A] Necessary action is needed

[B] Please take action

[C] Please take necessary action

[D] Do the needful

100. 'Against Public Interest' के लिए उपयुक्त हिन्दी पद होगा -

[A] जनता के लिए

[B] लोकहित में

[C] जनता के साथ

[D] लोक हित के प्रतिकूल

101. इनमें एक वाक्य शुद्ध है –

[A] सच सुनते ही उसका चेहरा उतर गया ।

[B] जबरदस्ती आप जो चाहें करें ।

[C] सोरठा हिन्दी का एक छंद है ।

[D] मैंने एक साल तक आपकी प्रतीक्षा देखी ।

102. विमति (असहमति) टिप्पणी के लिए अंग्रेजी में उपयुक्त पद है -

[A] No objection note

[B] Objection note

[C] Negative note

[D] Note of dissent

103. They ran past me and jumped into a car.

[A] Past Perfect

[B] Past Continuous

[C] Past Simple

[D] Present Simple

104. I was standing outside the post office.

[A] Present Continuous

[B] Past Continuous

[C] Past Simple

[D] Past Perfect

105. Note: Select the sentence with coordinating conjunction.

[A] He held my hand lest I should fall

[B] He is slow but he is honest.

[C] Rama will go if Hari goes

[D] A book is a book although there is nothing in it.

106. Note: Select the sentence with subordinating conjunction.

[A] Horses neigh and cats mew

[B] I was annoyed still 1 kept quiet

[C] He is slow but he is honest

[D] He ran away because he was afraid.

107. Note: Mark the passive voice which is correct:

The Principal read the report-

[A] The Principal is reading the report

[B] The report was read by the Principal

[C] The report was had been read by the Principal

[D] The Principal will not read the report.

108. Could we have ___ coffee, please?

[A] Some

[B] Few

[C] No

[D] a few

109. ___ the money goes into a special bank account.

[A] Every

[B] All

[C] Each

[D] Some

110. The agent has asked ___ of his customers to give money.

[A] Every

[B] a little

[C] a few

[D] each

111. ___ I get you a glass of water?

[A] Dare

[B] Need

[C] Can

[D] Would

112. ___ you like to stay the night?

[A] Dare

[B] Would

[C] Need

[D] Can

113. She ___ be able to drive to school.

[A] Dare

[B] Need

[C] Can

[D] will

114. ___ you pass me the salt?

[A] Could

[B] Need

[C] Dare

[D] Ought

115. I' m trying to phone her, but I can't ___.

[A] get up

[B] get through

[C] get on

[D] get away

116. The weather is ___.

[A] carrying on

[B] closing down

[C] clearing up

[D] come round

117. ___ and see me any time.

[A] drop up

[B] drop doing

[C] do up

[D] drop in

Identify the correct indirect speech

118. "I may not be at home."

[A] He said he might not be at home.

[B] He said I may not be at home

[C] He said he could not be at home.

[D] He said he should not be at home.

119. "You can pay me cash or give me a cheque".

[A] He told her she could pay in cash or cheque.

[B] He told her she could pay him cash or give him a cheque.

[C] He told her she would pay him cash or give him a cheque

[D] He told her she should not pay him cash or give him a cheque

120. "I do not think I will buy another car."

[A] She says she cannot buy another car.

[B] She says she will not buy another car.

[C] She says she would not think of going to buy a car.

[D] She says she does not think she will buy another car.

Answers

1	C	46	B	91	A
2	A	47	B	92	B
3	A	48	B	93	B
4	A	49	B	94	A
5	C	50	B	95	C
6	C	51	C	96	D
7	B	52	B	97	B
8	C	53	D	98	A
9	A	54	D	99	C
10	D	55	D	100	D
11	D	56	B	101	C
12	D	57	A	102	D
13	C	58	D	103	C
14	D	59	B	104	B
15	D	60	D	105	B
16	D	61	B	106	D
17	C	62	A	107	B
18	B	63	A	108	A

19	D	64	D	109	B
20	C	65	C	110	D
21	B	66	C	111	C
22	B	67	A	112	B
23	B	68	C	113	D
24	D	69	C	114	A
25	A	70	A	115	B
26	B	71	A	116	C
27	D	72	A	117	D
28	A	73	D	118	A
29	B	74	D	119	B
30	*	75	B	120	D
31	D	76	A		
32	D	77	D		
33	D	78	D		
34	C	79	D		
35	C	80	B		
36	A	81	B		
37	D	82	C		
38	C	83	A		
39	A	84	A		
40	C	85	A		
41	A	86	B		
42	D	87	D		
43	D	88	C		
44	D	89	A		
45	D	90	D		

---X---

Preliminary Examinations 2013-14

1. The Supreme Court has held that right to fly the National Flag with respect and dignity is a fundamental right of every citizen within the meaning of Article 19(1)(a) of the Constitution of India in the case of ___.

[A] Keshvananda Bharti vs. State of Kerala

[B] Abhay Singh vs. State of Uttar Pradesh

[C] Union of India vs. Naveen Jindal

[D] Shabnam Hashmi vs. Union of India.

2. Which of the following is a constitutional right but not a fundamental right?

[A] Protection of life and personal liberty

[B] Right to move freely throughout the territory of India.

[C] Right to assemble peaceably.

[D] Right to hold property.

3. Which of the statement is correct?

Statement No. 1- Directive Principles of State Policy are not enforceable by any Court.

Statement No. 2- Directive Principles of State Policy are fundamental in the governance of the country.

[A] Both the statements are true

[B] Both the statements are false

[C] Statement No. 1 is true but statement No. 2 is false

[D] Statement No. 2 is true but statement No. 1 is false

4. The Supreme Court of India has laid down the law relating to Alternative Dispute Resolution processes and Section 89 of the Code of Civil Procedure in the case of ___.

[A] Dinesh Kumar vs. Yusuf Ali

[B] Afcon Infrastructure Ltd. vs. Cherian Varkey Construction Co.

[C] Bimlesh vs. New India Assurance Co.

[D] Standard Chartered Bank vs. Noble Kumar

5. Under Order XXXII Rule 9 of the Code of Civil Procedure, a next friend of a minor can be removed ___.

[A] if he ceases to reside in India during the pendency of the suit

[B] where his interest becomes adverse to that of the minor

[C] where he does not do his duty

[D] for any of the above reasons

6. In the Code of Civil Procedure, an *ex parte* decree can be set aside ___.

[A] Under Order IX Rule 5

[B] Under Order IX Rule 10

[C] Under Order IX Rule 13

[D] Under Order IX Rule 11

7. The communication of an acceptance is complete as against the acceptor ___.

[A] as soon as acceptance is made by the acceptor

[B] when it is put in the course of transmission to the proposer

[C] when it comes to the knowledge of the proposer

[D] none of the above

8. An agreement in restraint of the marriage of any person other than a minor is ___.

[A] Void

[B] Voidable

[C] a contingent agreement

[D] none of the above

9. 'Bailee' is a person ___.

[A] to whom the goods are delivered

[B] who delivers the goods

[C] who fails to deliver the goods

[D] none of the above.

10. The rule of 'strict liability' propounded in the case of Rylands vs. Fletcher is not applicable ___.

[A] When the damage is due to vis major

[B] When the damage is due to wrongful act of stranger

[C] When the damage due to the plaintiff's own fault

[D] All of the above

11. The Rule of 'res ipsa loquitur' is related to the tort of ___.

[A] Negligence

[B] False Imprisonment

[C] Defamation

[D] Malicious Prosecution

12. The land, for the beneficial enjoyment of which easement exists, is called ___.

[A] Servant heritage

[B] Dominant heritage

[C] Extinct heritage

[D] None of the above

13. Under Section 173 of the Motor Vehicles Act, a person aggrieved by an award of the Tribunal can prefer an appeal to ___.

[A] The Supreme Court

[B] The High Court

[C] The District Court

[D] None of the above

14. Unless otherwise agreed by the parties, the arbitral proceedings, in respect of a particular dispute commence on the date ___.

[A] when the arbitrator is appointed by the parties

[B] on which a request for that dispute to be referred to arbitration is received by the respondent

[C] when the matter is referred to arbitrator for settlement

[D] when the arbitrator takes notice of the dispute for further proceedings.

15. In the arbitral proceedings, where a party fails to appear at an oral hearing or fails to produce documentary evidence ___.

[A] The Tribunal has no power to continue the proceedings and to give its award

[B] The Tribunal shall terminate the arbitral proceedings

[C] The Tribunal has power to continue the proceedings and to give its award

[D] None of the above.

16. Under the Rajasthan Rent Control Act, 2001, which of the following landlord is entitled to recover immediate possession of a residential premises ___.

[A] A retired member of any Armed Forces of the Union

[B] A retired employee of the Central Government

[C] A retired employee of the State-Owned Corporation

[D] All the above

17. Under which provision of the Rajasthan Land Revenue Act, 1956, any dispute concerning any boundaries can be decided by the Land Records Officer?

[A] Section 109

[B] Section 110

[C] Section 111

[D] Section 112

18. In the Rajasthan Tenancy Act, 1955, such provisions of the Code of Civil Procedure, 1908 which do not apply to the suit or proceedings under that Act are contained in ___.

[A] First Schedule

[B] Second Schedule

[C] Third Schedule

[D] Fourth Schedule

19. Where the plaintiff, in a suit for specific performance, proves the existence of the agreement and its non-performance by the defendant, the

Court ___.

[A] is bound to issue a decree for specific performance

[B] can refuse to issue a decree for specific performance on the ground of inadequacy of consideration

[C] is not bound to issue a decree for specific performance, since the relief is discretionary

[D] None of the above

20. If a person is dispossessed without his consent of immovable property otherwise than in due course of law, he may file a suit to recover possession under Section 6 of the Specific Relief Act within ___.

[A] three months from the date of dispossession

[B] six months from the date of dispossession

[C] twelve months from the date of dispossession

[D] three years from the date of dispossession

21. The principles in the case of Jijabai Vithalrao Gajre vs. Pathan Khan (AIR 1971 SC 315) are related with ___.

[A] Dissolution of Marriage

[B] Succession

[C] Adoption

[D] Minority and Guardianship

22. The prescribed period of limitation for preferring an appeal under Section 28 of the Hindu Marriage Act is ___.

[A] thirty days

[B] sixty days

[C] ninety days

[D] one hundred and twenty days

23. Under the Muslim Law, 'Khula' and 'Mubara at' are ___.

[A] the forms of marriage

[B] the forms of dissolution of marriage by agreement

[C] the forms of repudiation of gift on attaining majority

[D] the forms of demanding pre-emption

24. If the donee dies before acceptance of gift, then ___.

[A] the gift is voidable

[B] the gift is void

[C] the gift is valid

[D] the gift is converted into will

25. A lessee accepts from the lessor a new lease of the property leased, to take effect during the continuance of the existing lease. This ___.

[A] converts the former lease into exchange

[B] converts the former lease into a perpetual lease

[C] is an implied surrender of the former lease

[D] is a voidable agreement

26. Where the prescribed period of limitation for any application is expiring on a holiday, the application ___.

[A] should be made a day prior to holiday

[B] may be made on the day when the Court re-opens

[C] may be made within thirty days of reopening of the Court

[D] may be made on any day after the Court re-opens.

27. Under the Limitation Act, the period of limitation for filing a suit for compensation for false imprisonment begins to run from the time ___.

[A] when imprisonment ends

[B] when imprisonment begins

[C] when prosecution terminates

[D] none of the above

28. Under the Limitation Act, the period of limitation for filing an application for an order to set aside an abatement is ___.

[A] 60 days

[B] 90 days

[C] 120 days

[D] none of the above

29. Where in a case referred under Section 20(1) of the Legal Services Authorities Act, 1987, no award could be made by the Lok Adalat on the ground that no compromise could be arrived at between the parties, the Lok Adalat shall ___.

[A] return the record of the case to the Court which made the reference

[B] shall dispose of the case on merits

[C] shall send the record to the District Legal Services Authority

[D] shall adjourn the proceedings in the case sine die

30. Under the Protection of Women from Domestic Violence Act, 2005, besides passing orders for protection and residence, a Magistrate can pass ___.

[A] Custody orders

[B] Compensation orders

[C] Ex parte orders

[D] All the above

31. Under the Rajasthan Guaranteed Delivery of Public Services Act, 2011, the State Government may notify the service provided by ___.

[A] The State Government

[B] An institution established by any law made by the State Legislature

[C] Departments of the State Government

[D] All the above

32. Under the Rajasthan Right to Hearing Act, 2012, the power to make rules to carry out the purposes of the enactment has been conferred on ___.

[A] The State Government

[B] The Chief Information Commissioner

[C] The Board of Revenue

[D] None of the above

33. Under the Rajasthan Panchayati Raj Act, 1994, the functions and powers of Zila Parishad are specified in ___.

[A] First Schedule

[B] Second Schedule

[C] Third Schedule

[D] Fourth Schedule

34. If any dispute arises between a Panchayati Raj Institution and other Local Authority, the same shall be referred to ___.

[A] The Civil Court

[B] The Public Service Commission

[C] The State Government

[D] The Divisional Commissioner

35. Under the Rajasthan Municipalities Act, 2009 a person, against whom an order has been passed under Section 117 of the Code of Criminal Procedure in the proceedings instituted under Section 110 of the said Code; and such order has not been subsequently reversed, is disqualified for being chosen as member of a Municipality ___.

[A] Forever

[B] for a period of six years

[C] for a period specified by the State Government

[D] until expiry of the period for which he is ordered to furnish security

36. Which kind of agreement can be presumed by the Court under Section 85-A of the Indian Evidence Act?

[A] Written Agreement

[B] Oral Agreement

[C] Electronic Agreement

[D] None of the above

37. Which one document from the following is not a "Public Document"?

[A] Judgment of a Court

[B] Police Charge Sheet

[C] Postmortem report

[D] Will

38. A witness unable to speak, if gives his statement in writing before the Court, then such evidence shall be deemed to be ___.

[A] Oral evidence

[B] Documentary evidence

[C] Hearsay evidence

[D] Primary evidence

39. In a criminal case, the primary burden to prove a fact is upon ___.

[A] Accused

[B] Prosecution

[C] Police

[D] Court

40. A sues B for negligence in providing him with a carriage for hire not reasonably fit for use, whereby A was injured. The fact that B was habitually negligent about the carriages which he let to hire is ___.

[A] Relevant

[B] Irrelevant

[C] Neither relevant nor irrelevant

[D] Relevant as well as irrelevant

41. Under which provision of the Indian Evidence Act, an accused may plead alibi?

[A] Section 10

[B] Section 11

[C] Section 12

[D] Section 13

42. The doctrine of estoppel means ___.

[A] Not to make statement in consonance to the earlier statement

[B] Restriction to make statement contrary to the earlier statement/admission

[C] Res judicata

[D] Vague statement

43. An accused in police custody, informs to the Station House Officer that the key by which he opened the safe and committed theft is kept by him in the patio of his house. To what extent this information can be proved?

[A] For committing an offence of theft

[B] For opening lock of safe

[C] For committing theft by opening safe and destroying evidence

[D] For keeping the key in patio of house

44. In a trial, while explaining any circumstances appearing in evidence against him, an accused of committing murder states that due to grave and sudden provocation he was deprived of the power of self-control and thus, gave a single lathi blow to A, causing his death. The burden to prove grave and sudden provocation is on ___.

[A] The Prosecution

[B] The Investigating agency

[C] The Court

[D] The Accused

45. In the Indian Evidence Act, the expression "Court" means ___.

[A] All Judges

[B] All Magistrates

[C] All persons except Arbitrators, legally authorized to take evidence

[D] All of the above.

46. When the Court has to form an opinion as to the electronic signature of any person, the opinion of the certifying authority which has issued the electronic signature certificate is ___.

[A] Fact in issue

[B] Relevant fact

[C] Proved fact

[D] None of the above.

47. During the course of trial of a rape case, a person present in Court causes a knife injury to another person before the Court. The Judge before whom the incident took place ___.

[A] May not be called in evidence

[B] May be called in evidence only under special order of a higher Court

[C] May be examined as a witness

[D] May be called in evidence, only if the trial of that incident is going on before a higher Court

48. For the purpose of the Code of Criminal Procedure 1973, who from amongst the following, may determine the language of each Court in the State other than the High Court?

[A] The High Court of the State

[B] The Supreme Court of India

[C] The State Government

[D] The Legislature Assembly of the State

49. To whom as per Section 98 of the Code of Criminal Procedure, a complaint on oath for restoration of an abducted female child to the person having her lawful charge, may be presented?

[A] The District Magistrate

[B] The Sub Divisional Magistrate

[C] The Magistrate First Class

[D] All the above

50. In a summons case, when the accused appears or is brought before the Magistrate, it shall not be necessary to ___.

[A] State the particulars of the offence of which he is accused

[B] Ask whether he pleads guilty

[C] Ask whether he has any defence to

make

[D] Frame a formal charge

51. The offence affecting the- socio-economic condition of the country, to which plea bargaining is not applicable, shall be notified by ___.

[A] The State Government

[B] The Scheduled Castes/Scheduled Tribes Commission

[C] The Human Rights Commission

[D] The Central Government

52. In a criminal trial, without producing the Chemical Examiner to the Government, the report given by him upon a thing duly submitted for analysis in the course of any proceeding under the Code of Criminal Procedure ___.

[A] Cannot be used as evidence

[B] Can be used as evidence only in summons cases

[C] Can be used as evidence

[D] Can be used only to refresh memory of the Investigating Officer coming in evidence

53. On a busy junction of road, a huge poster/banner installed by an association is creating obstruction in traffic. Who from amongst the following, on having information, may remove such banner/poster by initiating proceedings under the provisions of the Code of Criminal Procedure?

[A] The District Judge

[B] The Chief Judicial Magistrate

[C] The Sub Divisional Magistrate

[D] The Collector

54. Section 304 of the Code of Criminal Procedure provides for ___.

[A] In certain cases making available a pleader to the accused at the expenses of State

[B] Tender of pardon to accomplice

[C] Power to adjourn proceedings

[D] Power to proceed against other persons appearing to be guilty of offence.

55. In cases tried by the Court of Sessions or a Chief Judicial Magistrate, the Court or such Magistrate, as the case may be, shall forward a copy of its or his finding and sentence, if any, to ___.

[A] The Superintendent of Police in the area of whom the crime concerned was committed

[B] The Police Station that conducted the investigation of the crime concerned

[C] The High Court to which the trial Court is subordinate

[D] The District Magistrate within whose local jurisdiction the trial is held

56. A statement under Section 164 of the Code of Criminal Procedure may be recorded by ___.

[A] An Executive Magistrate

[B] A Police Officer

[C] A Judicial Magistrate or a Metropolitan Magistrate

[D] All the officers named above

57. Which one of the following statements is not correct?

[A] A sentence of death passed by the Sessions Court is subject to confirmation by the High Court

[B] A sentence of death passed by the Sessions Court can be confirmed by the High Court only when a Bench hearing the case consists of at least two Judges, when such Court consists of two or more Judges

[C] No order of confirmation of death sentence shall be made prior to expiry of the period for preferring appeal

[D] The High Court, considering the death punishment for confirmation, if no appeal is preferred by the accused challenging the death sentence passed, cannot acquit the accused person

58. The term "unlawful assembly" means ___.

[A] An assembly of five or more persons

[B] An assembly of five or more persons armed with lethal weapons

[C] An assembly of five or more persons with a common object of doing a crime

[D] An assembly of minimum two persons having common intention to commit a crime.

59. A police officer has received a sum of Rs.5000/- against fine from the persons violating traffic rules. Instead of depositing the fine money with State Treasury, he utilized the same for his personal use. What offence under Indian Penal Code, the police officer has

committed?

[A] Criminal breach of trust

[B] Mischief

[C] Cheating the Government

[D] None of the above.

60. If a person, with a knowledge that the feelings of a group of people is likely to be wounded trespasses a place set apart for the performance of funeral rights, he commits a crime described under Section ___.

[A] Section 298 Indian Penal Code

[B] Section 297 Indian Penal Code

[C] Section 295 Indian Penal Code

[D] Section 296 Indian Penal Code

61. A person held guilty for commission of an offence described under Section 326-A of the Indian Penal Code, is liable to be punished with imprisonment which shall not be less than ten years, but which may extend to imprisonment for life with fine, required to be paid to the victim. Such fine shall be ___.

[A] Not less than Rs.1,00,000/-

[B] Not more than Rs.5,00,000/-

[C] Just and reasonable to meet the medical expenses of the treatment of victim

[D] Determined by the Court but in no case shall be less than Rs.5,00,000/-

62. A police officer detains a person in the lock-up despite production of a bail order from the Court. The police officer is guilty of ___.

[A] Abduction

[B] Wrongful confinement

[C] Wrongful restrain

[D] Kidnapping

63. A hotel situated at the bank of a water reservoir, despite objection, discharge its polluted water in the reservoir, causing fouls to reservoir water. For which offence under Indian Penal Code the Manager of the Hotel can be charged?

[A] Section 277

[B] Section 276

[C] Section 278

[D] Section 282

64. In Indian Penal Code the pronoun 'he' and its derivatives are used for ___.

[A] Male

[B] Female

[C] Any person whether male or female

[D] Such words are not used in the Code

65. In which of the following leading cases, Hon'ble Supreme Court held that benefit of Section 3 or Section 4 of the Probation of Offenders Act, 1958 is subject to the limitations laid down in these provisions and the words 'may direct' in Section 4 does not mean 'must direct'.

[A] State of Gujarat vs. V. [A] Chouhan (AIR 1983 SC 359)

[B] Phul Singh vs. State of Haryana (AIR 1980 SC 249)

[C] Ram Parkash vs. State of Himachal Pradesh (AIR 1973 SC 780)

[D] Smt. Devki vs. State of Haryana (AIR 1979 SC 1948)

66. Who is entitled for immunity from prosecution under Section 64-A of the Narcotic Drugs and Psychotropic Substances Act, 1985?

[A] An addict charged for the offence punishable under Section 27 of the Act, if he volunteers for de-addiction treatment

[B] An addict charged for the offence involving small quantities of Narcotic Drugs, if he volunteers for de-addiction treatment

[C] A person who is not addict, but is accused for an offence punishable under Section 27 of the Narcotic Drugs and Psychotropic Substances Act, 1985

[D] Both [A] and [B] above

67. An officer of the Company shall not be liable to punishment, for contravention of any of the provisions of the Information Technology Act, 2000, if he proves that ___.

[A] He was not having knowledge about the provisions of the Act

[B] The person affected by such contravention was also involved in similar activities

[C] The contravention took place without his knowledge or he exercised all due diligence to prevent such contravention

[D] None of the above

68. Mrs. 'R' lodges a first information report at Police Station with assertion that Mr. 'X' by sending her vulgar message either by forwarding e- mails or through Short Messaging Service (SMS) intrudes upon her privacy. For what offence, the case may be registered against Mr. 'X'?

[A] Section 509 Indian Penal Code and 66- A of the Information Technology Act, 2000

[B] Section 66-A of the Information Technology Act, 2000

[C] Section 509 Indian Penal Code and 66- E of the Information Technology Act, 2000

[D] None of the above

69. As per Section 147 of the Negotiable Instruments Act, 1881, every offence punishable under the Act is ___.

[A] Compoundable

[B] Non-compoundable

[C] Cognizable

[D] Both [B] and [C] above

70. 'Mens rea has no place while determining penal liability under Section 138 of the Negotiable Instruments Act, 1881'. This statement is ___.

[A] Correct

[B] Wrong

[C] Partly correct

[D] Depends upon facts of the case

71. हिन्दी भाषा की लिपि है –

[A] प्राकृत

[B] पाली

[C] देवनागरी

[D] सिंहली

72. अनुप्रास अलंकार का उदाहरण है–

[A] कनक कनक ते सौ गुनी मादकता अधिकाई

[B] चारू चन्द्र की चंचल किरणें, खेल रहीं हैं जल थल में

[C] सारी बिच नारी है कि नारी बिच सारी है

[D] आँख लगती है तब आँख लगती ही नहीं

73. अनुराग शब्द का विलोम है –

[A] पराग

[B] विराग

[C] राग

[D] वीतराग

74. घर शब्द का पर्धायवाची है –

[A] प्रासाद

[B] ग्रह

[C] सदन

[D] ग्राम

75. उच्चारण का संधि विच्छेद हैं –

[A] उच्च+च

[B] उत् +चारण

[C] उ+चारण

[D] उच्च+आरण

76. सत् + जन की संधि है –

[A] सद्जन

[B] सज्जन

[C] सत्जन

[D] सजन

77. यह, वह, तुम, आप हैं –

[A] क्रिया

[B] संज्ञा

[C] विशेषण

[D] सर्वनाम

78. शुद्ध शब्द चुनिए –

[A] आर्शीवाद

[B] आर्शिवाद

[C] आशीर्वाद

[D] आशिर्वाद

79. 'जानने की इच्छा रखने वाला' के लिये उपयुक्त शब्द है –

[A] विश्वासी

[B] सर्वज्ञ

[C] जिज्ञासु

[D] वाचाल

80. 'गुस्से से देखना' के लिये उपयुक्त मुहावरा है –

[A] आँख बिछाना

[B] आँख मारना

[C] आँख दिखाना

[D] आँख चुराना

81. भीतर से शत्रुता और ऊपर से मीठी बात करने के भाव को व्यक्त करने वाली लोकोक्ति है –

[A] आम के आम, गुठली के दाम

[B] मुँह में राम, बगल में छूरी

[C] दोनों हाथों में लड्डू

[D] दूर के ढोल सुहावने

82. निम्न में से शुद्ध वाक्य है –

[A] कृपया करके अपना स्थान ग्रहण करें

[B] अपना स्थान ग्रहण करने की कपा करें

[C] अपना स्थान ग्रहण करने की कृपया करें

[D] उपरोक्त समी

83. 'किसान ने भूमि पर हल चलाया' इस वाक्य में कर्ता एवं अधिकरण कमश: है

[A] किसान, हल

[B] भूमि, हल

[C] किसान, भूमि

[D] हल, भूमि

84. 'अन्तरिम कालीन' के लिये उचित शब्द है –

[A] स्थानापन्न

[B] तदर्थ

[C] एतद्द्वारा

[D] स्थायी

85. 'टोकरी में मीठे सन्तरे है' में 'मीठे' शब्द कौनसा विशेषण है?

[A] परिमाणवाचक

[B] संख्यावाचक

[C] सार्वनामिक

[D] गुणवाचक

86. He has not yet recovered ____ his illness.

[A] With
[B] Over
[C] From
[D] on

87. It has been raining ____ yesterday.

[A] By
[B] Since
[C] After
[D] in

88. This is a matter ____ little importance.

[A] Of
[B] For
[C] From
[D] with

89. There is a cow ____ the field.

[A] In
[B] At
[C] Over
[D] upon

90. He keeps ____ his friends through the internet.

[A] out of touch
[B] in touch with
[C] into touch with
[D] of touch with

91. I shall do it ____ pleasure.

[A] Over
[B] By
[C] Across
[D] with

92. The Chief Guest will ____ the prizes.

[A] give over
[B] given up
[C] give in
[D] give away

93. Identify the tense. She has worked out all the sums.

[A] Present Simple
[B] Past Simple
[C] Present Continuous
[D] Present Perfect

94. Identify the tense. I am reading a book.

[A] Present Perfect
[B] Past Continuous
[C] Present Continuous
[D] Present Simple

95. Meaning of the proverb. "A miss is as good as a mile"

[A] never criticize a gift

[B] one must learn how to do things gradually

[C] failure is failure

[D] nothing can be gained without effort

96. Meaning of the proverb. "Strike while the iron is hot"

[A] make the most of present opportunities

[B] it is never too late to improve

[C] only practice will bring success

[D] none of the above

97. Pick out the correct passive voice of the given sentence.

This shop sells books ___.

[A] Books are sold in this shop

[B] Shop is selling books

[C] Books are on sale

[D] None of the above

98. Pick out the correct passive voice of the given sentence.

Mother has cooked the dinner.

[A] Did mother not cook the dinner?

[B] The dinner has been cooking by mother.

[C] The dinner has been cooked by mother.

[D] Mother has not cooked the dinner.

99. Opposite. Extrovert

[A] Boaster

[B] Mixer

[C] Introvert

[D] Social

100. Opposite. Urban

[A] Rustic

[B] Rural

[C] Civil

[D] Domestic

12	B	57	D
13	B	58	C
14	B	59	A
15	C	60	B
16	D	61	C
17	C	62	B
18	D	63	A
19	C	64	C
20	B	65	C
21	D	66	D
22	C	67	C
23	B	68	A
24	B	69	A
25	C	70	A
26	B	71	C
27	A	72	B
28	A	73	B
29	A	74	C
30	D	75	B
31	D	76	B
32	A	77	D
33	C	78	C
34	C	79	C
35	D	80	C
36	C	81	B
37	D	82	B
38	A	83	C
39	B	84	B
40	B	85	D
41	B	86	C
42	B	87	B
43	D	88	A
44	D	89	A
45	D	90	B

---X---

Preliminary Examination 2015

1. Under the provisions of the Rajasthan Agricultural Credit Operations (Removal of Difficulties) Act, 1974, a Bank can recover its dues from any agriculturist or his heir or legal representative or his guarantor on account of financial assistance availed of by the agriculturist by making an application to ___.

[A] District Judge

[B] High Court

[C] Prescribed Authority

[D] None of the above

2. Under Section 35 of the Rajasthan Court Fees and Suits Valuation Act, 1961, in a suit for partition and separate possession of a share in joint family

Answers

1	C	46	B	91	D
2	D	47	C	92	D
3	A	48	C	93	D
4	B	49	D	94	C
5	D	50	D	95	C
6	C	51	D	96	A
7	C	52	C	97	A
8	A	53	C	98	C
9	A	54	A	99	C
10	D	55	D	100	B
11	A	56	C		

property by a plaintiff, who has been excluded from possession of such property, court fee shall be ___.

[A] paid at fixed rate

[B] computed on the market value of the plaintiff's share of the property

[C] at the discretion of the plaintiff

[D] based on written statement of the defendant

3. Under the Rajasthan Stamp Act, 1998, in case of a release-deed in the absence of an agreement to the contrary, the expense of providing the proper stamp shall be borne by ___.

[A] the beneficiary

[B] the person drawing, making or executing the release-deed

[C] by both the parties in equal shares

[D] none of the above

4. If an instrument has not been duly stamped and where such an instrument has been admitted in evidence, such admission ___.

[A] can be called in question at any stage of the same suit or proceeding

[B] shall not be called in question at any stage of the same suit or proceeding except as provided for by Section 71 of the Rajasthan Stamp Act, 1998

[C] at the discretion of the opposite party can be called in question

[D] none of the above

5. Under the Registration Act, 1908 a will can be presented for registration before the Registrar or sub-Registrar by ___.

[A] the testator

[B] after death of testator, any person claiming as executor or otherwise under a Will

[C] both (1) and (2)

[D] none of the above

6. Two parties entered into a contract. They later realized that the law as they understood as applicable was not in force in India. This makes their contract ___.

[A] illegal

[B] void

[C] voidable

[D] none of the above

7. Acknowledgement after the expiration of the period prescribed under the Indian Limitation Act, 1963, for a suit or application ___.

[A] is of no effect

[B] gives rise to an independent & enforceable contract

[C] is of great value

[D] none of the above

8. Time limit for disposal of a petition filed under Section 9 of Rajasthan Rent Control Act, 2001 is ___.

[A] within the period of two hundred and forty days from the date of service of notice on the tenant

[B] within the period of twelve months from the date of service of notice on the tenant

[C] within the period of six months from the date of service of notice on the tenant

[D] no limitation

9. Subject to contract between the partners, a firm is dissolved ___.

[A] if constituted for a fixed term, by the expiry of that term

[B] if constituted to carry out one or more adventures or undertakings, by the completion thereof

[C] by the death of a partner

[D] all the above

10. Finder of lost goods under Indian Contract Act, 1872 is a ___.

[A] Bailor

[B] Surety

[C] Bailee

[D] none of the above

11. Under Rajasthan Right to Hearing Act, 2012, a complaint can be filed regarding grievance relating to ___.

[A] the service matters of a public servant

[B] any matter in which any Court or Tribunal has jurisdiction

[C] any matter under Right to Information Act, 2005

[D] none of the above

12. In which of the following cases has the supreme Court ruled that the members of the Transgender Community

who are neither male nor female, at the time of birth, are recognized as 'third Gender' for the purpose of safeguarding and enforcing appropriately their fundamental and other legal, social and economic rights guaranteed under the constitution?

[A] Rambilas Singh vs. State of Bihar - AIR 1989 SCC 1593

[B] Lily Thomas vs. Union of India - (2013) 7 SCC 653

[C] National Legal Services Authority vs. Union of India - (2014) 5 SCC 438

[D] None of the above

13. Article 21-A providing for Right to Education was inserted in the constitution by ___.

[A] the Constitution (Eighty sixth Amendment) Act, 2002

[B] the Constitution (Ninety First Amendment) Act, 2003

[C] the Constitution (Ninety Second Amendment) Act, 2003

[D] the Constitution (Eighty Fourth Amendment) Act, 2001

14. Which of the following is correct statement in so far as Section 20 of the Code of Civil Procedure, 1908, is concerned?

[A] The suit has to be instituted in the court of the lowest grade competent to try it

[B] The suit has to be instituted in the court within the local limits of whose jurisdiction the defendant actually and voluntarily resides or carries on business or personally works for gain

[C] The suit has to be instituted in the court within the local limits of whose jurisdiction, the cause of action wholly or in part arises

[D] All the above are correct

15. In which of the following cases, did the Supreme Court uphold the validity of the Code of Civil Procedure Amendment Acts of 1999 and 2002?

[A] Delhi H.C. Bar Association Vs. UOI

[B] Allahabad H.C. Bar Association Vs. UOI

[C] Salem Advocate Bar Association Vs. UOI

[D] P & H H.C. Bar Association Vs. UOI

16. An Appeal under Order XLIII of Code of Civil Procedure shall lie from which of the following orders ___.

[A] Rule-11 of Order VII, rejecting the plaint

[B] Rule-9 of Order XXII, refusing to set aside the abatement or dismissal of suit

[C] Rule-1 of Order VIII, not permitting the defendant to present the written statement

[D] Rule-5 of Order XIV, refusing to strike out the issue at the instance of either of the parties

17. Statement 'A' - where the access and use of light or air to and for any building have been peaceably enjoyed therewith, as an easement, without interruption, and for twenty years, the right to such access and use of light or air shall be absolute.

Statement "B' - A right to the free passage of light or air to an open space of ground, cannot be acquired by prescription.

(1) Statement 'A' is correct

(2) Statement 'B' is correct

(3) Both statements are correct

(4) Both statements are incorrect

18. Which of the following statement is correct?

(1) In a suit for specific performance of a contract for transfer of immovable property, the court cannot grant partition and separate possession of the property

(2) In a suit for specific performance of a contract for transfer of immovable property, the plaintiff cannot alternatively ask for the refund of earnest money or deposit made by him

(3) The court while refusing to grant specific performance of the contract, cannot grant refund of earnest money paid by the plaintiff, unless it has been specifically claimed

(4) All the above are correct

19. Which of the following documents is not required to be compulsorily registered?

(1) Instruments creating or declaring right, title or interest to or in immovable property of rupees one hundred and upwards

(2) wills in respect of immovable property

(3) Leases of immovable property for a term exceeding one year

(4) Instruments transferring any decree of a court when such decree purports to create right in immovable property of rupees one hundred and upwards

20. In which of the following mortgages, the mortgagor is required to deliver possession of the mortgaged property to the mortgagee?

(1) English mortgage

(2) Mortgage by conditional sale

(3) Usufructuary mortgage

(4) Anomalous mortgage

21. Statement 'A' - Every transfer of immovable property made with intent to defeat or delay the creditors of the transferor is void.

Statement 'B' - Every transfer of immovable property made without consideration with intent to defraud a subsequent transferee is void.

[A] Statement 'A' is correct

[B] Statement 'B' is correct

[C] Both statements are correct

[D] Both statements are incorrect

22. Which of the following statement is correct, so far as Section 9 of the Arbitration and Conciliation Act, 1996 is concerned?

[A] A party may apply to the court for interim measures during the pendency of the arbitration proceedings only

[B] A party may apply to the court seeking appointment of receiver by way of interim measures even after the making of the arbitral award by the Arbitral Tribunal

[C] A party cannot apply for interim measures before the commencement of arbitral proceedings

[D] All the above are correct

23. The period of three years is prescribed under Article 137 of the Limitation Act, 1963, in case where no other period of Limitation is provided for filing any ___.

[A] Suit

[B] Appeal

[C] Application

[D] Proceeding

24. Statement "A' - In computing period of limitation for any appeal, the day from which such period is to be reckoned, shall be included.

Statement "B" - In computing period of Limitation for any appeal, the day on which the judgment complained of was pronounced and the time requisite for obtaining the copy of the decree shall be excluded.

[A] Statement 'A' is correct

[B] Statement 'B' is correct

[C] Both are correct

[D] Both are incorrect

25. Which of the following is correct as per Section 22-c of the Legal Services Authority Act, 1987?

[A] Any party to a dispute may, after the dispute is brought before any court, make an application to the Permanent Lok Adalat for the settlement of dispute

[B] The Permanent Lok Adalat shall not have the jurisdiction in respect of any matter relating to an offence not compoundable under any law

[C] The Permanent Lok Adalat shall have the jurisdiction only in such matter where the value of the property in dispute is more than ten lakh rupees

[D] All the above are correct

26. Under Section 11 of the Hindu Marriage Act, 1955, the marriage may be declared null and void if ___.

[A] the parties are within the degrees of prohibited relationship

[B] at the time of the marriage, one of the parties was incapable of giving a valid consent to it in consequence of unsoundness of mind

[C] at the time of the marriage, one of the parties was subject to recurrent attacks of insanity

[D] in all the above circumstances

27. After the Hindu Succession (Amendment) act, 2005, the daughter of a coparcener in a Joint Hindu family governed by the Mitakshara law ___.

[A] shall have no right in the coparcenery property

[B] cannot become a coparcener by birth

[C] shall become a corparcener by birth in her own right in the same manner as the son

[D] shall be entitled to dispose of the entire coparcenery property

28. Which of the following is incorrect?

[A] The husband is the natural guardian of a Hindu married girl

[B] After the adoption of Hindu minor son, his father continues to remain his natural guardian till he attains majority

[C] The natural guardian of a Hindu minor child is the father, and after him the mother, but custody of minor upto the age of five years shall ordinarily be with the mother

[D] The natural guardian of an illegitimate Hindu minor boy is the mother, and after her, the father

29. A Hindu wife is entitled to claim maintenance after the death of her husband from her father-in-law under ____.

[A] Section 25 of the Hindu Marriage Act, 1955

[B] Section 24 of the Hindu Marriage Act, 1955

[C] Section 19 of the Hindu Adoptions and Maintenance Act, 1956

[D] Section 10 of the Hindu Succession Act, 1956

30. As per Section 2(q) of the Protection of women from Domestic Violence Act, 2005, "respondent" means and includes ____.

[A] any person, who is in a domestic relationship with the aggrieved person and against whom the aggrieved person has sought relief under the act

[B] male partner when aggrieved female is living in a relationship with him in the nature of a marriage

[C] the female relatives of the husband of the aggrieved wife, seeking their removal from the shared household

[D] none of the above

31. As per Section 3 of the Rajasthan Rent Control Act, 2001, the Chapter II and III thereof do not apply to ____.

[A] the premises, let out after the commencement of the Act for a period of two years through a registered deed

[B] the premises, let out to the multinational company having paid up share Capital of less than rupees one crore

[C] the premises, let out for residential purposes, the monthly rent whereof is rupees four thousand in case of the premises situated in the Municipal area of Jaipur city

[D] the premises belonging to the Government company as defined under the Companies Act, 1956

32. Which of the following statements is not correct, so far as Section 242 of the Rajasthan Tenancy Act, 1955 is concerned?

[A] civil court can frame the issue with regard to the tenancy rights in agricultural land and submit the record to the appropriate revenue court for the decision on that issue only

[B] Civil court may or may not accept the finding of revenue court on the issue referred to it

[C] The finding of the revenue court on the issue referred to it, shall be deemed to be part of the finding of civil court for the purposes of Appeal

[D] Civil court cannot decide the issue which was referred to the revenue court

33. Which of the following is not the judicial matter under Section 23 read with the First Schedule to the Rajasthan Land Revenue Act, 1956?

[A] Regularization of unauthorized occupation

[B] A dispute with respect to the right of grazing cattle on pasturage land

[C] Settlement of boundary disputes

[D] Mutation upon succession

34. The General Rules (Civil), 1986 have been framed ____.

[A] by the Rajasthan High Court under Article 227 of the Constitution of India

[B] by the Governor under Article 166 of the Constitution of India.

[C] by the Chief Justice under article 229 of the Constitution of India.

[D] by the State Government under Article 309 of the Constitution of India.

35. Which of the followings is not an essential ingredient of gift under the Mohammedan law ____.

[A] a declaration of gift by the donor

[B] acceptance of gift, expressed or implied, by or on behalf of donee

[C] delivery of possession of the subject gift by the donor to the donee

[D] a written deed of gift

36. Which of the following is correct statement of Jaw as per Sections 82 and 83 of the Code of Criminal Procedure 1973?

[A] The court may order attachment of property belonging to an accused before declaring him a proclaimed person under Section 82

[B] The court may order attachment of property of a person after publication of a written proclamation under Section 82 requiring him to appear before it

[C] The court may order attachment of property of a person regardless of whether or not he has been declared proclaimed offender

[D] None of the above

37. Which of the following irregularities of a Magistrate, not empowered by law to do so, vitiates the proceedings?

[A] To hold inquiry under Section 176 code of criminal procedure

[B] To make over a case under Sub-Section (2) of Section 192 code of criminal procedure

[C] To take cognizance of an offence under clause (c) of sub-Section (1) of Section 190 of the code of criminal procedure

[D] To tender pardon to accomplice under Section 306 of the code of criminal procedure

38. Which of the following irregularities of a Magistrate not empowered by law to do so, does not vitiate the proceedings?

[A] calling of record to exercise powers of revision under Section 397 of code of Criminal Procedure

[B] taking cognizance of an offence under clause (a) or clause (b) of sub-Section (1) of Section 190 of Code of Criminal Procedure

[C] decision of an appeal

[D] revision of an order passed under Section 466 of Code of Criminal Procedure

39. Which of the following offences is cognizable, non-bailable and non-compoundable?

[A] voluntarily causing grievous hurt, punishable under Section 325 IPC

[B] attempt to murder punishable under Section 307 IPC

[C] voluntarily causing hurt to extort confession, or to compel! Restoration of property, punishable under Section 330 IPC

[D] voluntarily causing grievous hurt on provocation punishable under Section 335 IPC

40. Which of the following provisions of the Indian Penal Code defines culpable homicide?

[A] Section 302

[B] Section 300

[C] Section 301

[D] Section 299

41. Statement of an accused can be recorded on oath ___.

[A] is not a correct statement of law

[B] under Section 315 code of criminal procedure

[C] under Section 313 code of criminal procedure

[D] under Section 391 code of criminal procedure

42. Which of the following is correct statement according to law?

[A] An accomplice shall be competent witness against an accused person

[B] Leading question may be asked in cross-examination of a witness

[C] The court may permit a party, who, calls a witness, to put any question to him, which might be put in cross-examination by the adverse party

[D] All the above

43. Burden of proof under Section 101 of the Indian Evidence Act, 1872 ___.

[A] goes on shifting as the trial proceeds

[B] never shifts

[C] may shift

[D] both (1) and (3) are correct

44. Proceedings under Section 145 of the Code of Criminal Procedure are initiated by the Executive Magistrate on the report of which of the following?

[A] Judicial Magistrate

[B] Police Officer

[C] Revenue Officer

[D] Complainant

45. In which of the following judgments has the Supreme Court held that only those courts within whose territorial limits the drawee bank is situated, would have jurisdiction to try the cases for offence under Section 138 of the Negotiable Instruments Act, 1881?

[A] K. Bhaskaran Vs. Sankaran Vaidhyan Balan and Another - (1999) 7 SCC 510

[B] Dashrath Rupsingh Rathod Vs. State of Maharashtra and Another - (2014) 9 SCC 129

[C] State of Bihar and Others Vs. Kalyanpur Cement Limited - (2010) 3 SCC 274

[D] None of the above

46. Which of the following is a correct statement of law as per Sections 138 and 142 of the Negotiable Instruments Act, 1881?

[A] A cheque is to be presented to the bank within a period of six months from the date it is drawn or within the period of its validity, whichever is earlier

[B] Notice within thirty days of receipt of information from the bank regarding return of cheque as unpaid, has to be served upon drawer, demanding payment of amount of money

[C] On failure of drawer of such cheque to make payment within fifteen days of receipt of such notice, the payee or holder of cheque has to file complaint within one month thereof

[D] All the above

47. The delay in filing a complaint under Section 138 of the Negotiable Instruments Act, 1881, can be condoned ____.

[A] under Section 5 of the Indian Limitation Act, 1963

[B] under Section 138 of the Negotiable Instruments Act, 1881

[C] under Section 142 of the Negotiable Instruments Act, 1881

[D] under Section 143 of the Negotiable Instruments Act, 1881

48. In which of the following judgments has the Supreme Court struck down Section 66-A of the Information Technology Act, 2000?

[A] Shreya Singhal Vs. Union of India - AIR 2015 sc 1523

[B] Selvi and Others Vs. State of Karnataka - (2010) 7 Scc 263

[C] PUCL Vs. Union of India - (1997) 1 scc 301

[D] Amar Singh Vs. Union of India - (2011) 7 Scc 67

49. According to Section 25 of the Protection of Children from Sexual offences Act, 2012, statement of a child under Section 164 of the Code of Criminal Procedure to be recorded by the Magistrate ____.

[A] shall be recorded in presence of the advocate of the accused

[B] shall not be recorded in presence of the advocate of the accused

[C] shall be recorded in presence of the Investigating Officer

[D] shall be recorded in presence of woman Police officer

50. Which of the following is not the duty of Probation officer?

[A] To supervise probationers placed under his supervision and where necessary, endeavour to find them suitable employment

[B] To advise and assist offenders in payment of compensation or costs ordered by the court

[C] To inquire into the circumstances or home surroundings of any person accused of an offence

[D] To arrange for lodging and boarding of the probationers

51. Which of following conditions, as per provisions of the Protection of children from Sexual offences Act, 2012, has to be adhered to while examining or recording statement of the child ____.

[A] the statement of child shall be recorded at the residence of child or the place where he usually resides or the place of his choice

[B] as far as practicable the statement should be recorded by woman police officer not below the rank of Sub Inspector, who shall not be in uniform

[C] the Investigating officer shall ensure that at no point of time the child comes in contact in any way with the accused

[D] all the above

52. A private key and its mathematically related public key, which are so related that the public key, can verify a digital signature created by the private key, in an Asymmetric crypto system means ___.

[A] Key pair

[B] Both keys

[C] Soft keys

[D] Soft pair

53. A person, who sends, generates, stores or transmits any electronic message; or causes any electronic message to be sent, generated, stored or transmitted to any other person, is called ___.

[A] sender

[B] Originator

[C] Generator

[D] Intermediary

54. What is the minimum and maximum sentence that can be awarded to an accused guilty of second or subsequent offence of theft of electric lines and materials under Section 136 of the Electricity Act, 2003 ___.

[A] not less than 1 year but which may extend to 10 years and also fine which shall not be less than one lac rupees

[B] not less than 6 months but which may extend to 5 years and also fine which shall not be less than ten thousand rupees

[C] not less than 3 months but which may extend to 3 years and also fine which shall not be less than fifty thousand rupees

[D] not less than 9 months but which may extend to 3 years and also fine which shall not be less than one lac rupees

55. A police officer empowered to investigate cybercrime as per Section 78 of the Information Technology Act, 2000, must not be below the rank of ___.

[A] Sub Inspector

[B] Inspector

[C] Deputy Superintendent of Police

[D] Superintendent of Police

56. In which of the following judgments did the Supreme Court set aside the judgment of the High Court of Delhi which decriminalized Section 377 of the Indian Penal Code, 1860 ___.

[A] Sakshi vs. Union of India - AIR 2004 SC 3566

[B] Naz Foundation (India) Trust vs. Suresh Kumar Koushal - (2014) 3 SCC 220

[C] PUCL vs. Union of India - (2010) 14 SCC 245

[D] Suresh Kumar Kaushal vs. Naz Foundation (India) Trust (2014) 1 SCC I

57. Which of the following acts constitute 'Atrocity' as defined in Section 3(1) of the Scheduled Castes and Scheduled Tribes (Prevention of Atrocities) Act, 1989?

[A] Forcing to drink or eat any inedible or obnoxious substances

[B] Intentionally insulting or intimidating with intent to humiliate in any place within public view

[C] Forcing or intimidating not to vote or to vote for a particular candidate or vote in a manner other than provided by law

[D] All the above

58. Benefit of probation to a convict of offence under the Narcotic Drugs and Psychotropic Substances act, 1985 can be provided only if ___.

[A] he is under 21 years of age and is convicted for offence punishable under Section 26 or 27 of the Narcotic Drugs and Psychotropic Substances Act, 1985

[B] he is under 18 years of age or is convicted for offence punishable under Section 26 or 27 of the Narcotic Drugs and Psychotropic Substances Act, 1985

[C] to any accused, regardless of his age, sentenced to rigorous imprisonment up to 10 years

[D] none of the above

59. Who, as per Section 2(1) of the juvenile Justice (Care and Protection of Children) Act, 2000, is a 'Juvenile in conflict with Law"?

[A] A Juvenile who is alleged to have committed an offence and has not completed eighteen years of age as on the date of commission of such offence

[B] A Juvenile who is alleged to have committed an offence and has not completed twelve years of age on the date of commission of such offence

[C] A Juvenile who is alleged to have committed an offence and has not completed sixteen years of age on the date of commission of such offence

[D] A Juvenile who is alleged to have committed an offence and has not completed fourteen years of age on the date of commission of such offence

60. Which of the following statements is not correct?

[A] one or more Juvenile justice Boards shall be constituted by the State Government for every district

[B] each Juvenile justice Board shall consist of a Metropolitan Magistrate or a Judicial Magistrate and two social workers, of whom at-least one shall be a woman

[C] the order passed by the juvenile Justice Board in absence of any Member at any stage of proceedings shall be invalid

[D] power of the Juvenile Justice Board may also be exercised by the High court and the Court of Sessions, when the proceedings come before them in appeal, revision or otherwise.

61. Under Section 32 of the Indian Evidence Act, 1872, statement of a person, who is dead, is relevant ___.

[A] if it relates to cause of someone else's death

[B] if it relates to cause of his own death or someone else's death

[C] if it relates to the cause of his own death

[D] none of the above

62. Section 436-A of the Code of Criminal Procedure, 1973, provides for grant of bail to an accused pending trial if ___.

[A] he has undergone detention for one-fourth period of 'imprisonment specified for the offence for which he is being tried

[B] he has undergone detention for one-third period of imprisonment specified for the offence for which he is being tried

[C] he has undergone detention for one-half period of imprisonment specified for the offence for which he is being tried

[D] (1) and (2) above

63. Facts, which, though not in issue, are so connected with a fact in issue as to form part of the same transaction, whether they occurred at the same time and place or at different times and places ___.

[A] are irrelevant

[B] are relevant

[C] are partly relevant

[D] none of the above

64. Which of the following statements, as per provisions of the Indian Evidence Act, 1872, is not correct?

[A] Facts which are inconsistent with any fact in issue, shall not be relevant

[B] Facts not otherwise relevant are relevant if by themselves or in connection with other facts, they make the existence or non-existence of any fact in issue or relevant fact highly probable or improbable

[C] any fact is relevant, which shows or constitutes 4 motive or preparation for any fact in issue or relevant fact

[D] Admissions are not conclusive proof of the matters admitted, but they may operate as estoppels under the provisions of the Indian Evidence Act, 1872

65. Narcoanalysis, polygraph test and brain electrical activation profile test conducted against will of the person subjected to such tests, violates his right protected under Article 20(3), and right to personal liberty protected under article 21 of the Constitution of India, was held by the Supreme Court in which of the following cases?

[A] Wakkar and Another vs. State of Uttar Pradesh - (2011) 3 SCC 306

[B] Munna Kumar Upadhyay vs. State of Andhra Pradesh - (2012) 6 SCC 174

[C] Jagroop Singh vs. State of Punjab - (2012) 11 SCC 768

[D] Selvi and others vs. State of Karnataka - (2010) 7 SCC 263

66. Statement "A' – When a court of Sessions passes a sentence of death, the court shall, according to Rule 102 of the General Rules (Criminal) 1980, commit the prisoner by a warrant in the appropriate form to the jail from which he came to stand his trial, and shall submit its proceedings to the High Court at the latest on the fourth day after the sentence of death has been pronounced.

Statement 'B" – When a court of Sessions passes a sentence against a female prisoner to death, according to

Rule 104 of the General Rules (Criminal) 1980, it shall consider after enquiring from such prisoner herself, if necessary, whether she is pregnant and if it thinks that it is likely, it shall have her examined by the District Medical officer or such other doctor as 1t may consider fit and if it finds that she is in fact pregnant, it shall make a report to the High Court.

[A] Both the aforesaid statements are correct

[B] Statement 'A' is correct and Statement 'B' is incorrect

[C] Statement 'B' is correct and Statement 'A' is incorrect

[D] None of them is correct

67. How many kinds of punishment are provided in Section 53 of the Indian Penal Code, 1860?

[A] Six

[B] Four

[C] Five

[D] Seven

68. According to Sections 73 and 74 of the Indian Penal Code, 1860, a convict can be kept in solitary confinement for any portion or portions of imprisonment to which he is sentenced. Which of the following is incorrect?

[A] For period not exceeding three months in the whole

[B] For period not exceeding three months, if the term of the imprisonment exceeds six months and does not exceed one year

[C] For period not exceeding three months if the term of imprisonment exceeds one year

[D] The solitary confinement in no case shall exceed 14 days at a time

69. A knows Z to be behind a bush. B does not know it. A, intending to cause, or knowing it to be likely to cause Z's death, induces B to fire at the bush. B fires and kills Z. What offence has been committed by A and B?

[A] A and B both would be guilty of committing offence punishable under Section 302 IPC

[B] While A would be guilty of committing offence under Section 302 IPC, B would be guilty of committing offence under Section 304 Part II, IPC

[C] A would be guilty of committing offence punishable under Section 302 IPC, B would be guilty of no offence

[D] A and B both would be guilty of committing offence punishable under Section 304 Part-I of the IPC

70. A is in a house which is on fire, with Z, a chil[D] People below hold out a blanket. A drop the child from the house-top, knowing it to be likely that the fall may kill the child but not intending to kill the child, and intending, in good faith, the child's benefit, and the child dies. Which of the following offence has been committed by A?

[A] Section 304-A, of Indian Penal Code, 1860

[B] Section 304 part II, of Indian Penal Code, 1860

[C] Section 302, of Indian Penal Code, 1860

[D] A has committed no offence

71. वे शब्द जो किसी संस्कृत या प्राकृत मूल से निकले हुए नहीं ज्ञान पड़ते और जिनकी व्युत्पत्ति का पता नहीं लगता, कहलाते है :-

[A] तसत्सम

[B] व्यंजन

[C] देशज़

[D] खडी बोली

72. स्वर, व्यंजन, विसगे किसके विभिन्न प्रकार है -

[A] विशेषण

[B] संज्ञा

[C] सर्वनाम

[D] संधि

73. जिस सर्वनाम से वक्ता के पास अथवा दूर की किसी वस्तु का बोध होता हो, को कहते है :-

[A] निजवाचक सर्वनाम

[B] निश्चयवाचक सर्वनाम

[C] अनिश्चयवाचक सर्वनाम

[D] संबंधवाचक सर्वनाम

74. संज्ञा के सर्वनाम का क्रिया के साथ संबंध निर्धारित करने वाले तत्तव कहलाते है :-

[A] विशेषण

[B] अव्यय

[C] क्रिया

[D] कारक

75. दो या अधिक शब्दों के परस्पर संबंध बताने वाले शब्दों अथवा प्रत्ययों का लोप होने

पर, दो या अधिक शब्द मैं से जो एक स्वतंत्र शब्द बनता है, कहलाता है :-

[A] समास

[B] उपसर्ग

[C] विशेषण

[D] संज्ञा

76. 'हाय ! अब मैं क्या करूं।' किस प्रकार का अव्यय है :-

[A] क्रिया विशेषण

[B] संबंध सूचक

[C] समच्चययबौधक

[D] विस्मयादिबोधक

77. क्रिया के उस रूपान्तरण को, जिससे क्रिया के व्यापार का समय तथा उसकी पूर्ण अथवा अपूर्ण अवस्था का बोध होता है, को कहते है :-

[A] समास

[B] सर्वनाम

[C] काल

[D] कारक

78. निम्न में से कौनसा शब्द "चांदनी" का समानार्थी नहीं है ?

[A] चन्द्रिका

[B] कोमुदी

[C] ज्योत्स्ना

[D] कालत्र

79. निम्न में से कौनसा 'विज्लोभ- युग्म' सही है :-

[A] निष्काम-सकाम

[B] निकट-सन्जिकेंट

[C] नाश-विनाश

[D] मितव्ययी- अल्पव्ययी

80. मूल पत्र की प्रतिलिघि किसी विभाग को प्रेषित की जाती है, उसे क्या कहते है :-

[A] पृष्ठांकन

[B] प्रेस विज्ञप्ति

[C] परिपत्र

[D] प्रस्ताव

81. 'धर की मुर्गी दाल बराबर', कहावत का अर्थ है :-

[A] घर की मुर्गी को दाल के बराबर मूल्यवान समझना

[B] घर की मुर्गी को बराबर दात्र खिलाना

[C] मुर्गी व दाल खाना

[D] अपने आदमी को कम महत्व टेमा

82. "साध्वाचरण" शब्द का संधि विच्छेट किस क्रम में है :

[A] साधु + आचरण

[B] साध + आचरण

[C] साधव + चरण

[D] साधु + चरण

83. 'नीलोत्पलभ्' में समास है :-

[A] तत्पुरुष

[B] कर्मधारय

[C] बहुत्रीहि

[D] अवययीभाव

84. निम्नलिखितु में से कौनसा शब्द 'विध्युत' का पर्यायवाची नहीं है?

[A] तडित

[B] चपला

[C] कोदंट

[D] चंचला

85. 'जिन ढूँढा तिन पाइयों गहरे पाभी पैठ' लोकोक्ति का अर्थ है :-

[A] बिना प्रयास के लाभ होना

[B] काम करने में शीघ्रता करना

[C] परिश्रम का फल अवश्य मिलता है

[D] सांसरिकता में लिप्त रहकर ईश्वर को प्राप्त करना

Note: Identify the tense in the following sentence.

86. I am pleading for the preservation of trees

[A] Simple Present Tense

[B] Past Tense

[C] Present Continuous Tense

[D] Past Continuous Tense

87. Fill in the blank with correct form of verb.

My sister saw a snake while she ____ in the garden

[A] Was walking

[B] Walks

[C] Is walking

[D] Were walking

88. Pick up the correct synonym for the word.

STUBBORN

[A] Easy

[B] Obstinate

[C] Willing

[D] Pliable

89. Choose the word opposite in the meaning to the word.

ARBITRARY

[A] Dictatorial

[B] Autocratic

[C] High handed

[D] Mathodical

Note: In next two questions, choose the alternative which best expresses the meaning of the idiom/phrase.

90. 'A man of weight'

[A] A fat person

[B] To truthful and trustworthy man

[C] A man of importance

[D] A notorious man

91. 'A fool's paradise'

[A] Paradise of idiots

[B] A state of happiness for foolish reasons

[C] To live in the past

[D] To remain in the state of day dreaming

Note: In the next three questions, identify the correct indirect speech.

92. The Policeman said to us, 'where are you going'?

[A] The Policeman asked to us where we are going.

[B] The Policeman told us where we were going.

[C] The Policeman enquired where we were going.

[D] The Policeman said where were we going.

93. 'Call the first witness', said the Judge.

[A] The Judge asked for calling first witness.

[B] The Judge commanded them to call the first witness.

[C] The Judge said to call the first witness.

[D] The Judge requested to call for first witness.

94. She said to me, "I shall play now".

[A] She told me that she should play now.

[B] She told me that she should play then.

[C] She told me that she would play now.

[D] She told me that she would play then.

Note: In the next two questions mark the correct passive voice of the given sentence.

95. Someone gave her a bulldog

[A] She was given a bulldog

[B] A bulldog was given to her by someone.

[C] She has been given a bulldog.

[D] She is being given a bulldog by someone.

96. Mona was writing a letter to her father

[A] A letter was written to her father by Mona.

[B] A letter has been written to her father by Mona.

[C] A letter was being written by Mona to her father.

[D] A letter was written by Mona to her father.

Note: In the next three questions choose the correct option to fill in the blanks.

97. ___ rich should help ___ poor.

(1) A, a

(2) The, a

(3) The, an

(4) The, the

98. ___ pupil should obey his teacher.

[A] A

[B] The

[C] An

[D] X

99. Kalidas is ___ Shakespeare of In-

dia.

[A] a

[B] an

[C] the

[D] x

100. What do you mean by 'ACTUS CURIAE NEMINEM GRAVABIT'?

[A] A personal right of action dies with the person

[B] The law holds no man responsible for the act of God

[C] An act of the court shall prejudice no man

[D] None

Answers

No.	Ans.	No.	Ans.	No.	Ans.
1	C	47	C	93	B
2	B	48	A	94	D
3	B	49	B	95	B
4	B	50	D	96	C
5	C	51	D	97	D
6	B	52	A	98	A
7	A	53	B	99	C
8	A	54	B	100	C
9	D	55	B		
10	D	56	D		
11	C	57	D		
12	C	58	B		
13	A	59	A		
14	D	60	C		
15	C	61	C		
16	B	62	C		
17	C	63	B		
18	C	64	A		
19	B	65	D		
20	C	66	A		
21	D	67	A		
22	B	68	B		
23	C	69	C		
24	B	70	D		
25	B	71	C		
26	A	72	D		
27	C	73	B		
28	*	74	D		
29	C	75	A		
30	A	76	D		
31	D	77	C		
32	B	78	D		
33	A	79	A		
34	A	80	A		
35	D	81	D		
36	B	82	A		
37	C	83	B		

No.	Ans.	No.	Ans.
38	B	84	C
39	B	85	C
40	D	86	C
41	B	87	A
42	D	88	B
43	C	89	*
44	B	90	C
45	B	91	B
46	D	92	C

---X---

Preliminary Examination 2016

1. An arbitration agreement providing for arbitration by four arbitrators is, under the Arbitration & Conciliation Act, 1996, to be construed as an agreement for arbitration by ___.

[A] Sole arbitrator.

[B] Five arbitrators.

[C] Three arbitrators.

[D] Four arbitrators.

2. Specific performance of any contract may be ordered where ___.

[A] There exists no standard for ascertaining actual damage by non-performance of the act to be done.

[B] Compensation in money is adequate relief.

[C] The performance of the contract involves performance of continuous duty which the Court cannot supervise.

[D] The contract is by its nature determinable.

3. A partnership firm is ___.

[A] A distinct legal entity from its partners.

[B] An independent juristic person.

[C] An agent of its partners.

[D] None of the above.

4. In view of Section 105 of the Transfer of Property Act, 1882 a lease of immovable property is a transfer of ___.

[A] A right to enjoy such property in consideration of a price paid or promised or-of money, a share of crops, service or any other thing of value.

[B] An interest in specific immovable property for securing the payment of money advanced.

[C] Ownership in consideration of price paid or promised.

[D] Certain immovable property, made

voluntarily and without consideration.

5. Which Article of the Constitution of India provides that the law declared by the Supreme Court of India shall be binding on all Courts within the territory of India?

[A] Article 141

[B] Article 139-A

[C] Article 140

[D] Article 142

6. A lease of immovable property for any term exceeding one year can be made ___.

[A] Only by a registered instrument

[B] By oral agreement

[C] By oral agreement accompanied with delivery of possession

[D] Either by oral agreement or by a registered instrument

7. Provisions of Se[C] 5 of the Limitation Act, 1963 for extension of prescribed period are applicable to ___.

[A] A suit

[B] An application for execution of decree

[C] Both the above

[D] None of the above

8. A suit may be defeated due to ___.

[A] Non joinder of a proper party

[B] Misjoinder of a necessary party

[C] Non joinder of a necessary party.

[D] Misjoinder of a proper party.

9. Communication of acceptance is complete as against the proposer ___.

[A] When it comes to the knowledge of the proposer.

[B] When it is put in the course of transmission to the proposer so as to be out of power of the acceptor.

[C] When the acceptance is communicated to the proposer.

[D] All the above.

10. The Commissioner appointed under the provisions of Order XVIII of the Code of Civil Procedure for the purposes of recording of evidence cannot ___.

[A] Re-examine a witness

[B] Decide objections raised during the recording of evidence

[C] None of the above

[D] Both (1) & (2)

11. 'Premises' under the Rajasthan Rent Control Act, 2001 does not include ___.

[A] Out house appurtenant to a building

[B] Accommodation in a hostel

[C] Both (1) & (2)

[D] None of the above

12. 'Dominant heritages' under the Easements Act, 1882 means ___.

[A] The Land for the beneficial enjoyment of which the right exists

[B] The land on which the liability is imposed

[C] Both (1) & (2)

[D] Neither (1) nor (2)

13. 'Lok Adalats' are organised under which legislation?

[A] Motor Vehicles Act, 1988.

[B] The Legal Services Authorities Act, 1987

[C] Code of Civil Procedure, 1908

[D] None of the above

14. The Indian Evidence Act, 1872 applies to ___.

[A] all judicial proceedings in or before any Court

[B] affidavits presented to any Court or Officer

[C] proceedings before an Arbitrator

[D] all the above

15. The Hindu Marriage Act, 1955 is not applicable to ___.

[A] a follower of the Brahmo Samaj

[B] the person, who is a Sikh by religion

[C] any person, who is a convert to the Hindu religion

[D] the members of any Scheduled Tribe

16. The special provisions as to payment of compensation on structured formula basis under the Motor Vehicles Act, 1988 are contained in ___.

[A] Section 140

[B] Section 163

[C] Section 163-A

[D] Section 166

17. The Negotiable Instrument Act, 1881 provides for making which of the following presumptions as special rule of evidence, until the contrary is proved ___.

[A] that every negotiable instrument bearing a date was not made or drawn on such date

[B] that every transfer of negotiable instrument was not made before its maturity

[C] that a lost promissory note, bill of exchange or cheque was duly stamped

[D] all the above

18. A document registered under the Registration Act, 1908 operates ___.

[A] from the time of its registration

[B] from the time from which it would have commenced to operate, if no registration was required

[C] at the choice of executants

[D] all the above

19. Under the Rajasthan Tenancy Act, 1955, the sale, gift or bequest of Khatedari interests by a member of the Scheduled Caste in favour of a person, who is not a member of Scheduled Caste shall be ___.

[A] valid

[B] void

[C] voidable

[D] voidable at the instance of transferor.

20. Appeals from original decrees under the Rajasthan Tenancy Act, 1955 is provided under ___.

[A] Section 223

[B] Section 224

[C] Section 225

[D] Section 229.

21. If an instrument comes within several descriptions in the Schedule to the Rajasthan Stamp Act, 1998, where the duties chargeable are different, stamp duty is chargeable ___.

[A] with the lowest of such duties

[B] with the highest of such duties

[C] at the choice of the executants

[D] none of the above.

22. An instrument chargeable with the duty under the Rajasthan Stamp Act, 1998, unless such instrument is duly stamped ___.

[A] cannot be admitted in evidence for any purpose

[B] can be acted upon

[C] can be registered or authenticated

[D] all the above.

23. Under the provisions of Rajasthan Agricultural Credit Operations (Removal of Difficulties) Act, 1974, the prescribed authority on the application of a bank cannot make an order against ___.

[A] the agriculturist, who has availed financial assistance

[B] heirs or legal representative of the agriculturist

[C] Guarantor of the agriculturist

[D] tenant of the agriculturist

24. In a suit for partition and separate possession of joint family property or property owned jointly or in common by a plaintiff who is in joint possession of such property, if the value of plaintiffs share exceeds Rs.10,000/-, the Court fees payable in Rajasthan would be ___.

[A] computed on the market value of the plaintiffs share of the property

[B] computed on half of the market value of the plaintiffs share

[C] fixed Court fee of Rs.200/-

[D] computed on market value of the entire property

25. Which provision of the Rajasthan Court Fees and Suits Valuation Act, 1961 provides for refund of full amount of fee where a suit is settled by any one of the modes provided under Section 89 of the Code of Civil Procedure?

[A] Section 63

[B] Section 65-A

[C] Section 65-B

[D] Section 68

26. Under the provisions of Hindu Succession Act, 1956, any property inherited by a female Hindu from her father or mother shall devolve, in absence of any son or daughter of the deceased (including the children of any predeceased son or daughter) ___.

[A] Upon the heirs referred to in Section 15 (1) of the Act

[B] Upon the heirs of deceased female Hindu's father

[C] Upon the heirs of deceased female Hindu's husband

[D] None of the above

27. In which of the following cases has the Supreme Court ruled that under the Muslim Law a gift of immovable property fulfilling essential ingredients of a valid gift i.e., declaration of gift by donor, acceptance of gift by donee and delivery of possession, even if reduced into writing does not require compulsory registration?

[A] Hafeeza Bibi and others vs. Shaikh Far id & others, (2011) 5 SCC 654

[B] Abdul Basil vs. Moh[D] Abdul Kadir Chaudhary & others, (2014) 10 SCC 754

[C] Abdul Gani Bhat vs. Is lamia College Governing Board, (2011)12 SCC 640

[D] None of the above

28. Part IX-B of the Constitution of India containing Articles 243ZH to 243ZT pertaining to the Cooperative Societies was inserted by ___.

[A] Constitution (Seventy Third Amendment) Act, 1992

[B] Constitution (Ninety Seventh Amendment) Act, 2011

[C] Constitution (Ninety First Amendment) Act, 2003

[D] Constitution (Ninety Fifth Amendment) Act, 2010

29. Whether a valid adoption under the Hindu Adoption & Maintenance Act, 1956, can be cancelled by the adoptive father or mother or any other person?

[A] Yes

[B] No

[C] Only by adoptive mother

[D] None of the above.

30. Under which provision of the Rajasthan Land Revenue Act, 1956, power to stay execution of orders of lower Court, has been conferred on the appellate authority?

[A] Section 151

[B] Section 41

[C] Section 81

[D] Section 75.

31. Can a civil Court adjudicate in a civil suit, upon any question relating to registration of a person in an electoral roll for a constituency, under the Rajasthan Panchayati Raj Act, 1994?

[A] Yes

[B] No

[C] Both [A] and [B]

[D] None of the above.

32. Which provision of the Rajasthan Municipalities Act, 2009 deals with suits against Municipality or its officers?

[A] Section 302

[B] Section 304

[C] Section 182

[D] Section 199.

33. Which of the following Statutes regulates the amount of legal practitioner's fee to be taxed as costs under a decree or order of a Court?

[A] Code of Civil Procedure, 1908

[B] Rajasthan Court Fee & Suit Valuation Act, 1961

[C] General Rules (Civil), 1986

[D] Income Tax Act, 1961.

34. In the event of death of the person referred to in sub-clause (i) of Section 2 (i) of the Rajasthan Rent Control Act, 2001, in case of premises let out for residential purposes, who of the following ordinarily residing with the tenant as member of his family upto his death shall be included within the definition of tenant?

[A] surviving spouse, son, daughter, brother, sister, mother, father, grandfather and grand mother

[B] surviving spouse, son, daughter, brother, sister, mother and father

[C] surviving spouse, son, daughter, mother and father

[D] surviving spouse, son and daughter

35. The authority competent under Rajasthan Tenancy Act, 1955 to decide a dispute about ownership of a tree and a right to remove it is ___.

[A] Patwari

[B] SadarKanungo

[C] Tehsildar

[D] Sub-Divisional Officer

36. Which of the following statements is not correct ___.

[A] In a criminal act done by several persons in furtherance of common intention of all, each them will be held liable for that act.

[B] In an act done by several persons, the act being criminal only by reason of its being done with criminal knowledge or intention, all persons joining in the act, irrespective of such knowledge or intention, will be held liable for that act.

[C] In an offence done by means of several acts, all the persons intentionally cooperating in that act by doing any of those acts, will be held liable for that offence.

[D] In a criminal act done by several persons, all may be held liable for different offences by means of that act.

37. 'A', a public servant, having charge of translation of a document, makes an incorrect translation of a document with an intent to cause injury to 'B'. The offence committed by 'A' is ___.

[A] Non-Cognizable.

[B] Non-Bailable.

[C] Non-Compoundable.

[D] All of the above.

38. 'A' & 'B' orally agree to sell an estate. 'A' dishonestly induces 'B' to make advance payment of Rs.5 lacs and make final payment at the execution of conveyance. 'B' pays advance amount. Later on, at the request of 'B' to execute the conveyance, 'A' denies the agreement as well as the receipt of any amount. What offence has been committed by 'A'?

[A] Offence under Section 403 Indian Panel Code.

[B] Offence under Section 406 Indian Panel Code.

[C] Offence under Section 420 Indian Panel Code.

[D] Offence under Sections 420 & 465 Indian Panel Code.

39. 'A' & 'B' are good friends. 'A' proposes 'B' for marriage, but she denies 'A', in suspicion of B's love affair with somebody else, monitors the use mobile phone and email account by 'B'. What offence has been committed 'A'?

[A] Outrage the modesty.

[B] Voyeurism.

[C] Stalking.

[D] None of the above.

40. Which of the following case upheld the constitutionality of Section 499 & 500 of the Indian Penal Code?

[A] Subramanian Swamy vs. Union of India, Ministry of Law &Ors., 2016 (2) MLJ (Crl) 542

[B] Jacob Mathew vs. State of Punjab & Anr., (2005) 6 SCC 1

[C] Brij Bhushan vs. State of Delhi, AIR 1952 SC 329

[D] Manoj Narula vs. Union of India, (2014) 9 SSC 1.

41. The Court, after the commencement of prosecution evidence, allows the Assistant Public Prosecutor to withdraw the prosecution. The accused shall be ___.

[A] Released.

[B] Discharged.

[C] Acquitted.

[D] None of the above.

42. Which of the statement is correct?

Statement A – Bail granted under Section 167 (2) of the Code of Criminal Procedure, 1973 has same incidents as bail granted under Chapter XXXIII of the Code.

Statement B – Bail granted under Section 167 (2) of the Code of Criminal Procedure, 1973 cannot be cancelled under Section 437 (5) of the Code.

[A] Statement A is correct.

[B] Statement B is correct.

[C] Both the statements are correct.

[D] Both the statements are incorrect.

43. Any Court may take cognizance of an offence after expiry of the period of limitation, if it is satisfied on the facts and circumstances of the case that ___.

[A] An attempt has been made to explain the delay.

[B] It is necessary so to do in the interest of justice.

[C] The State Government has given instructions for taking such cognizance.

[D] In [A] and [B] both the conditions.

44. On a declaration of forfeiture of a

book by the State Government under Section 95 of Code of Criminal Procedure, the application to set aside lies to the ___.

[A] District Magistrate.

[B] Chief Judicial Magistrate.

[C] District & Sessions Judge.

[D] High Court.

45. Which of the following is correct?

[A] A person arrested by police officer without warrant shall be taken before a Magistrate without unnecessary delay.

[B] The detention of a person in police custody arrested without warrant, cannot exceed twenty-four hours even by a special order of Magistrate, excluding the time necessary for journey from place of arrest to the Magistrate's Court.

[C] The police officer shall discharge the person arrested of bailable offence without any bond or bail.

[D] All of the above.

46. The effect of error in stating the required particulars in the charge, shall be regarded material under which of the following circumstances ___.

[A] When co-accused dies.

[B] When the accused is misled by the error.

[C] When a material witness becomes hostile.

[D] When the accused is declared absconded.

47. Under Section 428 of Code of Criminal Procedure, which of the following period of detention undergone by the accused shall be set-off against the sentence of imprisonment in a case ___.

[A] Period of detention undergone in default of payment of fine.

[B] Period of detention undergone during investigation and trial of that case.

[C] Period of detention undergone during investigation and trial of a similar case.

[D] All of the above.

48. During the course of trial of a murder case, which of the following may be proved?

[A] Statement of confession of accused made in police custody during investigation.

[B] Recovery of the weapon of offence on basis of statement made by accused during investigation of another case.

[C] After recovery of dead body, the statement of accused as to the place where he threw the dead body.

[D] None of the above.

49. Which of the following statement is not correct?

[A] The non-examination of the doctor endorsing the dying declaration, does not always affect the evidentiary value of the dying declaration

[B] Non-signing of the dying declaration by a literate declarant unable to sign, does not render the veracity of dying declaration doubtful

[C] When the relatives of the declarant are present during dying declaration, the dying declaration would not be relevant

[D] The statements recorded in F.I.R. may be treated as dying declaration.

50. The report of a Medical Officer stating the injuries of the victim is ___.

[A] Conclusive in nature

[B] Relevant and admissible in evidence

[C] Irrelevant

[D] Substantive piece of evidence.

51. Under which of the following conditions, a leading question may be asked during examination-in-chief with the permission of the Court?

[A] In matters which are disputed or not introductory

[B] When matter in question is sufficiently proved

[C] Under both of the above conditions

[D] Under none of the above conditions.

52. Which of the statement is correct?

Statement A – The presumption under Section 113-A of Indian Evidence Act is not attracted if the marriage took place more than seven years prior to the suicide of woman, even if the cruelty is established by prosecution.

Statement B – By the introduction of Section 113-A of Indian Evidence Act, the prosecution is not required to prove the facts beyond reasonable doubt against the accused.

[A] Statement A

[B] Statement B

[C] Both statements A & B

[D] None of the statements.

53. During examination-in-chief of a case under Section 325 of Indian penal Code, the victim denies the prosecution case. Under what provision of Indian Evidence Act, the victim may be asked leading questions by the Public Prosecutor?

[A] Section 139

[B] Section 144

[C] Section 154

[D] Section 165

54. Which of the statement is correct?

Statement A – If an alteration to the electronic signature made after affixing such signature, is not detectable, then for the purpose of authentication, such electronic signature is reliable.

Statement B – During formation of a contract, the communication of proposals is expressed through electronic record. In such a case, that electronic record solely does not render the contract unenforceable.

[A] Statement A is correct

[B] Statement B is correct

[C] Both Statements are correct.

[D] Both Statements are incorrect.

55. The offence of theft of electricity is committed, if ___.

[A] the meter is dishonestly tampered with.

[B] The meter is dishonestly moved from one place to another without consent of owner

[C] The meter is dishonestly stored without consent of the owner

[D] All the above.

56. A material alteration in a negotiable instrument without the consent of the endorser, renders the negotiable instrument as ___.

[A] Voidable

[B] Void

[C] Invalid

[D] None of the above.

57. Which of the statement is correct?

Statement A – On failure to observe any of the conditions of the bond entered under Section 4 of the Probation of Offenders Act, 1958, the Court is at discretion to sentence the offender for the original offence, or to impose a penalty upto rupees fifty in case of first failure.

Statement B- An offender, above the age of twenty-one years, cannot be granted probation under Sections 3 & 4 of the Probation of Offenders Act, 1958.

Statement C – On failure of the offender to enter a fresh bond on an order of Court under Section 8 of the Probation of Offenders Act, 1958, the Court shall not sentence him for the offence of which he was found guilty.

Statement D – The amount of compensation imposed on the offender under Section 5 of the Probation of Offenders Act, 1958 can be recovered as fine in accordance with the provisions of Code of Criminal Procedure.

[A] Statements A & B

[B] Statements B & C

[C] Statements C & D

[D] Statements D & A.

58. Who of the following have powers to frame rules under Section 17 of the Probation of Offenders Act, 1958?

[A] State Government with the approval of Central Government

[B] Central Government with the consent of State Government

[C] High Court

[D] All the above.

59. Who of the following on acting in good faith are protected from prosecution under Section 84 of the Information Technology Act, 2000?

[A] The Subscriber

[B] The Controller

[C] The Originator

[D] All the above.

60. The Protection of Women from Domestic Violence Act, 2005 extends to whole of India, except ___.

[A] State of Jammu & Kashmir.

[B] State of Nagaland.

[C] Tribal areas of Assam as referred to in paragraph 20 of the sixth schedule to the Constitution.

[D] All the above.

61. A Magistrate directing the matter to be referred for counseling under Se[C] 14 of the Protection of Women from Domestic Violence Act, 2005, will fix the next date for hearing ___.

[A] After a period of two months.

[B] Within a period not exceeding two months.

[C] After a period of three months.

[D] After a period of four months.

62. An appeal to High Court against the judgment of special Court established under the Scheduled Castes and the Scheduled Tribes (Prevention of Atrocities) Act, 1989 should be preferred ___.

[A] Within a period of ninety days.

[B] Within a period of sixty days.

[C] Within a period of thirty days.

[D] Within a period of one hundred and twenty days.

63. In the prosecution for an offence of intentionally insulting the member of Scheduled Caste at a marriage function, it is proved that the victim is the neighbour of accused and they had good relations for past ten years, then what shall the Court presume?

[A] That accused has caused mental agony to victim.

[B] That accused was aware of victim's caste.

[C] Both of the above.

[D] That accused has promoted ill-will against members of Scheduled Castes.

64. A blood-stained shirt is produced in defence evidence by the accused. Which of the following exhibit will be marked on it?

[A] Exhibit P-1

[B] Exhibit D-1

[C] Exhibit Article-1

[D] Exhibit Article A-1

65. In a criminal case, the accused has been acquitted under Section 380 of Indian Penal Code. The papers of the file relating to the identification of stolen property can be destroyed ___.

[A] On expiration of fifty years, reckoned from 31st December next ensuing after the order disposing of the case.

[B] On expiration of five years, reckoned from 30th June or 31st December next ensuing after the order disposing of the case.

[C] On expiration of three years, reckoned from 31st December next ensuing after the order disposing of the case.

[D] On expiration of two years, reckoned from 30th June or 31st December next ensuing after the order disposing of the case.

66. The Chief Judicial Magistrate is duty bound to inspect the Court of his subordinate Judicial Magistrate, on which of the following basis?

[A] Weekly.

[B] Quarterly.

[C] Half yearly.

[D] Yearly.

67. Under Section 2(12) of the Juvenile Justice (Care and Protection of Children) Act, 2015, "child" means a person, who has not completed ___.

[A] 21 years of age.

[B] 18 years of age.

[C] 14 years of age.

[D] 16 years of age.

68. Who shall review the pendency of cases of Juvenile Justice Board, on quarterly basis?

[A] Chief Judicial Magistrate.

[B] High Level Committee consisting of the Executive Chairperson of the State Legal Services Authority.

[C] District Magistrate.

[D] Chairperson of Human Rights Commission.

69. Which of the statement is correct?

(A) A Judicial Magistrate First Class can authorize the detention in custody, of a person accused under an offence triable by Special Court established under The Narcotic Drugs and Psychotropic Substances Act, 1985, for a period not exceeding fifteen days.

(B) The Special Court established under The Narcotic Drugs and Psychotropic Substances Act, 1985, cannot exercise the power to authorize the detention of accused in custody, as enunciated under Section 167 of Code of Criminal Procedure.

(C) The definition of 'use' under Section 2(xxviii-a) of The Narcotic Drugs and Psychotropic Substances Act, 1985, excludes personal consumption of narcotic drugs and psychotropic substances.

(D) The High Court, by special order, may constitute as many Special Courts under The Narcotic Drugs and Psychotropic Substances Act, 1985, as necessary.

Which of the above statements are correct?

[A] A & B

[B] A & C

[C] B & C

[D] C & D

70. Who of the following police officers is empowered to record statement of a child under Section 24 of the Protection of Children from Sexual Offences Act, 2012?

[A] Constable.

[B] Any woman police officer.

[C] Woman police officer not below the rank of Sub-Inspector.

[D] Woman police officer not below the rank of Deputy Superintendent of Police.

Fill in the blank with correct form of verb (Q. No.71 to 73)

71. Look, that man is___ a photo of you.

[A] takes

[B] will take

[C] took

[D] taking

72. Someone has____ my books.

[A] steal

[B] stolen

[C] stole

[D] will steal

73. Slow and steady___ the race.

[A] win

[B] will win

[C] wins

[D] won

Choose the correct passive voice of the given sentence. (Q. No.74 and 75)

74. The child broke the mirror.

[A] The mirror is broken by the child.

[B] The mirror was broken by the child.

[C] The mirror was broken.

[D] The mirror has been broken.

75. Send these letters by Registered Post.

[A] The letters are sent by Registered Post.

[B] The letters were sent by Registered Post.

[C] Let these letters be sent by Registered Post.

[D] Let these letters sent by Registered Post.

Fill in the blanks with a grammatically correct and meaningful option from those given in each question. (Q.No.76 to 79)

76. ___ small shopkeepers are finding life increasingly difficult.

[A] A

[B] An

[C] The

[D] Any

77. ____ is known about the side effects of this drug.

[A] Few

[B] Some

[C] None

[D] Little

78. He is over eighty but___ still read without glasses.

[A] used

[B] can

[C] needs

[D] must

79. We ___ pay income tax without fail.

[A] should

[B] must

[C] may

[D] need not

Choose the correct option of the following as directed against each word/phrase (Q.No.80 to 83)

80. Illegible (opposite)

[A] Lawful
[B] Easy
[C] linkable
[D] Readable

81. Liability (opposite)

[A] Treasure
[B] Debt
[C] Assets
[D] Property

82. A bone of contention (Meaning)

[A] of submission
[B] area of agreement
[C] subject of dispute
[D] subject of intention

83. The accused was hiding important evidence. (Change to Negative)

[A] The accused not hiding important evidence.
[B] The accused was hiding not important evidence.
[C] The accused was not hiding important evidence.
[D] The accused not hiding was important evidence.

Fill in the blank with most appropriate option. (Q.No.84 and 85)

84. Tigers won't attack ____ they are hungry.

[A] because
[B] if
[C] unless
[D] although

85. Trust in God ____ do the right.

[A] but
[B] and
[C] or
[D] yet

86. उत्+हार की संधि है :-

[A] उद्गार
[B] उद्हार
[C] उद्धार
[D] उधार

87. 'कामचोर' में समास है :-

[A] अपादान तत्पुरुष
[B] अव्ययी भाव
[C] करण तत्पुरुष
[D] बहुब्रीहि

88. निम्नांकित में से 'पुत्री' शब्द का पर्यायवाची नहीं है :-

[A] तनया
[B] आत्मजा
[C] दुहिता
[D] अबला

89. 'सृजन' शब्द का विलोम है :-

[A] निर्माण
[B] संहार
[C] विजन
[D] दुर्जन

90. निम्नलिखित में से शुद्ध शब्द है :-

[A] कवयित्री
[B] कवियत्री
[C] कवित्री
[D] कवियत्रि

91. इनमें से निषेधवाचक वाक्य है :-

[A] वाह ! तुमने तो कमाल कर दिया।
[B] सदा सत्य बोलो।
[C] तुमने यह पुस्तक कब खरीदी ?
[D] विद्यार्थी कक्षा में उपस्थित नहीं था।

92. निम्नांकित में से शुद्ध वाक्य है :-

[A] तुलसीदास ने रामचरितमानस का प्रणयन किया।
[B] तुलसीदास ने रामायण का प्रणयन किया।
[C] तुलसीदास ने रामचरितमानस का पारायण किया।
[D] तुलसीदास ने रामचरितमानस का संयोजन किया।

93. "उंगलियों पर नचाना" मुहावरे का अर्थ-बोधक वाक्य है :-

[A] शीला अपने पति की उंगलियों पर नाचती है।
[B] शीला अपने पति की इच्छा के अनुसार काम करती है।
[C] शीला अपने पति से अपनी इच्छा के अनुसार काम करवाती है।

[D] शीला का पति अपनी इच्छा से सारे काम करता है।

94. 'मुट्ठी गरम करना' मुहावरे का अर्थ है :-

[A] रिश्वत देना।

[B] हाथ सेकना।

[C] बुखार चढ़ना

[D] सारा शरीर गरम होना

95. किस युग्म में विलोमता नहीं है?

[A] अभिज्ञ-अनभिज्ञ

[B] वियोग-संयोग

[C] ग्राह्म-त्याज्य

[D] हर्ष-विस्मय

96. किस शब्द की वर्तनी दोषपूर्ण है ?

[A] अनुगृहीत

[B] संग्रहीत

[C] उच्छृंखल

[D] गण्यमान्य

97. सत+जन की संधि है :-

[A] सद्जन

[B] सज्जन

[C] सत्जन

[D] सजन

98. 'जानने की इच्छा रखने वाला' के लिये उपयुक्त शब्द है :-

[A] बिस्वासी

[B] सर्वज्ञ

[C] जिज्ञासु

[D] वाचाल

99. भीतर से शत्रुता और ऊपर से मीठी बात करने के भाव को व्यक्त करने वाली लोकोक्ति है:-

[A] आम के आम, गुठली के दाम।

[B] मुँह में राम, बगल में छुरी।

[C] दोनों हाथों में लड्डू।

[D] दूर के ढोल सुहावने।

100. 'जिन ढूँढा तिन पाइयाँ गहरे पानी पैठ' लोकोक्ति का अर्थ है :-

[A] बिना प्रयास के लाभ होना।

[B] काम करने में शीघ्रता करना।

[C] जो प्रत्यन करते है, वे परिश्रम का कुछ न कुछ फल अवश्य प्राप्त करते है।

[D] सांसरिकता में लिप्त रहकर ईश्वर को प्राप्त करना।

Answers

1	A	47	B	93	C
2	A	48	B	94	A
3	D	49	C	95	D
4	A	50	B	96	B
5	A	51	B	97	B
6	A	52	A	98	C
7	D	53	C	99	B
8	C	54	B	100	C
9	B	55	A		
10	B	56	B		
11	B	57	D		
12	A	58	A		
13	B	59	B		
14	A	60	A		
15	D	61	B		
16	C	62	A		
17	C	63	B		
18	B	64	D		
19	B	65	A		
20	A	66	C		
21	B	67	B		
22	A	68	A		
23	D	69	B		
24	C	70	C		
25	C	71	D		
26	B	72	B		
27	A	73	C		
28	B	74	B		
29	B	75	C		
30	C	76	C		
31	B	77	D		
32	B	78	B		
33	C	79	B		
34	C	80	D		
35	C	81	C		

36	B	82	C
37	C	83	C
38	C	84	C
39	C	85	B
40	A	86	C
41	C	87	A
42	A	88	D
43	B	89	B
44	D	90	A
45	A	91	D
46	B	92	A

---X---

Preliminary Examinations 2017-18

1. Under provisions of Indian Succession Act, 1925 probate cannot be granted to ___.

[A] A married daughter

[B] A minor son

[C] Illegitimate child

[D] Half brother

2. Under the Hindu Adoptions and Maintenance Act, 1956 who among the following cannot be adopted ___.

[A] A Hindu

[B] Already adopted child

[C] A minor

[D] An unmarried child

3. Which of the following is not a 'Public Utility Service' for the purpose of the Legal Services Authority Act, 1987?

[A] Transport Service

[B] Postal, Telegraph or Telephone Service

[C] Insurance Service

[D] Banking Services

4. In a case where a party is added or substituted owing to assignment or devolution of any interest during the pendency of a suit, the suit shall as regard him, be deemed to have been instituted ___.

[A] On the date the suit was instituted.

[B] When he was so made a party.

[C] On the date when the application for addition or substitution is made.

[D] None of the above.

5. As per Schedule for compensation for third party fatal accidents under Section163A of the Motor Vehicles Act, 1988 the amount of compensation arrived at, inconsideration of the expenses, which a victim would have incurred, towards maintaining himself, had he been alive, shall be reduced by ___.

[A] 1/2

[B] 1/3

[C] 1/4

[D] 1/8

6. For an instrument of gift of immovable property, under the Registration Act,1908 ___.

[A] Registration is compulsory

[B] Registration is optional

[C] Registration is exempted

[D] None of the above

7. Where the time limit of a lease is of a year or number of years, which is expressed to be determinable before its expiration, and the lease omits to mention at whose option it is so terminable, who shall have such option ___.

[A] Lessee

[B] Lessor

[C] Transferor

[D] None of the above

8. The maxim 'Actus curiae neminem gravabit' means ___.

[A] An act of the Court shall prejudice no man.

[B] The act of God does wrong to no one.

[C] An act in law shall prejudice no man.

[D] An act does not constitute guilt unless done with a guilty intention.

9. Which of the following is not an internal aid to the construction or interpretation of statute?

[A] Long Title of an Act.

[B] Illustrations.

[C] Marginal Notes appended to a Section .

[D] Preamble of a statute.

10. Iddat period, in case of a divorced woman, if she is subject to menstruation, means ___.

[A] Three menstrual courses after the date of divorce.

[B] Six months period after the date of divorce.

[C] Nine menstrual courses after the date of divorce.

[D] Nine months period after the date of divorce.

11. For the purpose of Rajasthan Relief of Agricultural Indebtness Act, 1957, the term 'agriculture' does not include ___.

[A] Horticulture

[B] Breeding of cattle, camels, sheep or goats

[C] Bee farming and collecting honey

[D] Reserving of land for fodder grazing or thatching grass

12. Any person aggrieved by an order made by the Collector (Stamps) can apply for a revision under Section 65 of the Rajasthan Stamp Act, 1998, before ___.

[A] Rajasthan High Court

[B] Chief Controlling Revenue Authority

[C] Inspector General of Stamps

[D] State Government

13. The Supreme Court of India in the exercise of its jurisdiction may make such order as is necessary for doing complete justice in any case, such power is conferred by ___.

[A] Article 141 of the Constitution of India.

[B] Article 142 of the Constitution of India.

[C] Article 32 of the Constitution of India.

[D] Article 124 of the Constitution of India.

14. In which Judgment, Hon'ble Supreme Court has held Right to Privacy to be fundamental Right ___.

[A] Subramanium Swamy vs. Union of India & Ors.

[B] Lok Prahari vs. Union of India & Ors.

[C] Justice Sunanda Bhandare Founda-tion vs. Union of India & Ors.

[D] Justice K.S. Puttaswamy & Anr. vs. Union of India & Ors.

15. Which of the following is a valid defence against an action in tort?

[A] Mistake of fact

[B] Act of God

[C] Minority

[D] None of the above

16. When a marriage has been dissolved by a decree of divorce under Hindu MarriageAct,1955 and there is a right of appeal, the divorced persons may marry again ___.

[A] After expiry of 1 month from the decree of divorce.

[B] Immediately after passing of the decree of divorce.

[C] After expiry of 2 months from the decree of divorce.

[D] After expiry of the time for appealing, without any appeal having been presented.

17. Promissory estoppel is the extension of principle contained in which provision of the Evidence Act?

[A] Section 65

[B] Section 110

[C] Section 115

[D] Section 150

18. Prior to the Hindu Succession (Amendment) Act, 2005 coming into force, who amongst the following was not Class I heir of male Hindu dying intestate?

[A] Mother

[B] Widow

[C] Daughter

[D] None of the above

19. Under which provision of Rajasthan Land Revenue Act, 1956, a person without lawful authority occupying land, which is at the disposal of local authority, can be evicted ___.

[A] Section 91 of the Act

[B] Section 90-A of the Act

[C] Section 90-B of the Act

[D] Section 92 of the Act

20. 'Decree', as defined by Section 2 of

the Code of Civil Procedure, 1908 does not include ___.

[A] A preliminary decree

[B] Rejection of a plaint

[C] Determination of any question within Section 144 CPC

[D] Any order of dismissal for default

21. Against a decree passed in a suit after recording a compromise, an appeal on the ground that the compromise should not have been recorded, can be filed under ___.

[A] Section 151 CPC

[B] Order XXIII CPC

[C] Order XLII Rule 1-A CPC

[D] None of the above

22. Chapter II and III of Rajasthan Rent Control Act, 2001 applies to ___.

[A] Any premises let out to a citizen of a foreign country.

[B] Any premises belonging to or vested in a university established by any law for the time being in force.

[C] Any premises belonging to a Government Company as defined under Section617 of the Companies Act, 1956.

[D] Any premises situated in the municipal area of Jaipur City, let out for residential purposes, for a monthly rent of Rs. 8,000/-.

23. A suit against a municipality or its officers can be instituted otherwise than for the recovery of immovable property or for a declaration of title thereto ___.

[A] After six months of the accrual of cause of action.

[B] After eight months of the accrual of cause of action.

[C] Within six months next after the accrual of cause of action.

[D] None of the above.

24. The grant of and transfer of licences is governed by ___.

[A] The Transfer of Property Act, 1882.

[B] The Specific Relief Act, 1963.

[C] The Indian Contract Act, 1932.

[D] The Indian Easements Act, 1882.

25. Under Rajasthan Court fees and Suits. Valuation Act, 1961, all questions arising on a plea that the subject matter of the suit has not been properly valued or that the fee paid is not sufficient, are required to be heard and decided ___.

[A] At the final hearing of the suit.

[B] At the discretion of the trial court.

[C] Before the hearing of the suit as contemplated by Order XVIII CPC.

[D] None of the above.

26. Which of the contract is not specifically enforceable?

[A] A contract for the non-performance of which compensation in money is not an adequate relief.

[B] A contract which is in its nature determinable.

[C] A contract, the performance of which does not involve the performance of a continuous duty, which the Court can supervise.

[D] A contract which is not dependent on the personal qualification or volition of the parties.

27. The power of review on the Board of Revenue and other revenue courts is conferred by which provision of the Rajasthan Tenancy Act, 1955 ___.

[A] Section 207

[B] Section 224

[C] Section 229

[D] Section 230

28. Which of the following is not a negotiable instrument ___.

[A] Promissory note.

[B] Fixed Deposit Receipt.

[C] Bill of Exchange.

[D] A cheque.

29. Under the General Rules (Civil), 1986 all pleadings, applications and petitions filed in the course of civil judicial proceedings, shall be written in ___.

[A] Hindi

[B] English

[C] Any language specified in the Eighth Schedule of the Constitution of India

[D] None of the above

30. Under the Arbitration and Conciliation Act, 1996, in the case of interna-

tional commercial arbitration 'Court' means ___.

[A] The principal Civil Court of original jurisdiction.

[B] Small Causes Court

[C] The High Court

[D] None of the above

31. An order refusing to refer the parties to arbitration under Section 8 of the Arbitration and Conciliation Act, 1996 is appealable under ___.

[A] Section 34 of the Act.

[B] Article 227 of the Constitution of India.

[C] Section 37 of the Act.

[D] Section 11 of the Act.

32. The provisions for removal and suspension of any member or Chairperson of a Panchayati Raj Institution under the Rajasthan Panchayati Raj Act, 1994 are contained in ___.

[A] Section 119 of the Act.

[B] Section 38 of the Act.

[C] Section 117-A of the Act.

[D] Section 39 of the Act.

33. Under Section 10 of the Indian Partnership Act, 1932 every partner is under a duty ___.

[A] To render true accounts and full information.

[B] To indemnify the firm for any loss caused to it by his fraud in the conduct of the business of the firm.

[C] Not to carry on any business other than that of the firm.

[D] To be just and faithful to each other.

34. Under Sale of Goods Act, 1930, movable goods do not include ___.

[A] Stock and shares.

[B] Grass.

[C] Money.

[D] Growing crops.

35. Ina suit against a corporation, the summons may be served on ___.

[A] Any employee of the corporation.

[B] Relative of the director of the corporation.

[C] Principal officer of the corporation.

[D] None of the above.

36. The offences under Sections 66B, 66C, 66D and 66E of Information and Technology Act, 2000, are ___.

[A] Cognizable.

[B] Sessions Triable.

[C] Non-bailable.

[D] None of the above.

37. A complainant, of a Magistrate triable case instituted upon a complaint, can challenge the judgment of acquittal passed by the competent court, by filing ___.

[A] Revision in the Sessions Court.

[B] Revision in the High Court.

[C] Appeal before a Sessions Court.

[D] Application for grant of leave to appeal in the High Court.

38. An information, supplied by an accused under Section 27 of the Evidence Act, shall be recorded ___.

[A] In presence of two independent Panch witnesses.

[B] In presence of a Gazette Officer.

[C] In presence of two Police Officers.

[D] None of the above.

39. While assessing age of a person under the Juvenile Justice (care and protection of children) Act, 2015, the Court/Board is required to consider the documents/evidence in the following order of preference ___.

[A]	(i)	Birth Certificate issued by a Municipality.
	(ii)	School Certificate.
	(iii)	Ossification test report.
	(iv)	Aadhar Card.
[B]	(i)	Ossification test report
	(ii)	Birth Certificate issued by the Municipality
	(iii)	Aadhar Card
[C]	(i)	Birth Certificate issued from the school/matriculation certificate.
	(ii)	Date of birth certificate issued by the Municipality.
	(iii)	Ossification test report.
[D]		None of the above.

40. Which of the following orders may not be passed by the Juvenile Justice Board after conducting inquiry of a child in conflict with law ___.

[A] Direct the child to attend a school.

[B] Direct the child to attend a vocational training center.

[C] Sentence the child to imprisonment till he attains 18 years of age.

[D] Direct the child to perform community service.

41. A Children Court trying a child in conflict with law for a heinous offence, is not empowered to ___.

[A] Hold trial of a child as an adult.

[B] Hold inquiry of the child as a Juvenile Justice Board.

[C] Sentence the child to imprisonment for a term of 10 years.

[D] Send the child to a place of safety till he attains the age of 21 years.

42. Where, after inquiry under Section 15 of the Juvenile Justice (Care and Protection of Children) Act, 2015, the Juvenile Justice Board is satisfied that a child above 16 years of age, has committed a heinous offence and should be tried as an adult, it may ___.

[A] Commit the case to the Sessions Court concerned for trial of the child as an adult.

[B] Try the child as per the procedure provided in Cr.P.C.

[C] Return the charge-sheet to the Investigating Officer for presentation in the Court concerned.

[D] Transfer the case to the Children Court for trial of the child as an adult.

43. A private vehicle proceeding on a Highway, suspected to be carrying psychotropic drugs, may be searched by ___.

[A] A Head Constable posted in the Police Station concerned

[B] A Sub-Inspector posted in some other District

[C] The Deputy Superintendent of Police or officer-in-charge of police station of the area concerned.

[D] All of the above.

44. Before searching a suspect carrying a bag containing narcotic drugs in his hand, the Officer concerned is required to apprise him of his right to be searched in the presence of ___.

[A] A Magistrate or a Gazetted Officer.

[B] Two independent witnesses from the locality.

[C] Officer-in-charge of the Police Station of the area concerned.

[D] None of the above.

45. A vehicle, container or a receptacle used for commission of an offence punishable under the NDPS Act, 1985, shall not be liable to be confiscated ___.

[A] If the person using the same is acquitted by the Court after trial.

[B] If the prosecution fails to lead evidence about its ownership.

[C] If the owner proves that the vehicle was used in commission of the offence without his knowledge or connivance.

[D] None of the above.

46. A being the owner of a plot of land, sells the same to B through a registered sale deed in the year 2005. B however does not make full payment to A. A again sells the same land to C in the year 2010 without informing him of the earlier transaction of 2005.

Who would be the person aggrieved in these circumstances?

[A] B (the first purchaser).

[B] A (the seller).

[C] C (the subsequent purchaser)

[D] None of the above.

47. The bail application rejected by the Special Judge, 'SC/ST (Prevention of Atrocities) Act, in a case involving offence/s under the said Act, may be challenged in the High Court, by filing ___.

[A] Bail application under Section 439 Cr.P.C.

[B] Revision under Section 397 Cr.P.C.

[C] Petition under Section 482 Cr.P.C.

[D] An appeal

48. X knows that Y is a member of Scheduled Caste community. During the course of a free fight, X inflicts a grievous injury to Y by a sharp weapon. X is guilty of offence punishable under Section(s) ___.

[A] 326 IPC only.

[B] 3(2)(V) of SC/ST (Prevention of Atrocities) Act.

[C] 326 IPC and 3(2)(V) of SC/ST (Prevention of Atrocities) Act.

[D] None of the above.

49. A woman aged 30 years and her son aged 14 years, are witnesses to a murder. Their statements under Section 161 Cr.P.C. may be recorded by the Police Officer concerned at ___.

[A] The scene of the occurrence.

[B] The Women Police Station.

[C] At the Police Station where FIR is registered.

[D] The place where, such woman and her son reside.

50. In which of the following cases, the Court is required to record evidence before framing of charge?

[A] Summons trial cases.

[B] Session's trial cases.

[C] Warrant cases instituted upon a complaint.

[D] Warrant cases instituted upon a Police report.

51. Non-compliance of, which of the following orders passed under the Protection of Women from Domestic Violence Act, 2005, is an offence ___.

[A] Maintenance order.

[B] Custody order.

[C] Residence order.

[D] Protection order.

52. A woman subjected to rape, gives a statement under Section 164 Cr.P.C implicating the accused for the offence. She commits suicide sometime later but before her Statement could be recorded at the trial. Such statement recorded under Section 164 of Cr.P.C would be ___.

[A] Admissible as a substantive piece of evidence.

[B] Admissible under Section 32 of the Evidence Act.

[C] Admissible under Section 33 of the Evidence Act.

[D] Inadmissible in evidence.

53. A Court after holding trial, convicts and grants benefit of Probation of Offenders Act, 1958 to an accused. Which of the following orders is impermissible in law?

[A] Admonish the offender.

[B] Direct under Section 12 of the Act that the conviction shall not have an adverse effect on his service.

[C] Direct the offender to pay compensation and cost.

[D] Direct the offender to furnish bail and bonds to keep peace and good behaviour for three years.

54. Two friends A and B were sleeping in a room which was bolted from inside. In the morning, A is found murdered. Under which provision of the Evidence Act, prosecution can claim shifting of burden on B to prove the manner in which the murder took place ___.

[A] Section 114 of the Evidence Act.

[B] Section 103 of the Evidence Act.

[C] Section 106 of the Evidence Act.

[D] Section 101 of the Evidence Act.

55. An FIR in relation to the offence under Section 406 IPC is lodged on 1.1.2010. The Police conduct investigation and submits a negative Final Report in the Court concerned on 2.2.2012. The Court takes cognizance of the above offence on 3.3.2013. In these circumstances, which of the following is correct?

[A] The proceedings are barred by limitation.

[B] The proceedings are not barred by limitation as the offence under Section 406 IPC is a continuing offence.

[C] The proceedings are not barred by limitation as the FIR was lodged promptly.

[D] None of the above.

56. C being the wife of B, has obtained a decree of separation from the competent Court but they are still living in the same premises. B subjects C to intercourse. Their neighbour A watches the act and files an FIR. Which proposition is correct in these circumstances?

[A] B is guilty of the offence punishable under Section 376-B IPC.

[B] B is not guilty of any offence because C continues to be his legally wedded wife.

[C] A would be guilty of the offence punishable under Section 354-C IPC.

[D] None of the above.

57. 5 persons take illegal possession of a field. The owner (the complainant party) of the field collects his supporters and goes to the field for ousting the trespassers therefrom. In the free fight, which ensues, the trespassers kill one person from the complainant side. All

the accused can be convicted ___.

[A] With the aid of Section 34 of IPC.

[B] With the aid of Section 149 of IPC.

[C] For the individual injuries caused to the members of the complainant party.

[D] None of the above.

58. The Investigating Officer conducting investigation of a case under the Narcotic Drugs and Psychotropic Substances Act, 1985 collects the call details of the mobile phones held by the accused from whom, recovery of drug was affected and the conspirator, who supplied the drug. Such call details ___.

[A] Can be used as substantive evidence to prove the charge of conspiracy.

[B] Are inadmissible in evidence.

[C] Can be considered relevant only if the conversation held between the two accused is recorded and proved at the trial.

[D] None of the above.

59. In a case involving the offence punishable under Section 304 Part II of IPC, the accused, is arrested and the prosecution fails to comply with the requirements of Section 167(2) Cr.P.C The accused, who is a habitual offender, becomes entitled to compulsive bail on ___.

[A] 61st day from the date of his arrest.

[B] 91stday from the date of his arrest.

[C] The accused is not entitled to be released on compulsive bail

[D] None of the above.

60. A Patwari while preparing a revenue record, intentionally enters incorrect facts in the documents and signs & certifies the same with the intention of causing loss to the true owner of the land. The Patwari is guilty of ___.

[A] Offence of creating false/ forged documents punishable under Sections467 and 468 IPC.

[B] Offence of using a forged document punishable under Section 471 IPC.

[C] Offence of criminal breach of trust punishable under Section 406 IPC.

[D] None of the above.

61. An accused aged 20 years, having no previous criminal conduct, charged for the offence under Section 304 IPC, is convicted by the trial court. In these circumstances ___.

[A] The trial court is under a mandate of law to release the accused on probation.

[B] The trial court may release the accused on probation.

[C] The accused is not entitled to the benefit of probation because the offence is punishable with imprisonment upto 10 years.

[D] None of the above.

62. In which judgment, Hon'ble Supreme Court has laid down that the Police cannot refuse registration of an FIR on the ground of lack of jurisdiction ___.

[A] Manish Ratan vs. State of MP; 2007(1) SCC 336.

[B] Amrendu Jyoti vs. State of Chhattisgarh; 2014(6) Criminal 719

[C] Rasiklal Dalpatram Thakkar vs. State of Gujarat & Ors.; AIR 2010 SC 715

[D] Y. Abraham Ajith & Ors. vs. Inspector of Police, Chennai & Ors.: AIR 2004 SC4286

63. In which judgment, under the Negotiable Instruments Act, 1881 the Hon'ble Supreme Court held that though compounding requires consent of both the parties, but even in absence of such consent, the Court can, in the interest of justice, on being satisfied that the complainant has been duly compensated, in its discretion, close the proceedings and discharge the accused ___.

[A] Madhya Pradesh State Legal Service Authority vs. Prateek Jain; 2015(1) SCC(Cri) 211

[B] Meters and Instruments Private Limited vs. Kanchan Mehta; AIR 2017 SC4594

[C] JIK Industries Lt[D] vs. Amarlal V. Jumani & Anr.; AIR 2012 SC 1079

[D] Damodar S. Prabhu vs. Sayyed Bala Lal H.; AIR 2010 SC 1907

64. In which of the following judgments, the Hon'ble Supreme Court has laid down that the competent Magistrate can direct the Police to conduct thorough and fair investigation into an FIR ___.

[A] Hasan Bhai Wali Bhai Qureshi vs. State of Gujarat; AIR 2004 SC 2078

[B] Sakiri Vasu vs. State of U.P.; AIR 2008 SC 907

[C] Rashmi Behl vs. State of U.P. & Ors.; AIR 2015 SC 776

[D] Aziza Begum vs. Sate of Maharasthra; 2012 (2) SCC (Cri.) 61

65. In which judgment, the Hon'ble Supreme Court has laid down that a party, who is desirous of proving electronic evidence but does not have access to the device from which, the document was produced, is not required to produce and prove the certificate under Section 65-B of the Evidence Act ___.

[A] State of Delhi NCT Vs. Navjot Sandhu @ Afsan Guru; AIR 2005 SC 3826

[B] Harpal Singh @ Chhota Vs. State of Punjab; 2016(4) Crimes 154

[C] Anvar P.V. Vs. P.K.Bashir; AIR 2015 SC 180

[D] Shafi Mohd. Vs. State of Himachal Pradesh: SLP (Cri) No.3202/2017, decided on 30.1.2018

66. In which judgment, the Hon'ble Supreme Court has laid down that having taken cognizance of a case, the Magistrate cannot direct the Police to conduct further investigation ___.

[A] State of Haryana vs. Choudhary Bhajan Lal; AIR 1992 SC 604

[B] M/s. Jayanti Vitamin vs. Chaitanya Kumar; AIR 1992 SC 1930

[C] Amrutbhai Shambhubhai Patel vs. Sumanbhai Kantibhai Patel & Ors.; AIR 2017SC 774

[D] Hemant Dhasmana vs. CBI; AIR 2001 SC 2721

67. A competent Court, shall take cognizance of an offence punishable under the Electricity Act, 2003 ___.

[A] Upon a complaint in writing made by any general person.

[B] Upon an oral complaint made by a Chief Electrical Inspector.

[C] Upon a complaint in writing made by licencee or generating company.

[D] Upon none of the above.

68. Under the provisions of Protection of Children from Sexual Offences Act, 2012, can a report be published by the media, which discloses the identity of a sexually assaulted child ___.

[A] Cannot be published

[B] Can be published in public interest.

[C] Can be published, if permitted by competent Special Court.

[D] None of the above.

69. Police Officer, in all cases where the arrest of a person is not required under Section 41 (1) of Cr.P.C., against whom, a reasonable complaint has been made that he has committed a cognizable offence, then ___.

[A] Police Officer may without an order from a Magistrate and without a warrant, arrest such person.

[B] Police Officer shall issue a notice directing that person to appear before him or at such other place, as may be specified in the notice.

[C] Police Officer while recording his reasons in writing, can arrest such person.

[D] Police Officer can do all the above.

70. If a Magistrate of a Court, requiring to examine at his private residence, a record of a case in his Court, he ___.

[A] May take charge of such record without any permission.

[B] May take charge of such record with prior permission of concerned District &Sessions Judge.

[C] May take charge of such record with prior permission of concerned High Court.

[D] Cannot take charge of such record.

71. 'अभ्यन्तर' शद्ध में कौनसी संधि प्रयुक्त हुई है ?

[A] यण संधि ।

[B] वृद्धि संधि ।

[C] गुण संधि ।

[D] दीर्घ संधि ।

72. जिस समास में प्रथम पद संख्यावाचक अर्थात गणनाबोधक होता है तथा दूसरा पद प्रधान होता है, उसे कहते हैं :-

[A] द्वंद्व समास

[B] द्विगु समास

[C] तत्पुरुष समास

[D] कर्मधारय समास

73. निम्नलिखित में से एक से अधिक उपसर्ग वाला शब्द चुनिए:-

[A] निर्विरोध

[B] अंतरराष्ट्रीय

[C] संक्षेपण

[D] परिमार्जन

74. इनमें से कौनसा शब्द पर्वत का सही पर्याय नहीं है ?

[A] भूधर

[B] शैल

[C] वर्त्य

[D] नग

75. निम्नलिखित शब्द-युग्मों में से विलोम शब्द का सही विकल्प बताइए:-

[A] जड़-चेतना

[B] निर्दय--सदाशय

[C] शुभ-लाभ

[D] नैसर्गिक-कृत्रिम

76. 'जिजीविषा' शब्द का अर्थ प्रकट करने वाला वाक्यांश है:-

[A] जानने की इच्छा

[B] ग्रहण करने की इच्छा

[C] किसी को जीतने की इच्छा

[D] जिंदा रहने की इच्छा

77. निम्नलिखित में से शुद्ध शब्द बताइए :-

[A] ज्योत्सना

[B] द्वारका

[C] मंत्रीमंडल

[D] हरितिमा

78. निम्न शब्द-समूहों में वचन की दृष्टि से कौनसा विकल्प सही नहीं है?

एकवचन - बहुवचन

[A] लता - लताएँ

[B] गाथा - गाथाएँ

[C] क्षमा - क्षमाएँ

[D] कन्या - कन्याएँ

79. निम्नलिखित में से कौनसा वाक्य शुद्ध है?

[A] मैं मंगलवार के दिन व्रत रखता हूँ

[B] आपके प्रश्न का समाधान मेरे पास है

[C] वह उसका चश्मा भूल गया

[D] आज उसके रहस्य का राज खुल गया

80. LICENCE शब्द का सही हिंदी रूपांतरण बताइए:-

[A] पट्टा

[B] अनुज्ञप्ति

[C] अनुमति पत्र

[D] प्रत्याभूति

81. निम्न में से सही विकल्प बताइए:-

[A] HONORARIUM — मानदेय

[B] APPROVAL — संस्तुति

[C] ACKNOWLEDGEMENT — कार्यवाही

[D] OATH — संदेश

82. 'खूब मन लगाकर पढ़ो ताकि परीक्षा में प्रथमभ आओ' वाक्य में प्रयुक्त अव्यय कौनसा है?

[A] खूब

[B] ताकि

[C] में

[D] आओ

83. लिखते हुए किसी शब्द के छूट जाने पर उसे लिखने के लिए किस चिह्न का प्रयोग करते हैं:-

[A] कोष्ठक चिन्ह

[B] उद्धरण चिह्न

[C] अल्प विराम चिह्न

[D] हंसपद चिह्न

84. 'खग जाने खग ही की भाषा' का अभिप्राय है:-

[A] चालाक ही चालाक की बात समझ सकता है

[B] विद्वान् सभी भाषाओं का ज्ञाता होता है

[C] पक्षी ही पक्षी की बोली जानता है

[D] फालतू आदमी फालतू बात ही करता है

85. 'किये हुए उपकार को न मानने वाला' कहलाता है:-

[A] कृतज्ञ

[B] कृतार्थ

[C] कृतघ्न

[D] कुलांगार

86. Choose the correct alternative that expresses the 'Future Perfect' tense.

[A] She will be completing her assign-ment.

[B] She will complete her assignment.

[C] She is completing her assignment.

[D] She will have completed her assignment by midnight.

87. 'He has just___ out of the room in a rage.'

Supply the correct form of verb from the given alternatives.

[A] Flinged

[B] Flunged

[C] Flung

[D] Flanged

88. ____ man is the only animal that uses fire.

[A] X

[B] The

[C] A

[D] An

89. He has hardly ___ money for his survival.

[A] Few

[B] A few

[C] Some

[D] Any

90. 'As the enemy was closing in, we decided to stay away.'

The phrase 'close in' means ___.

[A] Shoot out

[B] Go away

[C] Come nearer

[D] Win

91. When someone says, "I am out of the woods now", he means that ___.

[A] He has come out of the forest.

[B] He has destroyed all the woods.

[C] He is no longer in danger or difficulty.

[D] He does not want to live in forest.

92. Choose the correct passive voice of the following sentence.

'We must not look down on the poor.'

[A] The poor must not looked down by us.

[B] The poor must not be looked on by us.

[C] The poor must not looked down on by us.

[D] The poor must not be looked down on by us.

93. Identify the sentence which is not written in passive voice ___.

[A] Utmost care has to be taken.

[B] Being a student, you must work hard.

[C] He was being chased.

[D] The case has been set aside by the court.

94. Complete the following sentence with the correct coordinating conjunction.

"I had studied a lot, ___ I did really well on the test."

[A] So

[B] For

[C] But

[D] Yet

95. Complete the following sentence with correct subordinating conjunction.

'You can only play outside ___ your father gets home.'

[A] Whereas

[B] Until

[C] In case

[D] Because

96. She said, "Merry Christmas!"

Which of the following is the correct indirect speech of the above statement?

[A] She told me Merry Christmas.

[B] She said that Christmas was Merry.

[C] She wished me a Merry Christmas.

[D] She called me a Merry Christmas.

97. Which of the following sentences uses the modal 'would' to express a wish or desire?

[A] Would that had made contact with him before his departure.

[B] Would you mind opening the window?

[C] She would look at the stars for hours when she was a child.

[D] She would not follow my advice.

98. Which of the following sentences expresses suggestion?

[A] Will I close the door?

[B] Shall I close the door?

[C] May I close the door?

[D] Could I close the door?

99. Pick the correct synonym for the word 'robust'.

[A] Strong

[B] Frail

[C] Infirm

[D] Noxious

100. Choose the word which is opposite in meaning to the word "Veracity".

[A] Truthfulness

[B] Probity

[C] Mendacity

[D] Integrity

Answers

1	*	38	D	75	D		
2	B	39	C	76	D		
3	D	40	C	77	B		
4	A	41	*	78	C		
5	B	42	D	79	*		
6	A	43	D	80	B		
7	A	44	D	81	A		
8	A	45	C	82	*		
9	C	46	C	83	D		
10	A	47	D	84	A		
11	C	48	C	85	C		
12	B	49	D	86	D		
13	B	50	C	87	C		
14	D	51	D	88	A		
15	B	52	D	89	D		
16	D	53	B	90	C		
17	C	54	C	91	C		
18	D	55	D	92	D		
19	A	56	C	93	B		
20	D	57	C	94	A		
21	C	58	C	95	B		
22	D	59	A	96	C		
23	C	60	D	97	A		
24	D	61	*	98	B		
25	C	62	C	99	A		
26	B	63	B	100	C		
27	C	64	B				
28	B	65	D				
29	A	66	C				
30	C	67	C				
31	C	68	C				
32	B	69	B				
33	B	70	A				
34	C	71	A				
35	C	72	B				
36	A	73	A				
37	D	74	C				

---X---

Preliminary Examination, 2018-19

1. Under the provisions of Rajasthan Rent Control Act, 2001, a landlord has a right to inspect the premises let out by him. Which of the following statement with reference to the inspection is incorrect?

[A] The inspection can be done during day time only.

[B] A prior intimation of at least three days to the tenant is necessary

[C] Such inspection can be carried out not more than once in three months

[D] None of the above.

2. A suit alleging 'public nuisance' can be instituted by ___.

(A) Advocate General of the State.

(B) By two or more persons, who have suffered the damage.

(C) By two or more persons, with the leave of the Court, even though no special damage has been caused to them.

(D) A member of the local body.

Which of the following combination is correct?

[A] (A) & (B)

[B] (A) & (C)

[C] (B) & (D)

[D] (C) & (D)

3. Ashok lets a house to Bharat for five years. Bharat underlets the house to Kishore at a monthly rent of Rs. 2,000/. The five years expire, but Kishore continues in possession of the house and pays the rent to Ashok. What is the status of Kishore?

[A] Tenant holding over

[B] Trespasser

[C] Possession is unauthorized

[D] None of the above

4. The executive power of the State is vested in ___.

[A] Chief Secretary of the State.

[B] Chief Minister of the State.

[C] Chief Executive Officer.

[D] The Governor.

5. Decree for payment of money passed against a woman cannot be executed ___.

[A] by proceeding against her legal representation, if she dies

[B] by attachment and sale of her property

[C] by appointing a receiver

[D] by her arrest and detention in prison

6. "Where a plaintiff omits to sue in respect of, or intentionally relinquishes am portion of his claim, he shall not afterwards sue in respect of the portion so omitted or relinquished". The genesis of this principle lies in ___.

[A] Section 115 of the Indian Evidence Act, 1872

[B] Section 11 of the Code of Civil Procedure, 1908

[C] Order II Rule 2 of the Code of Civil Procedure, 1908

[D] Order I Rule 2 of the Code of Civil Procedure, 1908

7. On rejection of plaint under provisions of Order VII Rule 11 Code of Civil Procedure, 1908, presenting of a fresh plaint in respect of the same cause of action, is ___.

[A] Barred by principles of Res judicata.

[B] On its own force, does not preclude the plaintiff from presenting a fresh plaint.

[C] Barred under Order XXIII.

[D] None of the above

8. 'Rule in Heydon's case' is also known as ___.

[A] Purposive construction.

[B] Casus omissus.

[C] Literal construction.

[D] Harmonious construction.

9. The Indian Evidence Act, 1872 applies to ___.

[A] Proceedings before an arbitrator.

[B] Departmental proceedings.

[C] Judicial proceedings before courts.

[D] None of the above.

10. Who amongst the following cannot be appointed as Advocate General?

[A] An advocate of 66 years of age.

[B] An advocate who has not practiced in such State.

[C] An advocate having 07 years of practice at Bar.

[D] All of the above.

11. Which of the following statement is incorrect?

[A] An agreement made without consideration is void irrespective of the circumstances.

[B] Every agreement in restraint of marriage of any person, other than minor, is void.

[C] Every agreement by which anyone is restrained from exercising a lawful profession, trade or business of any kind, is to that extent void.

[D] Agreements, the meaning of which is not certain or capable of being made certain, are void.

12. For the purpose of Limitation Act, 1963, a suit in the case of a pauper, is instituted ___.

[A] When the plaint is presented to the proper office

[B] When application for leave to sue as a pauper is made

[C] When the application seeking leave to sue as a pauper is granted.

[D] None of the above.

13. Which of the following contracts can be enforced?

[A] A contract for the non-performance of which compensation is an adequate relief.

[B] A contract which is in its nature determinable.

[C] A contract the performance whereof involves the performance of a continuous duty.

[D] Purchase of a share of a partner in a firm.

14. Section 43 of the Transfer of Property Act, 1882, which deals with transfer by unauthorized person who subsequently acquires interest in immovable property transferred, underlines doctrine of ___.

[A] Actionable claims.

[B] Estoppel by deed.

[C] Estoppel by election.

[D] Right of pre-emption.

15. Which provision in Code of Civil Procedure, 1908 bars entertainment of application to review an order made on an application for a review or a decree or order passed or made on a review ___.

[A] Section 11

[B] Section 10

[C] Order XLVI Rule 9

[D] Order IX Rule 9

16. Which provision of Rajasthan Rent Control Act. 2001 deals with permission to enter into the limited period tenancy and for grant of certificate for recovery of possession?

[A] Section 6

[B] Section 7

[C] Section 8

[D] Section 9

17. What is the remedy available to an aggrieved party against a final order passed by the Rent Tribunal constituted under the Rajasthan Rent Control Act, 2001?

[A] Writ petition under Article 226/227 of the Constitution of India

[B] Appeal to High Court under Section 96 of the Code of Civil Procedure.

[C] Appeal under Section 19 (6) of the Rajasthan Rent Control Act, 2001.

[D] No remedy, order is final.

18. 'A' and 'B' contract that 'A' shall build a house for 'B' at a fixed price. The order in which reciprocal promises are to be performed was not fixe[D] What shall be the order of performance?

[A] A's promise to build the house must be performed before B's promise to pay for the house.

[B] B's promise to pay for the house must be performed before A's promise to build the house.

[C] A & B should perform their promise simultaneously.

[D] None of the above.

19. The rule of construction 'Nocsitur a sociis' means ___.

[A] The meaning of a word is to be judged by the company it keeps.

[B] To reconcile incompatibility between the specific and general words.

[C] No word in a statute is superfluous.

[D] None of the above.

20. Which of the Acts & Regulations cannot be declared unconstitutional by High Courts and Supreme Court?

[A] Acts & Regulations concerning persons from Scheduled Castes & Scheduled Tribes.

[B] Acts & Regulations concerning Parliament & its members.

[C] Acts & Regulations enlisted in Schedule VII of the Constitution.

[D] Acts & Regulations enlisted in Schedule IX of the Constitution.

21. Special provisions as to evidence relating to electronics record were inserted in the Indian Evidence Act, 1872 ___.

[A] In the form of Section 65-B w.e.f. 17. 10.2000.

[B] In the form of Section 68-B w.e.f. 17.10.2000.

[C] In the form of Section 65-B w.e.f. 12.08.2002.

[D] In the form of Section 68-B w.e.f. 12.08.2002.

22. A mutual mistake of the parties in an instrument, which does not express their real intention, can be got rectified by either party to the instrument ___.

[A] By instituting a suit under Registration Act, 1908.

[B] By filing an application under Section 152 of the Code of Civil Procedure,1908.

[C] By instituting a suit under Section 26 of the Specific Relief Act, 1963.

[D] Cannot be rectified.

23. Power to amend the issue or frame additional issues prior to passing of a decree vest in a Court by virtue of which provision of the Code of Civil Procedure, 1908?

[A] Order XIV Rule 1

[B] Order XIV Rule 5

[C] Order XIV Rule 6

[D] Section 151

24. A Judge of a High Court may by writing under his hand, resign his office.

To whom such resignation should be addressed?

[A] Chief Justice of the High Court.

[B] Chief Justice of India.

[C] Governor of the State.

[D] President of India.

25. In case of repugnancy between the law made by the Parliament and the law made by the State Legislature, with respect to any matter enumerated in concurrent list ___.

[A] By virtue of Article 246 of Constitution of India, law made by Parliament shall prevail.

[B] by virtue of Article 246 of Constitution of India, law made by State Legislature shall prevail.

[C] by virtue of Article 254 of Constitution of India, law made by Parliament shall prevail.

[D] by virtue of Article 254 of Constitution of India, law made by State Legislature shall prevail.

26. Which provision of the Constitution of India abolished 'Untouchability' and forbids its practice in any form?

[A] Article 14

[B] Article 15

[C] Article 16

[D] Article 17

27. Complete the statement.

A Court cannot issue commission ___.

[A] to examine any person.

[B] to make a partition.

[C] to collect evidence.

[D] to examine or adjust accounts.

28. Which of the provision of the Code of Civil Procedure, 1908 provides that the objection regarding territorial or pecuniary jurisdiction has to be raised at the first available opportunity?

[A] Section 10

[B] Section 11

[C] Section 20

[D] Section 21

29. The words "SOCIALIST SECULAR" were inserted in the Preamble of the Constitution by which constitutional amendment?

[A] Forty First amendment.

[B] Forty Second amendment.

[C] Forty Fourth amendment.

[D] Forty Sixth amendment.

30. Which provision of the Constitution confers upon a High Court the power to punish for contempt of itself?

[A] Article 215

[B] Article 217

[C] Article 225

[D] Article 226

31. Which of the following facts are required to be proved?

[A] All law in force in the territory of India.

[B] Public festivals and holidays notified in official Gazette.

[C] The Rules of the road

[D] None of the above.

32. The period of limitation for filing a suit to set aside transfer of property made by a guardian of a ward, by the ward's legal representative, when the ward dies before attaining majority, is ___.

[A] Three years from the date when the ward would have become major.

[B] Three years from the date when such fact comes to the notice of the legal representative.

[C] Three years from the date of death of the ward.

[D] Twelve years from the date of the transfer.

33. Under which provision of Code of Civil Procedure, restoration or setting aside of orders passed ex parte can be sought regarding an application filed under Order XXI of CPC which has been dismissed for non-appearance or decided ex parte?

[A] Order IX Rule 13

[B] Order XXI Rule 58

[C] Order XXI Rule 106

[D] Order XXI Rule 100

34. The period of limitation for filing a Suit relating to tort against one who, having right to use property for specific Purpose, perverts it to other purpose is ___.

[A] One year from the date the Perversion first becomes known to the person injured,

[B] Two years from the date the Perversion first becomes known to the person injured,

[C] Three Years from the date the perversion first becomes known to the person injured,

[D] Four years from the date the Perversion first becomes known to the person injured.

35. The principle of 'force majeure' emanates from which provision of the Indian Contract Act, 1872?

[A] Section 52

[B] Section 54

[C] Section 56

[D] Section 58

36. Under which provision, can the Court issue a warrant of arrest against a person released on bail and require him to furnish sufficient sureties?

[A] Section 440 Cr.P.C.

[B] Section 446 Cr.P.C.

[C] Section 441 Cr.P.C.

[D] Section 443 Cr.P.C.

37. In which of the following, the Hon'ble Supreme Court held that in a case arising from Negotiable Instruments Act, successive sentences may be directed to run concurrently if both transactions are part of single transaction?

[A] (2010) 5 SCC 663, Damodar S. Prabhu vs. Sayed Babalal H.

[B] (2016) 3 SCC 1, Don Ayengia vs. State of Assam & Ors.

[C] (2009) 1 SCC 706, Mahindra & Mahindra Financial Services Lt[D] & Anr. vs. Rajiv Dubey.

[D] (2016) 10 SCC 761, Shyam Pal vs. Dayawati Besoya & Ors.

38. Which provision of Indian Evidence Act stipulates that the fact of a woman being habituated to sexual intercourse will not be relevant on the issue of consent in a Prosecution for rape or outraging the modesty of the said woman?

[A] Section 50

[B] Section 53-A

[C] Section 54

[D] Section 51

39. In reference to the trial of summons cases by a Magistrate, which of the following statements is correct?

[A] The Court shall frame charge after hearing the accused and the prosecution.

[B] The Court may discharge the accused after hearing the prosecution and the accused.

[C] There is no requirement for the Court to hear the accused and the particulars of the offence shall be stated to him.

[D] None of the above

40. Ram while going on pilgrimage, entrusted a box containing jewellery to his neighbor Shayam. Shayam dishonestly with the intent to commit mischief, breaks open the box without having any authority. Shayam has committed the offence of ___.

[A] Section 406 of Indian Penal Code.

[B] Section 379 of Indian Penal Code.

[C] Section 462 of Indian Penal Code.

[D] None of the above

41. In which of the following situations, the general principle of presumption of innocence of a child in conflict with law shall not be applicable?

[A] When the child is charged for the offence of murder punishable under Section 302 IPC

[B] When the child is charged for the offence of gang rape punishable Section 376(2)(g) of IPC.

[C] Where the Juvenile Justice Board has passed an order under Section 15 read with Section 18(3) of the Juvenile Justice (Care and Protection Children) Act that the child should be tried as an adult.

[D] None of the above.

42. A Police Officer receives a sum of Rs. 5000/- as fine from a traffic violator. He deposits the amount in the Treasury three months after the stipulated perio[D] He commits ___.

[A] Offence punishable under Section 407 IP[C]

[B] Offence punishable under Section 409 IPC.

[C] Offence punishable under Section 420 IPC.

[D] None of the above.

43. Under which provision of law, the Court while considering the case of a person convicted for an offence not punishable With death or imprisonment of life, is under an obligation to call for the report of Probation Officer?

[A] Section 9 of the Probation of Offenders Act

[B] Section 7 of the Probation of Offenders Act

[C] Section 4 of the Probation of Offenders Act

[D] None of the above.

44. A person (payee) signs a blank cheque and gives the same to another person (holder) and the holder fills up the blank space pertaining to amount and date and presents the same in his bank account and it is dishonoure[D] In such a situation, which of the following statement would be correct?

[A] The holder has committed forgery.

[B] The cheque will have to be treated as invalid.

[C] The Bank would not accept the cheque.

[D] The holder will be entitled to maintain a complaint filed upon the cheque being dishonored upon being presented in the bank.

45. In which celebrated judgment, did the Hon'ble Supreme Court classified the witnesses into three categories (i) wholly reliable, (ii) wholly unreliable, (ii) neither wholly, nor wholly unreliable?

[A] AIR 1987 SC 614, Vadivelu Thevar vs. State of Madras,

[B] AIR 1974 SC 276, Guli Chand & Ors. vs. State of Rajasthan.

[C] AIR 2012 SC 1357, Ramnaresh & Ors. vs. State of Chhattisgarh,

[D] (1994) 2 SCC 467, Bheru Singh vs. State of Rajasthan.

46. When a child in conflict with law is in custody while undergoing trial, is declared adult under Section 18(3) of the Juvenile Justice (Care and Protection of Children) Act upon crossing the age of 18 years during the course of trial, which of the following option is available to the trial court in such a situation?

[A] To allow the child to go home after advice or admonition.

[B] To drop the proceedings and release the child from custody forthwith,

[C] To direct the child to be released on probation of good conduct.

[D] Send the child to a place of safety.

47. Under which provision of law, a body incorporate is required to appoint an authorised representative for the purpose of inquiry or trial before a criminal court?

[A] Section 302 of Cr.P.C.

[B] Section 303 of Cr.P.C.

[C] Section 305 of Cr.P.C.

[D] None of the above.

48. Which of the following statements is correct?

(A) The presumption under Section 113-A of the Indian Evidence Act would be attracted, if the marriage of the accused and the deceased took place more than 7 years prior to the suicide of the woman and cruelty soon before death is established by the prosecution.

(B) That because Section 113-A of the Indian Evidence Act is attracted to a case, the prosecution is not required to prove its case beyond reasonable doubt against the accused.

[A] Statement (A).

[B] Statement (B).

[C] Both Statements (A) & (B).

[D] None of the above statements.

49. Which of the following cannot be a ground to deny bail to a person, who is apparently a child in conflict with law?

[A] When the offence alleged against such person is a heinous offence and the child has been ordered to be tried as an adult under Section 18(3) of the Juvenile Justice (Care and Protection of Children) Act.

[B] When there are reasonable grounds to believe that the child may come into association with known criminal if released on bail.

[C] That the person may be exposed to moral, physical or psychological danger.

[D] That the person released on bail would defeat the ends of justice.

50. Kalu prosecutes Khema for stealing a car from him, Khema is convicted. Kalu afterwards sues Ganesh for the

car which Khema had sold to him before his conviction. The Judgment of conviction of Khema in the suit between Kalu and Ganesh is ___.

[A] Relevant.

[B] Irrelevant.

[C] Relevant only with prior permission of court.

[D] None of the above

51. Which provision of Cr.P.C provides protection against double jeopardy?

[A] Section 305

[B] Section 300

[C] Section 188

[D] Section 203

52. In which judgment, the Hon'ble Supreme Court laid down that a complaint based on a second or successive dishonour of cheque is maintainable, if no complaint based on an earlier dishonour of cheque followed by statutory notice issued on the basis thereof had been filed ___.

[A] (2013) 1 SCC 177, M.S.R.Leathors vs. S.Palaniappan & Anr.

[B] (1998) 6 SCC 514, Sadanandan Bhadran vs. Madhavan Sunil Kumar.

[C] (1999) 4 SCC 567, Sil Import USA vs. Exim Aides Silk Exporters Bangalore.

[D] (2004) 13 SCC 498, Krishna Exports & Ors. vs. Raju Das.

53. Under which provision of law, the Sessions Court can make a reference to the High Court regarding the validity of any Act, Ordinance or Regulation, the determination of which is necessary for the disposal of the case?

[A] Section 396 of Cr.P.C.

[B] Section 368 of Cr.P.C.

[C] Section 366 of Cr.P.C.

[D] Section 395 of Cr.P.C.

54. Which of the following provisions of Indian Evidence Act permits evidence recorded in one case to be considered relevant in a subsequent proceeding?

[A] Section 32

[B] Section 37

[C] Section 38

[D] Section 33

55. Under which provision of law, can a court direct any person to write any words or figures for comparison of handwriting?

[A] Section 91 of Cr.P.C

[B] Section 54-A of Cr.P.C.

[C] Section 73 of Indian Evidence Act.

[D] Section 31 1 of Cr.P.C.

56. Which provision of Cr.P.C empowers a criminal court to recall and re-examine witnesses in a criminal case?

[A] Section 217

[B] Section 311

[C] Both (1) & (2)

[D] None of above

57. In which of the following cases, did the Hon'ble Supreme Court decide the issue of territorial jurisdiction of the court to entertain a complaint under the Negotiable Instruments Act in reference to the Amending Ordinance of 2015?

[A] (2016) 2 SCC 75, Bridgestone India Pvt. Ltd. vs. Inderpal Singh

[B] (2016) 11 SCC 105, K.S.Joseph vs. Philip Carbon Black Ltd. & Ors.

[C] (2016) 1 SCC (Cri) 173, Ultratech Cement Ltd. vs. Rakesh Kumar Singh & Anr.

[D] None of the above.

58. The right of private defence of the body does not extend to voluntary causing of death or of any other harm to the assailant, if the offence which occasions the exercise of the right to be of any of the descriptions hereinafter enumerated ___.

[A] An assault with the intention of committing rape.

[B] An assault with the intention of kidnapping or abducting.

[C] An assault with the intention of wrongfully confining a person under circumstances which may reasonably cause him to have recourse to the public authorities for his release.

[D] An assault of causing of grievous hurt on provocation.

59. A trial court in State of Rajasthan delivers' its judgment in English. Under which provision of law, can the accused seek a translated copy of the judgment in Hindi language?

[A] Section 353 of Cr.P.C.

[B] Section 362 of Cr.P.C.

[C] Section 364 of Cr.P.C.

[D] Section 363 of Cr.P.C.

60. Under which provision of law, a sentence of death passed by the Sessions Court is subject to confirmation by the High Court?

[A] Section 369 of Cr.P.C.

[B] Section 367 of Cr.P.[C]

[C] Section 366 of Cr.P.[C]

[D] Section 370 of Cr.P.C.

61. Which of the following irregularities vitiate the proceedings, if any Magistrate not being empowered by law in this behalf, does any of the following things?

[A] Makes an order under Section 133 of Cr.P.C as to a local nuisance.

[B] Makes an order under Part C or Part D of Chapter X of Cr.P.C.

[C] Holds an inquest under Section 176 of Cr.P.C.

[D] Makes an order for maintenance.

62. The trial court while recording evidence in a case wherein the accused is in custody, records the evidence of witnesses without ensuring presence of the accused in the court, which of the following statement would be correct?

[A] The judgment passed by trial court in such proceedings would be vitiated by virtue of Section 273 (1) of Cr.P.C.

[B] The judgment passed by trial court in such proceedings would be saved by virtue of Section 460 of Cr.P.C.

[C] The judgment passed by trial court in such proceedings would be saved by virtue of Section 465 of Cr.P.C.

[D] The judgment passed by trial court in such proceedings would be saved by virtue of Section 317 of Cr.P.C.

63. Which provision stipulates that lunatic can be a competent witness?

[A] Section 84 of Indian Penal Code

[B] Section 118 of Indian Evidence Act

[C] Section 119 of Indian Evidence Act

[D] None of the above.

64. In which of the following judgments, the Hon'ble Supreme Court held that where an act of domestic violence commenced prior to the enactment of The Protection of Women from Domestic Violence Act and continued even thereafter also, in such a situation, the aggrieved person is entitled to protec-

tion of the Act?

[A] (2014) 3 SCC 712, Sarswathy vs. Babu.

[B] (2015) 2 SCC 145, Meena Chaudhary vs. Commissioner of Delhi Police.

[C] (2013) 15 SCC 755, Indra Sarma vs. V.K.V. Sarma.

[D] None of the above.

65. Under which provision is the Court acquitting the accused, required to take a bond from him/her for appearance in the higher court?

[A] Section 439 Cr.P.C.

[B] Section 436-A Cr.P.C.

[C] Section 436 Cr.P.C.

[D] Section 437-A Cr.P.C.

66. Which of the following documents cannot be admitted in evidence in a criminal trial without formal proof?

[A] Certified copies of public documents.

[B] Report issued by a govt. scientist after chemical/serological examination of samples forwarded to him by the investigating agency.

[C] A report issued by a govt. handwriting expert after comparison of the disputed signatures with an admitted signature.

[D] A document which is admitted by the opposite party.

67. A Metropolitan Magistrate sentenced an accused of theft for three months simple imprisonment and a fine of Rs. 200/-. Accused can file an appeal against such judgment in ___.

[A] The Court of Sessions.

[B] The High Court.

[C] The Court of Chief Metropolitan Magistrate.

[D] No appeal can be filed.

68. Public Servant "A" while discharging his official functions, issues a document with incorrect particulars knowing that by this action, he is likely to harm another public servant "B". The public servant "A" is responsible for which of the following offence?

[A] Forgery.

[B] Creating of false document.

[C] Cheating

[D] None of the above.

69. Under which provision of Cr.P.C., can a party approach an Executive Magistrate and pray for dropping of the proceedings initiated under Section 145 of Cr.P.C?

[A] Section 145(2)

[B] Section 146(1)

[C] Section 148

[D] Section 145(5)

70. Under which provision of law, can the court award compensation to a person groundlessly arrested?

[A] Section 349 of Cr.P.C.

[B] Section 357 of Cr.P.C.

[C] Section 358 of Cr.P.C.

[D] None of the above.

71. Choose the correct Active voice sentence.

It is being said that too little money is being spent by the Government on roads.

[A] People are saying that the Government is spending too little money on roads.

[B] People were saying that too little money has been spent on roads by the Government.

[C] People said that too little money spent by Government on roading.

[D] People have said that Government have spent too little money on roads.

72. Fill in the blanks with the most appropriate option.

The last train ___ the station at 11.30 am.

[A] will leaving

[B] has been left

[C] leaves

[D] was left

73. Fill in the blanks with the most appropriate option.

The new witness ___ yesterday and the judge ___ the investigations early this morning.

[A] arrived, started

[B] arrived, starting

[C] have arrived, would be start

[D] had arrived, had start

74. The word similar in meaning to "Quote" is ___.

[A] sight

[B] sue

[C] sigh

[D] cite

75. Fill in the blanks with the most appropriate modal.

When I was a child, I ___ understand adults but now I don't.

[A] do

[B] should

[C] could

[D] must

76. Complete the following sentence with correct subordinating conjunction.

___ he worked hard, he did not win.

[A] However

[B] Though

[C] Nevertheless

[D] Moreover

77. The synonym of "Advise" is ___.

[A] Council

[B] Counsel

[C] Practice

[D] Proposal

78. "to make a long story short" means ___.

[A] paraphrase

[B] come to the point

[C] display composition skills

[D] have narrative excellence

79. Filling the blanks with the most appropriate phrasal verb.

The situation is difficult and calls ______ great tact.

[A] out

[B] up

[C] to

[D] for

80. Fill in the blanks with the most appropriate modal.

He ___ be lazy, but he is not stupid.

[A] needn't

[B] mustn't

[C] shall

[D] may

81. Fill in the blanks with the most appropriate modal.

He ___ have escaped by this window because it has been broken open.

[A] need

[B] dare

[C] ought

[D] must

82. Fill in the blanks with the most appropriate option.

We ___ just ___ the most extraordinary verdict today.

[A] to, hear

[B] have, heard

[C] will, hearing

[D] can, heard

83. Complete the following sentence with correct subordinating conjunction.

You must start at once ___ you will be late.

[A] therefore

[B] although

[C] otherwise

[D] because

84. Fill in the blanks with the most appropriate option.

___ of my friends advised me to take ___ taxi home.

[A] No, the

[B] One, a

[C] More, no article

[D] These, some

85. The antonym of "Proclaim'" is ___.

[A] suppress

[B] pretend

[C] attend

[D] distend

86. निम्न में से कौनसा अशुद्ध शब्द नहीं है?

[A] प्रमाणिक

[B] रचियता

[C] कवियत्री

[D] अन्त्याक्षरी

87. किस स्थिति में अवतरण चिह्न का प्रयोग सामान्यतः नहीं होता है?

[A] किसी के महत्त्वपूर्ण वचन उद्धृत करने में।

[B] अप्रचलित अथवा विशेष प्रचलित शब्दों में।

[C] व्यक्तियों के उपनामों में।

[D] रचना का अनुवाद करते हुए।

88. किस शब्द का संधि-विच्छेद त्रुटिपूर्ण है?

[A] अभीष्ट - अभी + इष्ट

[B] वाइमय - वाक् + मय

[C] अब्ज – अप् + ज

[D] महैश्वर्य - महा + एश्वर्य

89. निम्न में से कौनसा, वचन संबंधी त्रुटि वाला वाक्य है?

[A] महात्मा जी का दर्शन करके मैं धन्य हो गया।

[B] श्रोताओं में कई श्रेणियों के लोग थे।

[C] विद्रोहियों को कुत्तों की तरह घसीटा गया।

[D] हर एक ने टोपी पहन रखी थी।

90. निम्न में से किस विकल्प के सभी शब्द पर्यायवाची हैं?

[A] विमावरी, निशाचरी, रजनी

[B] मधुकरी, भिक्षा, भीख

[C] मान, सम्मान, मान्य

[D] अंबुधि, अर्णव, नीरद

91. किस मुहावरे का अभिप्राय गलत है?

[A] आकाश के तारे तोड़ लाना - असंभव कार्य कर डालना।

[B] आँख का काजल चुरा लेना - बड़ी बारीकी से चोरी करना।

[C] द्रौपदी का चीर होना - कभी समाप्त न होने वाली।

[D] ताल कटना - संगीत में बाधा उपस्थित होना।

92. 'अपने घर, गाँव या नगर में किसी का आदर नहीं होता', अभिव्यक्ति हेतु निकटतम लोकोक्ति है -

[A] घर की खाँड किरकिरी, बाहर का गुड़ मीठा।

[B] घर के पीरों को तेल का मलीदा।

[C] घर की बिल्ली घर में ही शिकार।

[D] घर आये नाग न पूजिए, बामी पूजन जाय ।

93. रग्गी को बहुत घबराहट हो रही थी। वाक्य में रेखांकित शब्द है;

[A] संज्ञा

[B] क्रिया

[C] क्रिया विशेषण

[D] अव्यय

94. 'वह आदमी आ रहा है', वाक्य में 'वह' की व्याकरणिक कोटि है;

[A] सज्ञा

[B] सर्वनाम

[C] विशेषण

[D] अव्यय

95. 'नौकर चिट्ठी लाया', वाक्य में क्रिया है;

[A] अकर्मक

[B] सकर्मक

[C] पूर्वकालिक

[D] प्रेरणार्थक

96. 'कसौटी' शब्द है;

[A] तत्सम

[B] तद्भव

[C] देशज

[D] विदेशी

97. निम्न में से कौनसा 'नि' उपसर्ग से निर्मित शब्द है?

[A] निरपराध

[B] निराकार

[C] न्यून

[D] निर्मम

98. निम्न में से कौनसा वाक्य अशुद्ध है?

[A] वह क्रोध में भरकर चिल्लाने लगा।

[B] अब मेरी बात मान लो

[C] वह राम का नाम लेकर चल पड़ा।

[D] धन से रहित जीवन व्यर्थ है।

99. निम्न में से कौनसा सही विलोम वर्ग नहीं है?

[A] भिज्ञ - अनभिज्ञ

[B] विघवा - सधवा

[C] वाचाल - मूक

[D] नैसर्गिक - कृत्रिम

100. निम्न में से कौनसा शब्द-युग्म अर्थ की दृष्टि से त्रुटिपूर्ण है?

[A] निर्झर - झरना

निर्जर - देवता

[B] प्रसाद - कृपा

प्रासाद - महल

[C] पष्टि - छह

पष्ठी - साठ

[D] अभिराम - सुंदर

अविराम – लगातार

Answers

1	B	47	C	93	A
2	B	48	D	94	C
3	A	49	A	95	B
4	D	50	*	96	B
5	D	51	B	97	C
6	C	52	A	98	A
7	B	53	D	99	A
8	A	54	D	100	C
9	C	55	C		
10	C	56	C		
11	A	57	A		
12	B	58	*		
13	*	59	C		
14	B	60	C		
15	C	61	*		
16	C	62	A		
17	C	63	B		
18	A	64	A		
19	A	65	D		
20	D	66	A		
21	A	67	D		
22	C	68	D		
23	B	69	D		
24	D	70	C		
25	C	71	A		
26	D	72	C		
27	C	73	A		
28	D	74	D		
29	B	75	C		
30	A	76	B		
31	D	77	B		
32	C	78	B		
33	C	79	D		
34	B	80	D		

35	C	81	D
36	D	82	B
37	D	83	*
38	B	84	B
39	C	85	A
40	C	86	D
41	D	87	D
42	B	88	D
43	C	89	A
44	D	90	B
45	A	91	D
46	D	92	B

---X---

Preliminary Examination, 2021

1. Under the provisions of the Specific Relief Act, 1963, when a part of a contract which, taken by itself, can and ought to be specifically performed, stands on a separate and independent footing from another part of the same contract which cannot' or ought not to be specifically performed, then___.

[A] The court may not direct the specific performance of the former part.

[B] It will be the discretion of the court to direct or not to direct the specific performance of the former part.

[C] The court may direct the specific performance of the former part.

[D] None of the above.

2. Under the Transfer of Property Act, 1882 'Attached to the earth' doesn't mean___.

[A] Trees

[B] Shrubs

[C] Growing crops

[D] Walls or Buildings

3. Under the Indian Contract Act, 1872, a Contract to perform the promise or discharge the liability of a third person in case of his default ___.

[A] is a contract of guarantee.

[B] is a contract of warranty.

[C] is a contract of Indemnity.

[D] None of the above

4. Which of the following statement with reference to Section 3 of Indian Evidence Act, 1872, is not correct?

[A] A map or plan is a document.

[B] An inscription on a metal plate is a document.

[C] A caricature is not a document.

[D] That a man said certain words, is a fact.

5. If for a period of ___, a member of a house of the legislature of a State, without permission of the house, is absent from all meetings thereof, the house may declare his seat vacant.

[A] 120 days

[B] 90 days

[C] 60 days

[D] 30 days

6. Under the Code of Civil Procedure, 1908, which of the following is not a supplemental proceeding?

[A] Appointment of a Receiver.

[B] Granting of a Temporary Injunction.

[C] Arrest and attachment before judgement.

[D] Granting of a Permanent Injunction.

7. Under the Code of Civil Procedure, 1908, in one situation the contract of engagement of a lawyer by the party to suit will be deemed to continue even after the death of that the party. Which is that situation?

[A] Till the pleader inform the court about death of party.

[B] Till the legal heirs engage a new lawyer.

[C] Till an application for impleadment of legal heirs is filed.

[D] Till the legal heirs are brought on record.

8. For the purpose of hearing any reference under Article 143 of Constitution of India, the minimum number of judges of Supreme Court who are to sit for the purpose, shall be ___.

[A] 3

[B] 5

[C] 7

[D] 11

9. In which of the following case, presumption or, contract to the contrary under Section 230 of the Indian Contract Act, 1872, shall not be presumed?

[A] Where the contract is made by an agent for the sale or purchase of goods for a merchant resident abroad.

[B] Where the principal does not disclose the name of his agent.

[C] Where the principal, though disclosed, cannot be sued.

[D] In all the above cases.

10. An Advertisement in a newspaper inviting tenders is___.

[A] Proposal

[B] Invitation for conversation

[C] Promise

[D] Invitation for proposal

11. What is meant by statutory interpretation?

[A] The interpretation of a statute by Parliament.

[B] The interpretation of a statute by the House of Commons.

[C] The interpretation of a statute by the courts.

[D] The interpretation of a statute by the House of Lords.

12. Under the Specific Relief Act, 1963, any person having the possession or control of a particular article of movable property, of which he is not the owner, may not be compelled specifically to deliver it to the person entitled to its immediate possession in which of the following cases?

[A] When the thing claimed is not held by the defendant as the agent or trustee of the plaintiff.

[B] When compensation in money would not afford the plaintiff adequate relief for the loss of the thing claimed.

[C] When it would be extremely difficult to ascertain the actual damage caused by its loss.

[D] When the possession of the thing claimed has been wrongfully transferred from the plaintiff.

13. Under the provisions of the Rajasthan Rent Control Act, 2001, which of the following is a requisite regarding inspection of a rented premise?

[A] A prior intimation of at least 7 days shall be given to the tenant.

[B] The premises shall be inspected in day time.

[C] Such inspection shall not be carried out more than once in 3 months.

[D] Such inspection shall be carried out only in the presence of tenant.

14. Any suit filed under the provisions of the Specific Relief Act, 1963 shall be disposed of by the court within a period of ___ from the date of service of summons to the defendant.

[A] 6 months

[B] 9 months

[C] 12 months

[D] 24 months

15. To enforce a right of pre-emption, period of limitation is ___.

[A] All of the above

[B] Twelve years

[C] Three years

[D] Two years

5. One year

16. *Ut Res Magis Valeat Quam Pereat* is also known as ___.

[A] Rule of harmonious construction

[B] Rule of reasonable construction

[C] Rule of ejusdem generis

[D] All of the above

17. Under the Code of Civil Procedure, 1908, in which of the following case 'Signed' does not include 'Stamped'?

[A] Summon

[B] Bailable Warrant

[C] Attachment Warrant

[D] Judgement

18. Which of the following statement regarding Chapter-VII of the Transfer of Property Act, 1882 relating 'Of transfer of actionable claims', is incorrect?

[A] This chapter applies to instruments which are for the time being by law or custom, negotiable.

[B] This chapter doesn't apply to any mercantile document of title of goods.

[C] The transferee of actionable claim shall take it subject to all the liabilities and equities and to which the transferor was subject in respect thereof at the date of the transfer.

[D] Every notice to transfer of an actionable claim shall be in writing.

19. The Writ Jurisdiction of High Court is wider than Writ Jurisdiction of Supreme Court.

Examine the Correct answer.

[A] Yes. Article 226 can be invoked to establish fundamental rights and any other right.

[B] No. Article 32 is wider.

[C] Both Jurisdictions are identical.

[D] None of the above option.

20. Under Section 15 of the Limitation Act, 1963, exclusion of time is not applicable to___.

[A] Suits

[B] Appeals

[C] Application for the execution of a decree

[D] All the above

21. According to ___ of interpretation, the meaning of a word is to be judges by the company it keeps.

[A] Mischief Rule

[B] Golden Rule

[C] Noscitur a Sociis

[D] Primary Rule

22. Under the Rajasthan Rent Control Act, 2001, an application made under Section 23 shall be disposed of by Rent Authority within ___ from the date of prosecution of the application.

[A] 120 days

[B] 90 days

[C] 60 days

[D] 30 days

23. Under the Code of Civil Procedure, 1908, which of the following statement is not correct?

[A] Decree includes the rejection of plaint.

[B] Decree includes the determination of any question under Section 144.

[C] Decree does not include any order of dismissal for default.

[D] Decree includes any adjudication from which an appeal lies as an appeal from an order.

24. The repealment of the Rajasthan Premises (Control of Rent and Eviction) Act, 1950 ("Act of 1950") by Section 32(1) of the Rajasthan Rent Control Act, 2001, affected which of the following?

[A] To anything duly done or suffered under the Act of J 950.

[B] To any right acquired under the Act of 1950.

[C] To any fine incurred under the provisions of the Act of 1950.

[D] None of the above option.

25. On application under Section 22-E of The Rajasthan Rent Control Act, 200[A] Court fee shall be payable___.

[A] Rs. 50

[B] Rs. 100/-

[C] Rs. 250/-

[D] Ad valorem

26. Which of the following statement with reference to Indian Evidence Act, 1872, is not correct?

[A] The contents of documents may be proved either by primary or by-secondary evidence.

[B] Primary evidence means the document itself produced 'for the inspection of the court.

[C] Counterparts of documents as against the parties who execute them, comes under secondary evidence.

[D] Oral evidence must be direct.

27. Under which Section it is provided that in all civil proceedings the husband or wife of any party to the suit shall be a competent witness?

[A] S. 120 of Indian Evidence Act. 1872

[B] S. 121 of Indian Evidence Act. 1872

[C] S. 122 of Indian Evidence Act. 1872

[D] S. 126 of Indian Evidence Act. 1872

28. Pending proceedings in a representative suit, the dispute is settled between plaintiff and defendants. They jointly filed an application to record settlement which was allowed. Suit was decreed in terms of the settlement. Is there any procedural irregularity?

[A] No

[B] Yes, Court ought to have conducted an enquiry about the genuineness of settlement.

[C] No, court could have granted leave to settle, being a representative suit.

[D] Yes, Court cannot grant permission without following due procedure, being a representative suit.

29. Which of the following Statement

regarding 'Gift' under the Transfer of Property Act 1882, is correct?

[A] Gift is the Transfer of Certain future movable or immovable property made voluntarily and without consideration.

[B] Transferor is known as donee and transferee is known as donor in gift.

[C] If the donee dies before acceptance, the gift is void.

[D] None of the above option.

30. Under the Constitution of India, provision to disqualification on ground of defection is made___.

[A] In Ninth Schedule

[B] In Tenth Schedule

[C] In Eleventh Schedule

[D] In Twelfth Schedule

31. Section 87 of Indian Evidence Act, 1872, provides___.

[A] Presumption as to certified copies of foreign judicial records

[B] Presumption as to books, maps and charts

[C] Presumption as to telegraphic messages

[D] Presumption as to due execution, etc., of documents not produced

32. Which of the following is not defined under Section 2 of the Limitation Act, 1963?

[A] Bill of exchange

[B] Bond

[C] Cheque

[D] Promissory note

33. Under the Indian Contract Act, 1872, requisite for a valid ratification is___.

[A] Knowledge of the correct facts of the case.

[B] Interest of the person ratifying, in the case.

[C] Right of the person ratifying, in the case.

[D] Liability of the person ratifying, in the case.

34. Under the Limitation Act, 1963, which of the following is not a correct definition?

[A] 'Tort' means a civil wrong which is exclusively the breach of a contract or the breach of trust.

[B] 'Suit' doesn't include an appeal or an application

[C] 'Foreign country' means any country other than India.

[D] None of the above option.

35. The concept of free legal aid takes its root from which Article of the Constitution India?

[A] Article 30

[B] Article 39

[C] Article 38

[D] Article 39-A

36. Order made under Section 144 of the Code of Criminal Procedure 1973, shall not remain in force for more than ___ from the making thereof.

[A] two months

[B] three months

[C] six months

[D] one month

37. Under Section 32 of the Protection of Children from Sexual Offences Act, 2012, a person shall be eligible to be appointed as a Special Public Prosecutor only if he had been___.

[A] In practice for not less than 3 years as an advocate.

[B] In practice for not less than 5 years as an advocate.

[C] In practice for not less than 7 years as an advocate.

[D] In practice for not less than 2 years as an advocate.

38. Under the Protection of Women from Domestic Violence Act, 2005, which of the following statement regarding Protection Officer, is correct?

[A] Protection Officer is not a public servant

[B] Penalty is prescribed for not discharging duty by protection Officer.

[C] A first information report can be lodged for the offence committed by protection officer.

[D] None of the above option.

39. Under the provision of Section 105-A of the code of Criminal Procedure, 1973, 'Identifying' includes___.

[A] Establishment of a proof that the

accused is related to commission of an offence.

[B] Establishment of a proof that the property was derived from the commission of an offence.

[C] Test Identification parade of accused and property

[D] None of the above option

40. While releasing the offenders after admonition under the Probation of Offenders Act, 1958, which of the following fact need not be taken into consideration by the court?

[A] Number of previously registered cases against the accused

[B] Nature of offence

[C] Character of offender

[D] Punishment provided for the offence

41. With reference to Section 90 of Indian Penal Code, 1860, 'Consent of child' means____.

[A] The consent given by a person who is under 15 years of age.

[B] The consent given by a person who is under 14 years of age.

[C] The consent given by a person who is under 13 years of age.

[D] The consent given by a person who is under 12 years of age.

42. Under Indian Penal Code, 1860 which of the following is not a punishable offence?

[A] Making preparation to commit murder.

[B] Making preparation to commit dacoity.

[C] Making preparation of waging war against the Government of India.

[D] Making preparation to commit depredation on territories of power at peace with the Government of India.

43. 'A' prosecutes 'B' for adultery with 'C', A's wife. 'B' denies that 'C' is A's wife, but the court convicts 'B' of adultery. Afterward, 'C' is prosecuted for bigamy in marrying 'B' during A's lifetime. 'C' Says that she never was A's wife. The judgment against 'B'____.

[A] Is irrelevant against 'C'

[B] Is relevant against 'C'

[C] Is a conclusive proof against 'C'

[D] Is a proved fact against 'C'.

44. Under the Juvenile Justice (Care and Protection of Children) Act, 2015, who may not be designated as a Child Welfare Officer?

[A] Head Constable

[B] Assistant Sub-Inspector

[C] Sub-Inspector

[D] All of the above

45. Under the provisions of the Protection of Women from Domestic Violence Act, 2005, which of the following statement regarding protection order, is wrong?

[A] A breach of protection order is an offence under the said act of 2005.

[B] Upon the sole testimony of the aggrieved person, the court may conclude that an offence under sub-Section (1) of Section 31 has been committed by the accused.

[C] Breach of protection order is a non-cognizable offence.

[D] Breach of protection order is a non-bailable offence.

46. Under Section 17 of the Probation of Offenders Act 1958, rules can be framed by____.

[A] Central Government

[B] State Government

[C] Central Government, with the approval of State Government

[D] State Government, with the approval of Central Government.

47. Z's Will contain these words: "I direct that all my remaining property be equally divided between 'A', 'B' & 'C'." 'A' dishonestly scratches out B's name, intending that it may be believed that whole was left to himself and 'C'. What offence 'A' has committed under Indian Penal Code 1860?

[A] Cheating

[B] Forgery

[C] Counterfeit

[D] None of the above option.

48. Evidence in the proceedings of 125 of the Code of Criminal Procedure, 1973 shall be recorded in the manner____.

[A] Prescribed for summons-cases.

[B] Prescribed for warrant-cases.

[C] As prescribed by the court in its discretion.

[D] Prescribed for summary trials.

49. The Indecent Representation of Women (Prohibition) Act, Gazette of India on___.

[A] 23 December 1986

[B] 1 April 1987

[C] 25 September 1987

[D] 2 October 1987

50. For the purposes of Section 141 of Negotiable Instruments Act, 188), 'company' doesn't mean___.

[A] Body Corporate

[B] Firm

[C] Group of individuals

[D] Association of individuals

51. Where an offence under the Juvenile Justice (Care and Protection of Children) Act, 2015 is punishable with imprisonment for less than three years, then such offence shall be___.

[A] Cognizable, bailable and triable by Magistrate of the First Class.

[B] Cognizable, non-bailable and triable by Magistrate of the First Class.

[C] Non cognizable, bailable and triable by any Magistrate.

[D] Non cognizable, non bailable and triable by any Magistrate.

52. Offence under Section 232 of Indian Penal Code, 1860 is___.

[A] Cognizable, Non Bailable and triable by the court of Sessions.

[B] Cognizable, Non Bailable and triable by the Magistrate of first class.

[C] Non-Cognizable, Bailable and triable by the Magistrate of first class,

[D] Non-Cognizable, Bailable and triable by any Magistrate.

53. Provisions of Section s 3 to 13 of the Protection of Children from Sexual Offences Act, 2012, shall not apply in case of medical examination or medical treatment of a child when___.

[A] Such medical examination or medical treatment is undertaken with the consent of child himself.

[B] Such medical examination or medical treatment is undertaken with the consent of the court.

[C] Such medical examination or medical treatment is undertaken with the consent of his parents.

[D] Such medical examination or medical treatment is undertaken under direction and presence of police.

54. Under the Code of Criminal Procedure, 1973, security for good behaviour from the persons disseminating seditious matters can be demanded by___.

[A] Magistrate of the First Class

[B] Chief Judicial Magistrate

[C] Sessions Judge

[D] Executive Magistrate

55. Which of the following statement in respect of Section 320 of the Code of Criminal Procedure, 1973, is not correct?

[A] The composition of an offence before charge shall have the effect of the accused.

[B] No offence shall be compounded if the accused is, by reason of a previous conviction, liable to enhanced punishment.

[C] When an appeal is pending, no composition for the offence shall be all without the leave of the appellate court.

[D] The person competent to compound an offence is dead, the legal representative of such person may, with the consent of the court, compound such offence.

56. How many fundamental principles are provided in Section 3 of the Juvenile Justice (Care and Protection of Children) Act, 2015?

[A] 12

[B] 14

[C] 16

[D] 18

57. Under Indian Penal Code, 1860, when the imprisonment awarded for solitary confinement shall exceed three months, the solitary confinement shall not exceed ___ in any one month of the whole imprisonment awarded.

[A] seven days

[B] fourteen days

[C] fifteen days

[D] ten days

58. For the purpose of Section 23 of the Protection of Children from Sexual Of-

fences Act, 2012, which among the following is not correct?

[A] No report in any media shall disclose the identity of a child.

[B] The publisher or the owner of the media shall be jointly and severally liable for the acts and omissions of his employee.

[C] On contravention of the provisions of subSection (1) or (2) of Section 23, the accused shall be liable to be punished with imprisonment of either description for a period which shall not be less than 1 year but which may extend to 2 years or with fine or with both.

[D] None of the above options.

59. Which statement with reference to Section 101 of the Juvenile Justice (Care and Protection of Children) Act, 2015, is wrong?

[A] An Appeal shall lie against an order of the Board before the Children's Court.

[B] A Second Appeal shall lie from any order of the Court of Sessions, passed in appeal under Section 101 (2) before the High Court.

[C] Any person aggrieved by an order of the Children's Court may file an appeal a before the High Court.

[D] No appeal shall lie from any order made by a committee in respect of finding that a person is not a child in need of care and protection.

60. For the purpose of Section 363-A of Indian Penal Code 1860, 'Minor' means___.

[A] A person under 18 years of age

[B] A person under 21 years of age

[C] A female under 18 years of age

[D] A male under 18 years of age.

61. Under Section 13 of Indian Penal Code, 1860, definition of 'Queen' was repealed by___.

[A] Adaptation Order 1937

[B] Adaptation Order 1950

[C] Adaptation Order 1938

[D] Adaptation Order 1951

62. Under the Sexual Harassment of Women at Workplace (Prevention, Prohibition and Redressal) Act, 2013, in the constitution of 'Internal Complaints Committee, at least ___ of the total members so nominated shall be wom-

en.

[A] One-fourth

[B] One-third

[C] One-half

[D] Two-third

63. 'A', a soldier, fires on a mob by the order of his superior officer, in conformity with the commands of the law. Work done by 'A' comes under which General Exception of Indian Penal Code, 1860?

[A] Act done by a person believing himself bound by law.

[B] Act done by a person believing himself justified by law.

[C] Accident in doing a lawful act.

[D] Act likely to cause harm, but done without criminal intent.

64. Which provision of the code of Criminal Procedure, 1973 deals with identification of person arrested?

[A] Section 53-A

[B] Section 54

[C] Section 54-A

[D] Section 55-A

65. Under Section 65 of Indian Penal Code, 1860, the term for which the court directs the offender to be imprisoned in default of payment of a fine shall___.

[A] Not exceed one-fourth of the term of imprisonment which is the maximum fixed for the offence.

[B] Not exceed one-third of the term of imprisonment which is the maximum fixed for the offence.

[C] Not exceed half of the term of imprisonment which is the maximum fixed for the offence.

[D] None of the above option.

66. Under Section 41 of the Code of Criminal Procedure, 1973, whom among the followings, police can arrest without warrant?

[A] Who commits in presence of a police officer, a non-cognizable offence.

[B] Who commits in presence, of a police officer, a cognizable offence.

[C] Who, Commits in presence of a Magistrate, a non-cognizable offence

[D] None of the above option.

67. Sections 143 to 147 of Negotiable Instruments Act, 1881 came into force on___.

[A] 6 February 2002

[B] 6 February 2003

[C] 1 April 2002

[D] 1 April 2003

68. "Being in possession of false weight or measure" is a punishable offence___.

[A] Under Section 264 of Indian Penal Code, 1860

[B] Under Section 265 of Indian Penal Code, 1860

[C] Under Section 266 of Indian Penal Code, 1860

[D] Under Section 267 of Indian Penal Code, 1860

69. 'A' is tried for the murder of 'B' by 'Intentionally "shooting him dead. In trail, the irrelevant fact is ___.

[A] 'A' was in the habit of Shooting al People With intent to murder them.

[B] 'A' on other occasions shot at 'B'

[C] Both (1) & (2) are relevant.

[D] Both (1) & (2) are not irrelevant.

70. The judgment passed by Hon'ble Supreme Court in Hardeep Singh vs. State of Punjab (2014) 3 SCC 92, deals with___.

[A] Section 311 of the Code of Criminal Procedure, 1973

[B] Section 41 of the Code of Criminal Procedure, 1973

[C] Section 313 of the Code of Criminal Procedure, 1973

[D] Section 319 of the Code of Criminal Procedure, 1973

71. निम्न वाक्य की पूर्ति स्थानवाचक क्रियाकिशेषवण से कीजिये

मैं ___ चला गया था।

[A] कल

[B] दस बजे

[C] दिल्ली

[D] अकेले।

72. "अपना अपना सामान उठाओ और चलते बनो" वाक्य में सवनाम है

[A] अपना अपना

[B] सामान

[C] उठाओ

[D] चलते बनो

73. अध्यादेश शब्द में उपसर्ग है

[A] अध्य

[B] अधि

[C] अ

[D] देश

74. "निषेध" शब्द का संधि विच्छेद है

[A] निः + षेध

[B] निः + सेध

[C] नि+ षेध

[D] निष + एध

75. शुद्ध वाक्य बवाइए:-

[A] यह बुद्धिमान स्त्री है।

[B] आदरणीय यावाणी से निवेदन कीणिए

[C] युणवान स्त्री सर्वत्र पूणी जाती है।

[D] सीता की आँखों से आँसू बह रहे हैं

76. "कान में फूंक मारना" मुहमवरे का अर्थ है:

[A] प्रभावित करना

[B] बुगली करना

[C] ध्यान से सुनना

[D] ध्यान न देना

77. "'अकारण" शब्द का विलोगार्थी शब्द है:-

[A] विकारण

[B] सकारण

[C] नकारण

[D] कारण

78. निम्न में से अशुद्ध वाक्य है:-

[A] मुझे आपका काम पसंद है।

[B] मोहन और उसके पिता घर पर ही हैं

[C] वह अनेकों भाषाएँ जानता है।

[D] यह कहानी प्रेमचंद की लिखी हुई है।

79. निम्न में से कर्मवाच्य का उदाहरण है

[A] रोगी को दवा दे दी यई है।

[B] पत्र भेजविया गया था।

[C] रोगियों को छोड़।दिया णाएगा।

[D] यौरव पुस्तक पढ़ता है।

80. निम्न में से सी एकक्चन व बढ़ुवचन का मेल बताइए

एकक्चन बहुक्चन

[A] देवी देवियों

[B] गुडिया गुड़ियाँ

[C] बात बाते

[D] याचना याचनाएं

81. अनुप्रास अलंकार का कौन सा उदाहरण है।

[A] निधियाँ न्यारी

[B] योल करेया

[C] लहरकर यदि चूसे

[D] सब यजरे

82. निम्न में से बहुवचन शब्द है:

[A] चाँदी

[B] क्रोध

[C] अहंकार

[D] आसूं

83. 'ढक्कन' शब्द में प्रत्यय है:

[A] अन

[B] कन

[C] न

[D] ज

84. "अक्ल का पतला" मुहम्मवरे का अर्थ है:-

[A] मुर्ख

[B] बुद्धिमान

[C] बुद्धिहीन

[D] निठल्ला

85. निम्न में से शब्द व उसके संधि-विच्छेद का सही मेल बताइये

शब्द संधि- विच्छेद

[A] जलोर्मि जल + ओर्मी

[B] महोदधि महो + दधी

[C] लंकेश लंका + ेश

[D] गंगोदक गंगा + उदक

86. Fill in the blank with appropriate article. India will become ____ super power shortly.

[A] a

[B] an

[C] no article

[D] the

87. Choose the word which is opposite in meaning to the word — Extraneous

[A] Unusual

[B] Dispirited

[C] Relevant

[D] Intrusive

88. Choose the Correct synonym of the word — Lethargy

[A] Laxity

[B] Impassivity

[C] Listlessness

[D] Serenity

89. Choose correctly spelt word.

[A] Monotonuous

[B] Monotonous

[C] Monotonauos

[D] Monatonous

90. Fill in the blank with appropriate phrasal verb.

Before finally launching of the missile many experiments were ____.

[A] carried off

[B] carried out

[C] carried over

[D] carried through

91. Choose the correct active/passive voice, which best expresses the following sentence.

Help the needy.

[A] The needy will help

[B] Let the needy be helped.

[C] The needy are to be helped.

[D] The needy shall be helped.

92. Fill in the blank with appropriate phrasal verb.

He will go to Mumbai and ____ in a hotel.

[A] put off

[B] put out

[C] put up

[D] put in

93. Choose the correct active/passive

voice, which best expresses the following sentence.

Scientists successfully conducted a water detection test on Mars.

[A] A water detection test on Mars conducted successfully.

[B] A water detection test on Mars is conducted successfully.

[C] A water detection test on Mars has been conducted successfully.

[D] A water detection test on Mars was conducted successfully by scientists.

94. Fill in the blank with appropriate article.

I couldn't believe my eyes when I saw ___ elephant crossing the road in front of my school yesterday.

[A] a

[B] an

[C] the

[D] No article

95. Choose the correct synonym of the word — Verbose

[A] Talkative

[B] Natural

[C] Effortless

[D] Random

96. Fill in the blank with appropriate option.

The Chief Guest, with his wife, ___.

[A] has left

[B] are leaving

[C] have left

[D] left

97. Choose the correct indirect/direct speech which best expresses the following sentence.

He said, "I was writing an application to the mayor about pathetic condition of road".

[A] He said that he was writing an application to the mayor about the pathetic condition of road.

[B] He said that he has been writing an application to the mayor about the pathetic condition of road.

[C] He said that he had been writing an application to the mayor about the pathetic condition of road.

[D] He said that he had written an application to the mayor about the pathetic ic condition of road.

98. Choose the correct indirect/direct speech which best expresses the following sentence.

Mother told her son, "Why are you leaving the house early today?".

[A] Mother asked her son why was he leaving the house early that day.

[B] Mother asked her son why he was leaving the house early today.

[C] Mother said her son why he was leaving the-house early that day.

[D] Mother asked her son why he was leaving the house early that day.

99. Choose the word which is opposite in meaning to the word — Congenial

[A] Accord

[B] Snug

[C] Engaging

[D] Unpleasant

100. Choose the correct sentence.

[A] When | woke up, he has already eaten breakfast.

[B] When I woke up, he had already eaten breakfast.

[C] When I had woken-up, he had already ate breakfast.

[D] When I had woken up, he has already ate breakfast.

Answers

1	C	31	B	61	B	91	D
2	C	32	C	62	C	92	C
3	A	33	A	63	A	93	D
4	C	34	A	64	C	94	B
5	C	35	D	65	A	95	A
6	D	36	A	66	B	96	A
7	A	37	C	67	B	97	C
8	B	38	B	68	C	98	D
9	B	39	B	69	A	99	D
10	D	40	D	70	D	100	B
11	C	41	D	71	C		
12	A	42	A	72	A		
13	D	43	A	73	B		
14	C	44	A	74	B		
15	D	45	C	75	D		
16	B	46	D	76	A		
17	D	47	B	77	B		
18	A	48	A	78	C		
19	A	49	C	79	A		
20	B	50	C	80	B		

21	C	51	C	81	A
22	C	52	A	82	D
23	D	53	C	83	A
24	D	54	D	84	B
25	B	55	A	85	D
26	C	56	C	86	A
27	A	57	A	87	C
28	D	58	C	88	C
29	C	59	B	89	B
30	B	60	C	90	B

---X---

Preliminary Examination 2024

1. "A" sues "B" for compensation on account of trespass. "B" holds a promissory note for Rs. 50000/- from "A". Under Order 8 Rule 6 of the Code of Civil Procedure, 1908, to setoff that amount of Rs. 50000/- from any sum to be recovered from "A" in the suit, "B" ____.

[A] cannot claim because the different characters of "A" & "B" regarding payment of amount

[B] cannot claim because as soon as "A" recovers, "B" has two different characters

[C] can claim because as soon as "A" recovers, both sums are definite pecuniary demands

[D] cannot claim because the both sums are not definite

2. Which of the following statement is not correct regarding the notice in writing given under Section 80 the Code of Civil Procedure, 1908?

[A] It is necessary to state the cause of action and the relief.

[B] It is necessary to state the name, description and the place of residence of the plaintiff.

[C] If the defendants are other than Central Government /State Government, then, it is necessary to state the name, description and the place of residence of all the defendants.

[D] The plaint can be presented after expiration of two months from the delivery of such notice.

3. Which of the following is an illustration of Section 116 of the Transfer of Property Act, 1882?

[A] A lessee accepts from his lessor a new leader of the property leased, to take effect during the continuance of the existing lease.

[B] A "A", the lessor, gives, "B", the lessee, notice to quit the property leased. The notice expires. "B' tenders "A" accepts, rent which has become due in respect of the property since the expiration of the notice.

[C] "A" lets a farm to "B" for the life of "C". "C" dies, but "B" continues in possession with "A's" assent.

[D] None of the above

4. Which of the following statements is not correct?

[A] A member holding office as Deputy Chairman of the Council of States shall vacate his office if he ceases to be a member of the council.

[B] A member holding. office as Deputy Chairman of the Council of States may at any time by writing under his hand addressed to the chairman, resign his office.

[C] A member holding office as Deputy Chairman of the Council of States may be removed from his office by resolution of the Council passed by majority of all the then members of the Council.

[D] A member office as Deputy Chairman of the Council of States shall not be removed from his office except by an order of the President of India passed after an address by Council of States supported by a majority of the total members on the ground of proved incapacity.

5. According to the provisions of Limitation Act, 1963, match correctly the suit and article thereof in which period of limitation is prescribed.

	Suit	Article wherein period of limitation is prescribed
1	For money payable for money lent	[A] Article 54
2	For arrears of rent	[B] Article 19
3	For specific performance of a contract	[C] Article 52
4	For foreclosure by a mortgagee	[D] Article 63

[A] 1 - b, 2 - c, 3 - d, 4 - a

[B] 1 - b, 1 - c, 3 - a, 4 - d

[C] 1 - c, 2 - d, 3 - a, 4 - b

[D] 1 - d, 2 - b, 3 - a, 4 - c

6. Which of the following powers is not

vested in the court to which the decree was sent for execution?

[A] Power to send the decree for execution to another court under Section 39 of the Code of Civil Procedure, 1908

[B] Power to execute the decree against the legal representative deceased judgement debtor under Section 50 of the Code of Civil Procedure, 1908

[C] Power to order execution at the instance of the transferee of the decree

[D] Power to order attachment of a decree

7. Which of the following cases is related to the ambit of judicial review in the matter of appointment of judges to High Courts under Article 217 of the Constitution of India?

[A] Anna Mathews Vs. Union of India

[B] Anna Mathews Vs. Supreme Court of India

[C] Anna Mathews Vs. President of India

[D] Anna Mathews Vs. State of Kerala

8. Which of the following communications is not protected from disclosure under Section 126 of the Indian Evidence Act, 1872?

[A] The client says to his advocate that he has murdered "A" by shooting and he wishes that advocate is to defend him.

[B] The client says to his advocate that he has obtained the possession of the property on the basis of forged documents and he wishes that advocate is to defend him.

[C] The client says to his advocate that he wishes to obtain possession of the property on the basis of forged will, on which he requests to sue.

[D] All of the above

9. Which of the statements is not correct according to the provisions of Rule 43 and Rule 68 of Order 21 of the Code of Civil Procedure, 1908?

[A] When the property seized is subject to speedy and natural decay, then, it may be sold at once.

[B] The sale of Immovable property shall not take place until after the expiration of at least 15 days calculated from the date on which the copy of the proclamation has been affixed on the courthouse of the Judge ordering the same.

[C] The sale of movable property shall not take place until after the expiration of at least 7 days calculated from the date on which the copy of the proclamation has been affixed on the courthouse of the Judge ordering the same.

[D] The sale of Immovable property shall not take place until after the expiration of at least 1 month calculated from the date on which the copy of the proclamation has been affixed on the courthouse of the Judge ordering the same.

10. Civil Procedure Code is included in which of the lists of the Constitution of India?

[A] State List

[B] Concurrent List

[C] Union List

[D] All of the above

11. In which illustration of the following illustrations, the surety discharged from his liability?

[A] "C" the holder of an overdue bill of exchange drawn by "A" as surety for "B", and accepted by "B" contracts with "M" to give to "B".

[B] "B" owes to "C" a debt guaranteed by "A". The debt becomes payable. "C" does not sue "B" for a year after the debt has become payable.

[C] "C" contract to lend "B" Rs. 5000/- on the 1* March. "A" guarantees repayment. "C" pays Rs. 5000/- to "B" on 1** of January.

[D] In all of the above

12. "A" obtains a decree against "B" for Rs. 25000/-. "C", who is a trustee for "B", obtains a decree on behalf of "B" against "A" for Rs. 25000/-. Which of the following statements is correct with regard to the above illustration?

[A] "B" can treat "C's" decree as a cross decree.

[B] "B" cannot treat "C's" decree as a cross decree.

[C] "C" can deny to treat his decree as a cross decree.

[D] None of the above

13. The statutes of limitation are premised on which fundamental legal maxim?

[A] *Vigilantibus non dormientibus jura subveniunt*

[B] *Actori incumbit onus probandi*

[C] *Frustra probatur quod probatum non relevant*

[D] *Nemo potest esse tenens et dominus*

14. Which of the following statements is correct for the purposes of Section 21 of the Specific Relief Act, 1963?

[A] Compensation can only be awarded in those 'matters, where specific performance is not granted.

[B] The compensation cannot be awarded, where, plaintiff has not claimed the compensation in the suit.

[C] The compensation cannot be awarded, where the contract has become incapable of specific performance.

[D] If the plaintiff has not claimed the compensation at the time of filing of the suit, he cannot amend his plaint, demanding compensation.

15. Which of the following statement is not correct with regard to mortgages of immovable property and charges under the Transfer of Property Act, 18827

[A] The transferor is called a mortgagor and the transferee a mortgagee.

[B] The instrument by which the transfer is affected, is called a mortgage deed.

[C] In simple mortgage, the possession of the mortgaged property is delivered.

[D] The provision with regard to accession to mortgaged property is envisaged in Section 63 of the Act of 1882

16. In which of the following judgements, Hon'ble Supreme Court declared that Right to Privacy is a Fundamental Right?

[A] Association for domestic reforms Vs. Union of India

[B] Rajeev Kumar Gupta Vs. Union of India

[C] Navtej Singh Johar Vs. Union of India

[D] Justice K.S. Puttaswamy (Retd.) and Anr Vs. Union of India and Ors.

17. No attachment under a precept sent under Section 46 of the Code of Civil Procedure, 1908 shall continue for more than ___ months.

[A] One

[B] Two

[C] Three

[D] Six

18. "When specific words are followed by general words, the meaning of those general words should be taken in the context of those specific words and the general words should be constructed as limited as the specific words." The above rule is ___.

[A] Rule of harmonious interpretation

[B] Golden Rule of interpretation

[C] Rule of homogeneous interpretation

[D] Rule of Association

19. In which of the following cases, the Hon'ble Supreme Court held that there is no unqualified right to marriage and that same sex couples claim this as a fundamental right?

[A] Supriyo @ Supriya Chakraborty and Anr. Vs. Union of India

[B] Subhash Desai Vs. Chief Secretary & Anr.

[C] Dr. Jaya Thakur Vs. Union of India

[D] Dev Gupta Vs. Union of India

20. The judgement debtor shall secure to the decree holder such periodical payments. The above order can be passed by the court in execution of which type of decree?

[A] In execution decrees of restitution of conjugal rights

[B] In execution decrees of immovable property

[C] Execution of decree for execution of document

[D] Execution of decree against firm

21. Under the Code of Civil Procedure, 1908, "The first hearing of the suit" means ___.

[A] The presentation of the plaint in the court

[B] The presentation of written statement by the defendant

[C] The examination under Order 10 Rule 2

[D] The framing of issues

22. Match correctly.

Decree	**Order & Rule**

(1) Decree in Administration Suit	(a) Order 20 Rule 14
(2) Decree in Pre-emption Suit	(b) Order 20 Rule 18
(3) Decree in Suit for partition of Property	(c) Order 20 Rule 12
(4) Decree for Possession and mesne Profits	(d) Order 20 Rule 13

[A] (1) - (d), (2) - (a), (3) - (b), (4) - (c)

[B] (1) - (b), (2) - (c), (3) - (d), (4) - (a)

[C] (1) - (a), (2) - (b), (3) - (c), (4) - (d)

[D] (1) - (c), (2) - (d), (3) - (a), (4) - (b)

23. With regard to the Doctrine of Estoppel, which of the following statements is wrong?

[A] The Doctrine of Estoppel is recognised by Rule of Equity.

[B] The Doctrine of Estoppel deals only relating to the aspect of public policy.

[C] The Doctrine of Estoppel arises from the conduct of parties.

[D] The Doctrine of Estoppel is not applicable against a minor.

24. The legal maxim *"Ur Res Magis Valeat Onam Pareatis"* is also known as ___.

[A] Rule of harmonious construction

[B] Rule of Reasonable construction

[C] Rule of ejusdem generis

[D] Golden Rule of Interpretation.

25. "A" is a decree holder and "B" is a judgement debtor. "B" took loan from "A". At that time, it was the condition mentioned in the agreement that all moneys payable under a policy of life insurance of "B" will also be liable to pay the amount of loan and for attachment.

[A] Such agreement is voidable at the instance of "B"

[B] Such agreement is Lawful

[C] Such agreement is void ab initio

[D] Looking to the facts and circumstances of the case the court will pass the order regarding such agreement being void, legal or voidable

26. In which of the following cases, Hon'ble Supreme Court observed that presumption U/S 90 of the Indian Evidence Act, 1872 with regard to the genuineness and regularity of documents which are more than 30 years old, is inapplicable when it comes to a Will?

[A] Ramakrushna Mohapatra and others Vs. Gangadhai

[B] Ashutosh Samante (D) by LRs and others Vs. SM. Ranjan Bala Dasi and others

[C] Lupin Limited Vs. Johnson & Johnson

[D] Rani Purnima Devi & Anr. Vs. Kumari Khagendra Narain Dev & Anr.

27. Which of the following statements is correct, when the reference of question has been made to the High Court under Order 46 Rule 1 of the Code of Civil Procedure, 1908?

[A] After making the reference, the court who made the reference will not proceed in the case until the receipt of the copy of the judgement of the High Court upon the reference.

[B] After making the reference, the court who made the reference can proceed in the case and may pass a decree contingent upon the decision of the High Court on the point referred.

[C] After making the reference, the court who made the reference shall return the file to the party with the direction to re-present on receipt of the copy of the judgement of the High Court upon the reference.

[D] All of the above statements are correct.

28. The agreement executed on 01.01.2024 between landlord and the tenant to increase the rent of the let-out premises by 4% per annum. Under Section 7 of the Rajasthan Rent Control Act, 2001, such agreement ___.

[A] is lawful

[B] is voidable at the instance of the tenant

[C] is voidable at the instance of the landlord

[D] is void ab initio

29. A law made by one legislature affects the scope of the other legislature in a related manner, then which of the following doctrine of interpretation is applied?

[A] Doctrine of Separation

[B] The doctrine of imbibing essence

[C] Doctrine of colorable legislation

[D] Doctrine of rigidity

30. Which of the following is not correct under the provisions of the Transfer of Property Act, 1882?

[A] An interest in property restricted in its enjoyment to the owner personally can be transferred by him.

[B] Instrument means a non-testamentary instrument,

[C] An easement cannot be transferred apart from the dominant heritage.

[D] A transfer of property may be made without writing in every case in which a writing is not expressly required by law.

31. Under Section 20(3) of Rajasthan Rent Control Act, 2001, "mesne profit" denotes ___.

[A] Rent as agreed as envisaged in Section 4 of the Act, 2001

[B] Compensation depriving landlord from the use of the premises

[C] Revision of Rent as envisaged in Section 7 of the Act, 2001

[D] Revision of Rent as per Section 7 of the Act, 2011

32. In which order of the Code of Civil Procedure, 1908, under the expression "Decree" includes the final order?

[A] Order 41

[B] Order 43

[C] Order 45

[D] Order 47

33. Article 39A of the Constitution of India deals with ___.

[A] Equal Pay for Equal Work

[B] Equal Justice and free legal aid

[C] Uniform Civil Code for the Citizens

[D] Living wage et[C] for workers

34. The object behind the oral examination of parties under Order 10 Rule 2 of the Code of Civil Procedure, 1908 is ___.

[A] To elucidating matters in controversy

[B] To Pre-examining the Witnesses

[C] To find out the issues of facts & law

[D] To find out the admitted facts

35. Which of the following is not an appealable order?

[A] An Order under Rule 34 of Order 21 of the Code of Civil Procedure, 1908

[B] An Order under Rule 17 of Order 6 of the Code of Civil Procedure, 1908

[C] An Order under Rule 10 of Order 22 of the Code of Civil Procedure, 1908

[D] An Order under Rule 2 of Order 25 of the Code of Civil Procedure, 1908

36. Ramlal purchase a motorcycle and get it insured. Thereafter, he causes to same cast away, with the intention of causing damages to the insurance company. Which offence, Ramlal has committed?

[A] Mischief

[B] Cheating

[C] Criminal Misappropriation

[D] Criminal Breach of Trust

37. Who among the following does not include in the definition of "Domestic Worker" under the Sexual Harassment of Women at workplace (Prevention, Prohibition and Redressal) Act, 2013?

[A] Women employed on temporary basis

[B] Women employed on permanent basis

[C] Women employed on part time basis

[D] Any member of the family of the employer

38. Which of the following does not come under the exception to the offence of Defamation?

[A] Imputation of truth which public good requires to be made or published

[B] Public conduct of Public Servants

[C] Merits of case decided in Courts or conduct of witnesses and other concerned

[D] Censure passed in good faith by the person not having lawful authority over another

39. There was an argument between Ramesh and Suresh over some issues. Ramesh started abusing Suresh badly, which caused sudden and grave provocation to Suresh. Suresh had a stick lying beside him. Under the effect of sudden and grave provocation, he picked up the stick with his right hand. Vijay, who has an old enmity with Ramesh and wants to kill Ramesh at

any cost, was standing nearby and watching all this. He suddenly reached there and says to Suresh, what kind of a person are you, you are standing and listening to abuses against your mother and sister, the stick is not going to do anything, take this revolver, saying this he hands over a revolver to Suresh and Suresh takes the revolver and fires at Ramesh, which causes Ramesh's death. What offences have Suresh and Vijay committed?

[A] Both have committed the offence of culpable homicide not amounting to murder.

[B] Suresh has committed the offence of murder and Vijay has committed the offence of culpable homicide not amounting to murder.

[C] Vijay has committed the offence of murder of murder and Suresh has committed the offence of culpable homicide not amounting to murder.

[D] Both have committed the offence of murder.

40. While committing any case exclusively triable by the Court of Sessions, Magistrate shall remand the accused for how much period?

[A] For a period of 15 days

[B] Until the date of framing of charge by the Court of Sessions

[C] During and until the conclusion of trial

[D] Remaining period of 60 and 90 days, as the case may be, as prescribed under Section 167 of the Code of Criminal Procedure

41. Under the Juvenile Justice (Care and Protection of Children) Act, 2015, which of the following statement is wrong in relation with the eligibility of prospective adoptive parents?

[A] The prospective adoptive parents shall be physically fit, financially sound, mentally alert and highly motivated to adopt a child for providing a good upbringing to him,

[B] Incase of a couple, the consent of both the spouses for the adoption shall be required,

[C] A single male is eligible to adopt a girl child.

[D] A single or divorced person can also adopt, subject to fulfilment of the criteria and in accordance with the provision of adoption regulation framed by

the Authority.

42. Who among the following is not competent to conduct investigation?

[A] Station House Officer of Police Station

[B] A Magistrate

[C] Any person, other than Magistrate, who is authorised by a Magistrate in this behalf

[D] Director General of Police of the State

43. U/s 33 of Indian Evidence Act, 1872, a criminal trial regarding relevancy of certain evidence for proving, in subsequent proceeding, truth of facts there in stated shall be deemed to be ——.

[A] a proceeding between the complainant and the accused

[B] a proceeding between the prosecutor and the accused

[C] a proceeding between the witness produced for the complainant and the accused

[D] All of the above are correct

44. When one fact is declared by the Indian Evidence Act, 1872 to be the conclusive proof of another, the court ——.

[A] shall, on disproving one fact, regard the other as proved, and shall not allow evidence to be given for the purpose of disproving it.

[B] shall, on proof of one fact, regard the other as proved, and shall not allow evidence to be given for the purpose of disproving it.

[C] hall, on proof of one fact, regard the other as proved, and shall allow evidence to be given for the purpose of disproving it.

[D] shall, on proof of one fact, regard the other as disproved, and shall not allow evidence to be given for the purpose of disproving it.

45. Accused prays before the court 1o see the report of Probation Officer made under Section 4(2) or 6(2) of the Probation of Offenders Act, 1958. In this regard, which of the following statement is correct?

[A] A copy of such report is to be made available to the accused so that he may produce reasonable evidence in his defence.

[B] Such report must be made available for perusal to the accused or his advocate, whereupon, he will put signature after making endorsement that he has perused the report.

[C] Such report is a confidential document, although, the court may, it it so thinks fit, communicate the substance thereof to the accused.

[D] Accused may submit the application for copy as per rule and may get certified copy.

46. Ramswaroop is charged and convicted for the theft of the golden chain of Savita. 'Which of the following statement is correct regarding above illustration?

[A] Ramswaroop can subsequently be charged with and tried for robbery on the same facts.

[B] Ramswaroop can neither subsequently be charged nor tried for robbery on the same facts.

[C] However, Ramswaroop can subsequently be charged with for robbery on the same facts but shall be acquitted without trial as per the provisions prescribed under Section 300 of the Code of Criminal Procedure, 1973

[D] After getting prior permission in writing from the District & Sessions Judge concerned, only thereafter, Ramswaroop can subsequently be charged with and tried for robbery on the same facts.

47. Distribution of which of the following samples under the Indecent Representation of Women (Prohibition) Act, 1986 comes under the definition of "Distribution"?

[A] Distribution of free samples only

[B] Distribution of paid samples only

[C] Distribution by way of samples whether free or otherwise

[D] Distribution of samples does not come under the definition of Distribution

48. Which of the following case cannot be tried summarily under the provisions of the Code of Criminal Procedure, 1973?

[A] Offences not punishable with death, imprisonment for life and imprisonment for a term exceeding 02 years.

[B] Offence punishable under Section 454 of the Indian Penal Code.

[C] Offence punishable under Section 414 of the Indian Penal Code, where the value of property concealed is Rs. 5000/-

[D] Any offence constituted by an act, in respect of which a complaint may be made under Section 20 of the Cattle-trespass Act, 1871.

49. Who among the following is not entitle to get maintenance under Section 125 of the Code of Criminal Procedure, 1973?

[A] Wife who has obtained divorce from her husband and nor remarried

[B] Illegitimate minor child

[C] Mother or Father

[D] Married daughter who has attained majority and by reason of any physical or mental abnormality or injury unable to maintain herself

50. In order to commit theft, Vinay put his hand in the pocket of Dinesh but came to know that Dinesh's pocket is empty. What offence has Vinay committed?

[A] Due to the missing of the object proposed to be stolen, Vinay has not committed any offence.

[B] Vinay has committed the offence of attempt to theft.

[C] Due to the act of Vinay, people came to know that Dinesh's pocket is empty, Vinay has committed the offence the defamation of Dinesh.

[D] Vinay has committed the offence of attempt to Criminal Misappropriation.

51. Which of the following is such an offence, if commission thereof would be the object of the assembly, then, it does not come under the purview of unlawful assembly?

[A] To overawe by criminal force any public servant in the exercise of his lawful duties

[B] To resist the execution of any legal process

[C] To commit criminal trespass

[D] To commit cheating

52. Chetna and Vijayta works in similar office. Chetna finds a Government Promissory Note belonging to Vijayta bearing endorsement. Chetna knowing that the note belongs to Vijayta, pledges it with banker as a security for a loan, intending at a future time to restore it to Vijayta. Which of the following

statement is correct?

[A] Chetna has not committed any offence because she intending at a future time to restore it to Vijeyta.

[B] Chetna has committed the offence of Dishonest Misappropriation of Property.

[C] Chetna has committed the offence of Criminal Breach of Trust of Government Promissory Note.

[D] Chetna has committed the offence of Cheating.

53. In which of the following circumstance, a private person can arrest any person?

[A] When such person commits a non-bailable and non-cognizable offence in his presence.

[B] When such person commits a bailable and cognizable offence in his presence.

[C] When such person commits a non-bailable and cognizable offence in his presence.

[D] When such person commits a bailable and non-cognizable offence in his presence.

54. In which of the following case, Hon'ble Supreme Court has held that mere death of the deceased being unnatural in the matrimonial home within 7 years of marriage will not be sufficient to convict the accused under Section 304-B and 498-A of Indian Penal Code if the cruelty or harassment has not been proved to be soon before the death?

[A] Phulel Singh Vs. State of Haryana

[B] Manoj Kumar Soni Vs. State of M.P.

[C] Charan Singh Vs. State of Uttarakhand

[D] Poonam Sharma Vs. Union of India

55. Under the Juvenile Justice (Care and Protection of Children) Act, 2015, "Aftercare" means making provision of support, financial or otherwise, to persons, who ___ and have left any institutional care to join the mainstream of the society.

[A] not completed the age of 18 years

[B] completed the age of 21 years

[C] completed the age of 18 years but have not completed the age of 21 years

[D] completed the age of 15 years but have not completed the age of 18 years

56. Which of the following is not an essential ingredient of the offence of Theft?

[A] Dishonest intention

[B] Movable property

[C] Property in possession of owner

[D] Fear of causing injury

57. Hariom is sentenced for an offence of theft for simple imprisonment of two years and a fine of Rs. 500/-, In default of payment of fine, he is ordered to undergo further imprisonment for a period of one month. During imprisonment of two years, Hariom died due to some illness. Hariom is only having a house of his sole ownership. Which of the following statement is correct regarding the recovery of such payment of fine?

[A] Due to the death of Hariom, he is discharged from the liability of fine.

[B] Amount of fine shall be recovered from his house.

[C] It is the matter of the discretion of the Court. Court can discharge from liability or can recover the amount of fine from his house.

[D] Payment of fine cannot be recovered from his house. Although, if court desires, then such fine can be ordered to be recovered from his legal representatives.

58. Under the Protection of Children from Sexual Offences Act, 2012, the Special Court, from the taking of cognizance ___.

[A] The evidence of the child shall be recorded within 30 days and trial shall be completed within one year.

[B] The evidence of the child shall be recorded within three months and trial shall be completed within one year.

[C] The evidence of the child shall be recorded within 30 days and trial shall be completed within six months.

[D] The evidence of the child shall be recorded within two months and trial shall be completed within one year.

59. Which option is correct with relation to the proceedings conducted in camera, under the Protection of Women from Domestic Violence Act, 2005?

[A] All the proceedings must be in camera.

[B] This statement is not correct, all the

proceedings must be conducted in open court.

[C] This is the question of the discretion of the court. If Magistrate thinks fit that it is necessary, then proceeding may be conducted in camera.

[D] If both the parties give consent in writing then proceedings can be conducted in open court otherwise it mandatorily be conducted in camera.

60. The Sarpanch of a village Mohan was being tried for Rape with the secretary of village assembly Savita. A question is asked to Savita during cross examination that did she voluntarily have illicit relation with ex-Sarpanch Amit? Such Question is ___.

[A] permissible

[B] permissible with prior permission of Public Prosecutor

[C] permissible with prior written permission of ex-Sarpanch Amit

[D] not permissible

61. Search warrant under Section 94 of the Code of Criminal Procedure, 1973 is issued by ___.

[A] District Magistrate or Session Judge only

[B] Chief Judicial Magistrate or Session Judge only

[C] District Magistrate, Magistrate of first class or Tehsildar only

[D] District Magistrate, Sub-Divisional Magistrate or Magistrate of first class only

62. Offence of breach of a protection order passed under the Protection of Women from Domestic Violence Act, 2005 is ___.

[A] Non-Cognizable and Bailable.

[B] Non-Cognizable and Non-Bailable.

[C] Cognizable and Non-Bailable.

[D] Cognizable and Bailable.

63. Court issues a Non Bailable Warrant under Section 70 of the Code of Criminal Procedure, 1973 in a matter. Such warrant shall remain in force -

[A] Till next date of hearing in the matter

[B] Till it is cancelled by the court which issued it or it is executed

[C] Till final disposal of the matter

[D] Till the officer signed the warrant remain posted in the court

64. In which of the following matter, Section 306 of the Code of Criminal Procedure, 1973 does not apply to?

[A] Any offence triable exclusively by the Court of Sessions

[B] Offence punishable with imprisonment of three years

[C] Any offence triable exclusively by Court of Special Judge appointed under the Criminal Law Amendment Act, 1952 (46 of 1952)

[D] Any offence punishable with imprisonment which may extend to seven years or with a more severe sentence

65. Suresh, Ramesh and Jagdish are kept in judicial custody in a house, declared as Jail under special circumstances. There are stern guard of armed forces around the house. Jagdish is murdered, for which Suresh and Ramesh are prosecuted. Direct evidence of murder is not found. Prosecution wants to prove that entry of anybody was not possible due the guard of armed forces and commission of murder of Jagdish was not possible by anybody else, then Suresh and Ramesh. This fact is ___.

[A] relevant

[B] irrelevant

[C] neither relevant nor irrelevant

[D] a conclusive proof

66. There is an old rivalry between Rachit and Vikas. Vikas goes to Rachit's house with an automatic Pistol to kill him. On reaching there, he puts the Pistol on his head and says you have troubled me a lot, today your life will end. Rachit suddenly snatched the Pistol from Vikas's hand. Upon which Vikas immediately starts running away from there. While running, Rachit fires several rounds of Pistol at Vikas, due to which he dies on the spot. What offence has Rachit committed?

[A] Rachit has self-defend him therefore has not committed any offence.

[B] Rachit has committed the offence of culpable homicide amounting to murder.

[C] Rachit has committed the offence of culpable homicide not amounting to murder.

[D] Rachit has committed offence of causing death by negligence.

67. Under the Negotiable Instruments Act, 1881, "director" in relation to a firm means ___.

[A] A partner in the firm

[B] Any employee of the firm who is involved in the activities of the firm

[C] Manager of the firm

[D] All of the above

68. Under the Protection of Children from Sexual Offences Act, 2012, the Magistrate or the police officer, as the case may be, shall record the statement as spoken by the child in the presence of ___.

[A] Special Public Prosecutor

[B] Reader of the Court

[C] Member of Child Welfare Committee

[D] Parents of the child or any other person in whom the child has trust or confidence

69. Trial of a murder committed in Jaipur, is inadvertently conducted by District and Sessions Judge, Dausa and the accused has been convicted. Which of the following statements is correct?

[A] Such trial and conviction is void ab initio, due to the reason, it took place in the wrong Sessions Division.

[B] Such trial and conviction is liable to be quashed due to the reason, it took place in the wrong Sessions Division.

[C] Such trial and conviction can be quashed only in the condition when it appears that such error has in fact occasioned a failure of justice.

[D] None of the above statements is correct.

70. For the purposes of making an inquiry under Sub Section (1) of Section 11 of the Sexual Harassment of Women at Workplace (Prevention, Prohibition and Redressal) Act, 2013, the internal committee shall have the same powers for summoning of any person and examining him on oath, as ___.

[A] vested in a civil court under the Code of Civil Procedure, 1908 when trying a suit.

[B] vested in a civil court under the Indian Evidence Act, 1872 when trying a suit.

[C] vested in a criminal court under the Code of Criminal Procedure, 1973 when trying a complaint.

[D] vested in a criminal court under the Indian Evidence Act, 1872 when trying a complaint.

71. अशुद्ध शब्द है -

[A] अभ्यार्थी

[B] स्वातन्त्रय

[C] नि रपराध

[D] उच्छ्वास

72. पारि भाषि कता की दृष्टि से गुमेलन नहीं है-

[A] विधिमान्य VALID

[B] विधिपूर्वक LAWFULLY

[C] विधिपूर्ण VALIDATE

[D] विधिसम्मत LEGITIMATE

73. अपने आप को स्वयं मारने वाला वाक्यांश हेतु उपयुका शब्द है ___.

[A] आत्मघात

[B] आत्महाया

[C] आरबंधक

[D] आत्मघाती

74. संज्ञा से बनने वाला क्रि या नहीं है ___.

[A] बतियाना

[B] अपनाना

[C] हथियाना

[D] स्वीकारना

75. तत्सम शब्द नहीं है ___.

[A] छटा

[B] महार

[C] चीता

[D] कान

76. बहुवचन में यथावत प्रयोग हेतु उपयुक्त शब्द वाला विकल्प है ___.

[A] लड़की

[B] प्राण

[C] घोडा

[D] बकरी

77. उपयुक्त विलोमता वाला विकल्प नहीं है ___.

[A] असूया - अनसूया

[B] अनिवार्य - निवार्य

[C] अभिज्ञ - भिज्ञ

[D] आर्द्र - अनार्द्र

78. किस विकल्प में सभी शब्द पुल्लिंग हैं?

[A] गुलाब, सेब, शरबत

[B] टकसाल, धनिया, शराब

[C] सौदामिनी, रुपया, संदूक

[D] मखमल, पुस्तक, मौसम

79. 'ईन' प्रत्यय से निर्मित शब्द नहीं है।

[A] कुलीन

[B] ग्रामीण

[C] शालीन

[D] प्रवीण

80. शुद्ध वाक्य है

[A] देश में सर्वस्व शांति है।

[B] पुस्तक विद्वतापूर्ण लिखी गयी है।

[C] बजट के ऊपर बहस होगी।

[D] राष्ट्र की उन्नति और शक्ति उसकी एकता पर निर्भर है।

81. विस्मयादि बोधक चिह्न के अशुद्ध प्रयोग वाला विकल्प है -

[A] वाह! तुम्हारे क्या कहने!

[B] हे ईश्वर! सबका कल्याण हो।

[C] भगवान! तुम्हारा भला करे।

[D] वाह! कितना अच्छा गीत गाया तुमने!

82. अनु उपसर्ग से निर्मित शब्द नहीं है -

[A] अन्वेषण

[B] अनुपस्थित

[C] अन्वय

[D] अनुष्ठान

83. "दाल में कुछ गिर गया है।" वाक्य में 'कुछ' शब्द में सर्वनाम का प्रकार है -

[A] अनिश्चयवाचक

[B] निश्चयवाचक

[C] प्रश्नवाचक

[D] संबंधवाचक

84. व्यंजन संधि से निर्मित शब्द रूप नहीं है -

[A] सुषुप्ति

[B] शरच्चन्द्र

[C] वाङ्मय

[D] समुद्रोर्मि

85. दमड़ी की सर्दी, सवा मन मलीदा लोकोक्ति का निकटतम अर्थ है

[A] थोड़े से लाभ के लिए बहुत अधिक खर्च करना

[B] छोटी से वस्तु के लिए बेईमानी करना

[C] खुशामद से प्रसन्न होना

[D] जरा से काम को बहुत बढ़ाकर दिखाना

86. Choose the correct passive of the following sentence.

We ought to keep our surroundings clean.

[A] Clean surroundings ought to be kept.

[B] Our surroundings ought to be kept clean.

[C] Keep the surroundings clean.

[D] Ought we to keep our surroundings clean.

87. Choose the correct option to fill in the blank with the model auxiliaries suitable to the meaning indicated in the bracket.

I ____ punish you if you don't behave yourself. (Threat)

[A] may

[B] will

[C] dare

[D] might

88. "Tell me where you live".

In the given sentence, noun clause is used as ____.

[A] Subject to verb

[B] Object of a Transitive verb

[C] Object of a Preposition

[D] Complement of a Verb of incomplete predication

89. Fill in the blank with correct form of verb.

He ____ in his father's firm till his father died.

[A] stay

[B] had stayed

[C] will stay

[D] stayed

90. Fill in the blank with a suitable Article/Determiner.

The Economist is ____ magazine.

[A] an

[B] a

[C] the

[D] Zero Article

91. Synonym of 'Impeccable' is ___.

[A] Flawless

[B] Fearful

[C] Furious

[D] Fictitious

92. Fill in the blank with a suitable Article/Determiner.

___ of the staff can speak Japanese.

[A] Each

[B] Some

[C] Any

[D] Either

93. Fill in the blank with suitable Article/Determiner.

___ beauty of Cleopatra is famous all over the world.

[A] A

[B] An

[C] The

[D] Those

94. Antonym of the 'Prospect' is ___.

[A] Introspect

[B] Inspect

[C] Retrospect

[D] Suspect

95. Fill in the blank with correct form of verb.

The builders say they ___ the roof by Tuesday.

[A] finish

[B] will have finished

[C] will finished

[D] finishing

96. Choose the option which is the correct indirect transformation of the sentence given below.

He said, "Alas! I have lost my mobile phone."

[A] He exclaimed with sorrow that I have lost my mobile phone.

[B] He exclaimed with sorrow whether he has lost his mobile phone.

[C] He exclaimed with sorrow that he had lost his mobile phone.

[D] He exclaimed with sorrow whether he had lost his mobile phone.

97. Complete the sentence with the correct phrasal verb/Idiom from the option given below.

My plans to go to Germany ___ because the journey tuned out to be very exorbitant.

[A] felling

[B] fell through

[C] fall behind

[D] fall out

98. Fill in the blank with correct form of verb.

I ___ all my childhood in Denmark.

[A] had spenting

[B] will have spent

[C] will spending

[D] spent

99. Complete the sentence with the correct phrasal verb/Idiom from the option given below.

He always ___ his rivals.

[A] runs down

[B] run up to

[C] run through

[D] run for

100. Choose the correct Passive Transformation of the given sentence.

We have already given him a notice to vacate our house.

[A] He has already been given a notice to vacate our house.

[B] He has already given a notice to vacate our house.

[C] He has already given a notice to be vacated our house.

[D] He was already been given a notice for the house to be vacated by him.

ANSWERS

1	C	36	A	71	A
2	C	37	D	72	C
3	C	38	D	73	D
4	D	39	C	74	B
5	B	40	C	75	C
6	C	41	C	76	B
7	B	42	B	77	C
8	C	43	B	78	A
9	D	44	B	79	D
10	B	45	C	80	D
11	C	46	A	81	C
12	B	47	C	82	B

13	A	48	C	83	A
14	B	49	D	84	D
15	C	50	B	85	A
16	D	51	D	86	B
17	B	52	B	87	B
18	C	53	C	88	B
19	A	54	C	89	B
20	A	55	C	90	B
21	D	56	D	91	A
22	A	57	B	92	B
23	B	58	A	93	C
24	B	59	C	94	C
25	C	60	D	95	B
26	B	61	D	96	C
27	B	62	C	97	C
28	A	63	B	98	D
29	B	64	B	99	A
30	A	65	A	100	A
31	B	66	C		
32	C	67	A		
33	B	68	D		
34	A	69	C		
35	B	70	A		

---X---

EXPLANATIONS

R.J.S. Preliminary Examination 2011

1. C - The ban on smoking in public places is not a violation of Article 14, 20, or 25, as it is a reasonable restriction for public health. However, it may infringe on personal liberty under Article 21, as smoking is a personal choice.

2. A - In Peoples' Union for Civil Liberties vs. Union of India, the Supreme Court held that unauthorized telephone tapping violates the right to privacy under Article 21, setting guidelines for lawful interception.

3. A - The right to strike is not a Fundamental Right but is recognized by the Supreme Court as essential for collective bargaining. Article 19(1)(c) protects forming unions, but not striking.

4. A - Parliament can expand the Supreme Court's jurisdiction under Article 138 by enacting a law to grant additional appellate powers beyond those defined in the Constitution.

5. C - A State law on the Concurrent List prevails over a Central law if it received the President's assent before the enactment of the Central law, as per Article 254(2).

6. C - The Speaker of the Lok Sabha nominates the Chairman of the Public Accounts Committee, which scrutinizes public expenditure and government financial transactions.

7. B - State legislature laws are not subordinate legislation; they are supreme within their jurisdiction unless overridden by Parliament or unconstitutional.

8. C - Under Section 9 CPC, a court cannot try a second suit on the same cause of action while another is pending, preventing duplicate litigation.

9. A - A decree from another State on reciprocity can be executed in the same manner as a domestic decree, with full enforcement powers.

10. D - A transferee of a decree cannot initiate execution separately; execution must be carried out by the court to which the decree was transferre[D]

11. D - The transferee of a decree acquires the same rights as the original decree holder, including any equities the judgment debtor could enforce.

12. D - A commission under Section 75 CPC, unless a civil court judge, cannot impose fines, penalties, or initiate contempt proceedings; it assists in evidence collection.

13. C - An ex-parte order or decree can be set aside under Order 9, Rule 7, and Order 9, Rule 13 CPC, subject to sufficient grounds being establishe[D]

14. D - An interpleader suit cannot be filed if a pending suit exists where all parties' rights can be decided, avoiding duplicate proceedings.

15. D - A revision under CPC does not automatically stay proceedings unless the court explicitly grants a stay.

16. D - A caveat under CPC can be lodged when a suit is instituted or about to be, ensuring prior notice to the caveator before an adverse order is passe[D]

17. C - A suit by an unregistered partnership firm is barred under Section 69 of the Partnership Act, preventing enforcement of contractual rights in court.

18. B - A contract to sell and buy a residential building is specifically enforceable, unlike personal service contracts, as immovable property transactions qualify for such enforcement.

19. D - A crossword competition is a valid agreement as it is a mutual understanding between participants and the organizer, enforceable if legal.

20. C - An auction advertisement is an invitation to offer, not a proposal; bids made by participants constitute offers subject to acceptance.

21. B - A contract of bailment does not require consideration; it involves the temporary transfer of goods with the obligation to return or dispose of them per instructions.

22. B - The agreement becomes impossible as B was to marry C, but C married D, making the contract's condition unfulfillable.

23. B - There was neither a proposal nor acceptance; B's response did not confirm the sale but indicated a minimum price, making it a negotiation rather than an offer.

24. D - A quasi-easement arises by presumed grant or law, unlike an easement of necessity, which exists due to essential nee[D]

25. A - In Donoghue v. Stevenson, Lord Atkin's neighbor principle established a duty of care, forming the foundation of modern negligence law.

26. B - Davies v. Mann laid down the "last opportunity rule," making a party liable if they had the last chance to prevent harm but failed to act.

27. D - Publishing a false newspaper report about a minister's involvement in kidnapping is defamatory as it harms their reputation.

28. A - Joint tort-feasors are liable jointly and severally, meaning each can be sued for full damages, with contributions among them later determine[D]

29. B - The bus owners are not joint tort-feasors but may be vicariously liable for their drivers' negligence under employer liability principles.

30. C - Donoghue v. Stevenson did not establish that manufacturers must always compensate consumers for damages caused by their products but set a duty of care principle.

31. A - Under Section 166 of the Motor Vehicles Act, only the injured person, property owner, or deceased's legal representative can seek compensation, not public interest individuals.

32. D - If arbitrators are not appointed within 30 days, the Chief Justice or a designated entity appoints an arbitrator to ensure fair arbitration proceedings.

33. D - The Chief Justice or a designated institution appoints an arbitrator if the parties fail to do so within the stipulated time, ensuring impartiality.

33. (D) Chief Justice or a person/institution designated by him. If parties fail to appoint arbitrators within 30 days, or if arbitrators fail to appoint the third arbitrator, the Chief Justice or a designated entity makes the appointment. This ensures fairness when parties cannot agree.

34. (C) Compensation is not an adequate relief. Specific performance is ordered when monetary compensation is insufficient, often in contracts involving unique goods or real estate.

35. (C) Either before or after partition. Under Hindu law, a son must repay his father's lawful debts, irrespective of partition, as part of pious obligation.

36. (A) Voi[D] Hindu law requires the adoptive parent to be at least 21 years older than the adopted child, which is not satisfied here.

37. (D) Persons belonging to Scheduled Tribe. The Hindu Marriage Act, 1955 applies to Hindus, Jains, Buddhists, and Sikhs, but not specifically to Scheduled Tribes.

38. (C) Vali[D] While same-gotra marriages are traditionally discouraged, the Hindu Marriage Act does not declare them voi[D]

39. (A) On the ground of not taking permission from the Court. Selling a minor's immovable property without court permission makes the sale voidable upon attaining majority.

40. (C) Above fifteen years of age. Hindu law permits adoption of minors, but there is no mandatory requirement that adoptees must be above 15 years.

41. (A) Mahar. Maina Bibi vs. Choudhary Vakil Ahmed deals with the Muslim law concept of Mahar, a husband's obligatory payment to the wife.

42. (D) Non-payment of Mahar. The Dissolution of Muslim Marriage Act, 1939 does not list non-payment of Mahar as a ground for divorce.

43. (D) A secured debt. A secured debt, backed by collateral, is not an actionable claim since enforcement does not require a lawsuit.

44. (D) All the above. Exceptions to the rule against perpetuity include permanent transfers for gifts, personal covenants, and pre-emption rights.

45. (D) Acts of parties and process of law. A charge can be created by an agreement between parties or by operation of law under the Transfer of Property Act.

46. (B) Section 18, Limitation Act, 1963, which gives a fresh period of limitation. Acknowledgment of debt in writing restarts the limitation perio[D]

47. (B) Matter relating to an offence compoundable under any law. Permanent Lok Adalats can take cognizance of disputes, including compoundable offenses.

48. (B) Magistrate of the First Class. Victims of domestic violence can seek residential orders under the Protection of Women from Domestic Violence Act, 2005.

49. (B) Procedural law. The Code of Civil Procedure, 1908 governs civil litigation procedures without defining substantive rights.

50. (B) A Magistrate can under Section 156(3), Code of Criminal Procedure, 1973 send a complaint of non-cognizable offence to the police. A Magistrate cannot order police to investigate non-cognizable offenses under Section 156(3).

51. (C) Theft. Plea bargaining is available for theft but not for serious offenses like murder or those affecting women/children.

52. (B) Frame the charge and transfer

the case to the Chief Judicial Magistrate/Magistrate of the First Class. If a Sessions Court finds a case not exclusively triable by it, it can transfer it.

53. (D) Police, Magistrate, or Court during investigation, enquiry, or trial. Bail can be granted at different stages depending on legal authority.

54. (D) His family and one member of the locality, and countersigned by the arrested person. The memorandum of arrest must have signatures to ensure transparency.

55. (D) On any one or all of the above grounds. An Executive Magistrate may issue ex-parte orders under Section 144 CrPC for immediate prevention.

56. (B) Do all these mentioned things. The High Court cannot review its own judgment, act as an appellate court without jurisdiction, or grant police custody from judicial custody under Section 482 CrP[C]

57. (A) Habitually commits offenses. A habitual offender frequently engages in criminal activity.

58. (D) In charge Police Station. For cognizable offenses, the Station House Officer (SHO) can investigate without Magistrate approval.

59. (B) Explanation of the nature of the transaction. The cries of a mob in a riot case are relevant to understanding the event.

60. Police custody refers to the physical detention of an accused by the police for investigation or legal proceedings. It involves surveillance, confinement in lockups, monitoring movements, and investigative procedures. This control may be direct or through third persons, ensuring the accused remains under police supervision.

61. A retracted confession, though admissible, has weak evidentiary value. Courts view it cautiously since retractions often indicate coercion, inducement, or fear. It must be corroborated by other evidence to be relied upon for conviction, as its credibility is generally questionable.

62. The judgment against B for adultery is irrelevant in C's bigamy trial. Bigamy requires proving C's first marriage's validity, which the adultery conviction does not establish. The court must independently assess evidence of C's marital status before determining guilt.

63. A newspaper report is hearsay evidence since it is based on secondhand information, not direct testimony. It is generally inadmissible unless corroborated by reliable sources. Courts treat such reports cautiously, as their credibility depends on the reporter's accuracy.

64. A hostile witness is one who testifies against the party that called them. They may be uncooperative, give false or contradictory statements, or show bias. The calling party can cross-examine them to challenge their credibility and contradict their testimony.

65. (C) Cheating. A prostitute misrepresenting her health while knowingly having a communicable disease constitutes cheating under Section 415 IP[C] The false representation induces the victim to engage in sexual intercourse, making it a deceptive act.

66. (C) Section 78. A hangman executing a court's order is exempt from criminal liability under IP[C] This provision ensures protection when acting in good faith.

67. (A) Murder. A knowingly inflicted a fatal blow on B, aware of his heart condition, making it murder under Section 300 IP[C]

68. (C) Every murder is culpable homicide. Murder is a specific form of culpable homicide as defined under IPC Sections 299 and 300.

69. (C) Abettor and principal offender may be differently liable. Abettors under Section 107 IPC may face distinct liability based on their role in the offense.

70. (A) In theft, property is dishonestly taken; in extortion, delivery is coerce[D] Theft (Section 378 IPC) involves taking property, while extortion (Section 383 IPC) involves compelling delivery.

71. (A) Section 36. A caused Z's death by omission (denying food) and commission (beating), making him liable under IP[C]

72. (A) Forgery. A misrepresented himself on a bill of exchange, falsifying a document under Section 463 IP[C]

73. (D) Cannot be held liable. Instigation outside India does not attract Indian jurisdiction unless specified by law.

74. (D) Cognizable and non-bailable. NDPS Act offenses are serious, permitting arrest without warrant and requiring judicial discretion for bail.

75. (B) Chief Justice's concurrence. A Sessions Court is designated a Special Court under the SC/ST Act with the High Court Chief Justice's approval.

76. (A) Sessions Court. The Juvenile

Justice Act allows appeals against competent authority orders in the Sessions Court.

77. (D) Amount of damage is irrelevant. Probation under the Probation of Offenders Act depends on the offense's nature and the offender's character.

78. (D) Using electricity as per the license. Theft occurs when electricity is used without authorization, not when consumed lawfully.

79. (D) IT Act applies if a crime involves an Indian computer network. Jurisdiction extends beyond borders if India's cyber resources are involve[D]

80. (B) Ex-P-1 (prosecution) and Ex-D-1 (defense). Criminal trial documents are marked distinctly for clarity.

81. (B) Both are true, but (R) is not the correct explanation. Equality before law ensures equal treatment under similar conditions, irrespective of personal differences.

82. (C) (A) is true, but (R) is false. Rajasthan language's non-inclusion in the Eighth Schedule is a central policy matter, not a violation of Article 14.

83. (A) Both (A) and (R) are true, and (R) explains (A). Accomplice testimony requires scrutiny as they may favor the prosecution for leniency.

84. (A) Both (A) and (R) are true, and (R) explains (A). Dishonor of cheques is a strict liability offense, not requiring mens rea.

85. The correct option is (A) 'आच्छादन' शब्द में 'आः' उपसर्ग है। उपसर्ग शब्द के पहले भाग में पाया जाता है और इसका उपयोग शब्द के अर्थ और मान में परिवर्तन लाने के लिए किया जाता है। इस प्रकार, 'आच्छादन' शब्द में 'आः' उपसर्ग के रूप में उपयोग होता है जो इसके अर्थ को प्रभावित करता है।

86. The correct option is (B) 'ग्रामागत' शब्द का समास विच्छेद 'ग्राम को आया हुआ' होगा। यहाँ 'ग्राम' शब्द प्रधान पद होता है और 'आगत' शब्द सम्बन्धी पद होता है। जब ये दोनों पद एक साथ मिलकर एक नये शब्द का निर्माण करते हैं, तो उसे समास कहा जाता है। इस प्रकार, 'ग्रामागत' शब्द में समास विच्छेद के रूप में 'ग्राम को आया हुआ' होगा।

87. The correct option is (D) 'रसोत्पत्ति' शब्द संधि से बना है जिसका निर्माण 'अ+उ' वर्णों के मिलने से हुआ है। यहाँ 'अ' और 'उ' का संयोजन होने से 'ओ' ध्वनि का निर्माण हो जाता है। इस प्रकार, 'रसोत्पत्ति' शब्द में संधि से बने हुए 'अ+उ' वर्णों का उपयोग होता है।

88. The correct option is (C) दिए गए विकल्पों में 'रात' का पर्यायवाची (समानार्थी) शब्द 'उर्मि' नहीं है। 'निशा', 'यामिनी' और 'विभावरी' विकल्प रात के समानार्थी हैं और रात की परिभाषा में प्रयुक्त हो सकते हैं।

89. 'निष्कर्ष', 'उपकर्ष', 'उत्सर्ग' आदि शब्द अशुद्ध हैं, किंतु 'अपकर्ष' 'उत्कर्ष' का विलोम शब्द है।

90. 'विदेशज' शब्द का अर्थ होता है 'विदेशी', अर्थात एक व्यक्ति या वस्तु जो विदेश से है या विदेशी होती है। इसलिए, 'विदेशज' शब्द का सही उत्तर है 'जलेबी' (जलेबी विदेशी स्वाद की मिठाई के रूप में मशहूर है)।

91. गिरा का पर्यायवाची शब्द सरस्वती, गिरा, शारदा, भारती, वीणापाणि, विमला, वागीश, वागेश्वरी होता है।

92. 'पूर्ण भूतकाल' का धोतक वाक्य है 'मैं तो कब की अपना काम कर चुका था।' इस वाक्य में क्रिया 'कर चुका था' भूतकाल में हो रही है और इसे पूर्ण भूतकाल का धोतक कहा जाता है। धोतक क्रिया द्वारा क्रिया का पूर्वाग्रह, काल, और पुरुष का पता चलता है। इस प्रकार, यह वाक्य 'पूर्ण भूतकाल' का उदाहरण है।

93. महावरा 'बाल बाँका न होना' व्यक्ति की स्थिति का वर्णन करता है जब उसे भारी मुसीबत में भी कोई अनिष्ट नहीं होता है। इस महावरे में 'बाल बाँका न होना' का अर्थ होता है कि बाल बाँधने वाले के लिए उसकी बाँधने की चीज़ की उपयोगिता नहीं होती है, यानी यह कहना है कि कार्य करने में व्यक्ति को कोई परेशानी नहीं होती है।

94. "तबेल की बला बंदर के सिर" लोकोक्ति का अर्थ है कि किसी दोषी व्यक्ति का परिणाम स्वतः होता है और वह खुद ही फँस जाता है। इस लोकोक्ति के अनुसार, जैसे कि जब तबेल (मछली पकड़ने की जाल) पर एक बंदर चढ़ जाता है, तो वह खुद ही फँस जाता है और बाहर निकलने के लिए उसे दूसरे की मदद की आवश्यकता होती है। इसलिए, यह लोकोक्ति एक दोषी व्यक्ति को संकट में दिखाने का एक मार्ग प्रदर्शित करती है।

95. साक्ष्य या गवाही के लिए अंग्रेजी का उपयुक्त शब्द है "[C] Evidence" (साक्ष्य)। यह शब्द उस संदर्भ में प्रयोग होता है जब हम किसी विवाद या मामले के समर्थन में प्रमाण प्रस्तुत करने के लिए उदाहरण, तथ्य या शास्त्रीय साक्ष्य का उपयोग करते हैं। यह शब्द साक्ष्य या प्रमाण की भूमिका को दर्शाता है और किसी विचार या दावे की सत्यता को समर्थित करने के लिए प्रयोग होता है।

96. अंग्रेजी के "SINE DIE" पद के लिए हिंदी में उपयुक्त पद है "[D] अनिश्चित काल के लिए"। "SINE DIE" शब्द का अर्थ होता है किसी कार्य को अनिश्चित समय तक स्थगित कर देना, यानी इसे किसी निश्चित तारीख तक टाल देना। यह एक विधानसभा या सभा के अधिवेशन के दौरान प्रयोग होता है जब किसी कार्य को अनिश्चित समय तक स्थगित किया जाता है और तारीख तय करने के लिए बाद में फिर से बुलाया जाता है। इसलिए, "अनिश्चित काल के लिए" हिंदी में "SINE DIE" को

उपयुक्त रूप से प्रकट करता है।

97. अंग्रेजी के "Autonomous" शब्द के लिए हिंदी का सही पद है "[B] स्वायत्त"। "Autonomous" शब्द का अर्थ होता है स्वतंत्र या स्वायत्त, यानी किसी संगठन या संस्था का स्वतंत्रता या स्वायत्तता रखने की क्षमता। यह शब्द एक ऐसे संगठन या संस्था को विशेष रूप से वर्णित करता है जिसकी आपातकालीनता और निर्णायक शक्ति उसके अपने आप में होती है। "स्वायत्त" शब्द इस अर्थ को सही रूप से प्रकट करता है और अंग्रेजी शब्द "Autonomous" के हिंदी अनुवाद के रूप में उपयोग किया जाता है।

98. "कानूनी प्रक्रिया" के लिए अंग्रेजी में उपयुक्त पद 'Legal process' है। यह शब्द संबंधित कानूनी प्रक्रियाओं और न्यायिक प्रक्रियाओं को संकेतित करता है जो किसी मामले के न्यायिक या कानूनी निर्णय तक पहुंचने के लिए अनुशासित तरीके से अवलंबित होती है।

99. "कृपया आवश्यक कार्यवाही करें" के अनुवाद के लिए उपयुक्त विकल्प है 'Please take necessary action'। यह वाक्य विशेषतः किसी संदेश या अनुरोध में उपयोग किया जाता है जब किसी व्यक्ति से अपेक्षित कार्यवाही या कार्रवाई की अनुरोध की जाती है।

100. 'Against Public Interest' के लिए उपयुक्त हिंदी पद है 'लोक हित के प्रतिकूल'। यह प्रयोग उस स्थिति को व्यक्त करने के लिए होता है जब किसी कार्रवाई, नियम, या निर्णय का लोक हितों के प्रतिकूल माना जाता है या उसे जनसाधारण के हितों के खिलाफ माना जाता है।

101. सही वाक्य है 'सोरठा हिन्दी का एक छंद है।' इस वाक्य में 'सोरठा' शब्द का प्रयोग सही रूप से हुआ है, जो कि हिंदी का एक विशेष छंद है जिसमें 13 अक्षर होते हैं।

102. "विमति" (असहमति) के लिए अंग्रेजी में उपयुक्त पद 'Note of dissent' है। यह शब्द विशेषतः ऐसे दस्तावेज़ों के लिए प्रयुक्त होता है जिनमें कोई व्यक्ति या सदस्य साझा राय या सहमति के खिलाफ अपने मत का व्यक्त करता है।

103. [C] Past Simple. The verbs "ran" and "jumped" describe completed past actions, which is the function of the Past Simple tense.

104. [B] Past Continuous. The verb "was standing" indicates an ongoing action in the past, fitting the Past Continuous tense.

105. [B] He is slow but he is honest. "But" is a coordinating conjunction that connects two independent clauses of equal importance.

106. [D] He ran away because he was afrai[D] "Because" is a subordinating conjunction that introduces a dependent clause.

107. [B] The report was read by the Principal. The sentence is in passive voice, where the subject receives the action.

108. [A] Some. "Some coffee" refers to an unspecified quantity, commonly used in polite requests.

109. [B] All. "All the money" refers to the entire amount, indicating total inclusion.

110. [D] Each. "Each of his customers" emphasizes individual members of a group separately.

111. [C] Can. "Can I get you a glass of water?" is a polite way to offer assistance.

112. [B] Woul[D] "Would you like to stay the night?" is a polite invitation using "would."

113. [D] Will. "She will be able to drive" expresses a future ability.

114. [A] Coul[D] "Could you pass me the salt?" is a polite request using "could."

115. [B] Get through. "I can't get through" means struggling to establish communication.

116. [C] Clearing up. "The weather is clearing up" means the weather is improving.

117. [D] Drop in. "Drop in and see me" means visiting informally.

118. [A] He said he might not be at home. "May" changes to "might" in reported speech.

119. [B] He told her she could pay him cash or give him a cheque. The pronouns and modals change in indirect speech.

120. [D] She says she does not think she will buy another car. The verb tense adjusts for indirect speech.

R.J.S. Preliminary Examination

2013-14

1. The correct answer is 3. In Union of India vs. Naveen Jindal, the Supreme Court held that flying the National Flag with dignity is a fundamental right under Article 19(1)(a).

2. The correct answer is 4. The right to hold property is a constitutional right, not a fundamental right, unlike the other options.

3. The correct answer is 1. Directive Principles of State Policy (DPSPs) are not enforceable in court but guide governance.

4. The correct answer is 2. Afcon Infrastructure Lt[D] vs. Cherian Varkey Construction Co. clarified ADR under Section 89 CP[C]

5. The correct answer is 4. A next friend of a minor can be removed under Order XXXII Rule 9 CPC for various reasons.

6. The correct answer is 3. An ex parte decree can be set aside under Order IX Rule 13 CPC on showing sufficient cause.

7. The correct answer is 3. Acceptance is complete against the acceptor when it comes to the proposer's knowledge.

8. The correct answer is 1. Agreements restraining marriage (except minors) are void and against public policy.

9. The correct answer is 1. A bailee receives goods under an agreement and must return or dispose of them per terms.

10. The correct answer is 4. Rylands vs. Fletcher's strict liability rule has exceptions like vis major or plaintiff's fault.

11. The correct answer is 1. Res ipsa loquitur shifts the burden in negligence cases where the cause is unclear.

12. The correct answer is 2. The land benefiting from an easement is called the dominant heritage or tenement.

13. The correct answer is 2. Under Section 173 of the Motor Vehicles Act, Tribunal awards can be appealed in the High Court.

14. The correct answer is 2. Arbitration starts when the respondent receives a request for dispute resolution.

15. The correct answer is 3. Arbitral tribunals can continue proceedings and issue awards even if a party is absent.

16. The correct answer is 4. The Rajasthan Rent Control Act allows certain retired officials to recover immediate possession.

17. The correct answer is 3. Under Section 111 of the Rajasthan Land Revenue Act, boundary disputes are settled by the Land Records Officer.

18. The correct answer is 4. The Fourth Schedule of the Rajasthan Tenancy Act lists CPC provisions that do not apply.

19. The correct answer is 3. Specific performance is discretionary even if contract existence and breach are proven.

20. The correct answer is 2. Section 6 of the Specific Relief Act allows a dispossessed person to sue within six months.

21. The correct answer is 4. Jijabai Vithalrao Gajre vs. Pathan Khan established principles on minority and guardianship.

22. The correct answer is 3. Appeals under Section 28 of the Hindu Marriage Act must be filed within ninety days.

23. The correct answer is 2. Khula and Mubara'at are mutual divorce methods under Muslim law.

24. The correct answer is 2. A gift is void if the donee dies before accepting it.

25. The correct answer is 3. Accepting a new lease during an existing lease implies surrender of the former lease.

26. If the prescribed period of limitation expires on a holiday, the application may be filed on the next working day when the court reopens. This ensures applicants aren't deprived of filing opportunities due to holidays.

27. The limitation period for filing a compensation suit for false imprisonment starts when the imprisonment ends, meaning from the time of release or legal intervention.

28. To set aside an abatement, an application must be filed within 60 days from the date the case is abated, which occurs upon the death of a party.

29. If no compromise is reached in a Lok Adalat case, the record is returned to the court that referred the case. The court then continues the proceedings.

30. A Magistrate can pass orders for protection, residence, custody, compensation, and ex parte orders under the Protection of Women from Domestic Violence Act, ensuring comprehensive relief for victims.

31. Under the Rajasthan Guaranteed Delivery of Public Services Act, 2011, the State Government can notify services provided by the State Government, institutions, and various departments.

32. The Rajasthan Right to Hearing Act, 2012, authorizes the State Government to create rules for effective implementation, ensuring guidance on procedural aspects.

33. The Third Schedule of the Rajasthan Panchayati Raj Act, 1994, de-

fines the functions and powers of Zila Parishad, guiding district-level governance and development.

34. Disputes between Panchayati Raj Institutions and Local Authorities are referred to the State Government, which resolves conflicts based on its administrative powers.

35. Under the Rajasthan Municipalities Act, 2009, a person disqualified under Section 117 of the CrPC is ineligible to be chosen as a Municipality member until the security period expires.

36. Under Section 85-A of the Indian Evidence Act, an electronic agreement can be presumed, recognizing the evidentiary value of electronic records in legal proceedings.

37. A "Will" is not a public document under the Indian Evidence Act, as it is a private document, unlike public records such as court judgments or police charge sheets.

38. A written statement from a witness unable to speak is treated as oral evidence by the court, as it represents their personal testimony, despite not being spoken.

39. In criminal cases, the burden of proof lies with the prosecution, which must prove the accused's guilt beyond a reasonable doubt to secure a conviction.

40. In negligence cases, B's habitual negligence is irrelevant to A's injury. The focus is on the specific negligence that led to the injury in the current instance.

41. Under Section 11 of the Indian Evidence Act, an accused can plead alibi by presenting evidence to prove they were not at the crime scene when the offense occurred.

42. Estoppel prevents a party from contradicting their earlier statements or actions, ensuring fairness by not allowing individuals to deny previous admissions that harm another party.

43. The information about the accused keeping a key in the patio is admissible to establish that fact but doesn't directly prove theft or other crimes without further evidence.

44. In criminal cases involving grave and sudden provocation, the burden of proof lies with the accused to demonstrate they were provoked to the extent of losing self-control.

45. "Court" in the Indian Evidence Act refers to judges, magistrates, and other persons authorized to take evidence, ensuring uniformity in the application of evidentiary rules.

46. The certifying authority's opinion regarding an electronic signature is relevant when forming an opinion on its authenticity, especially in legal matters involving digital records.

47. In a trial, a Judge who witnesses an injury or crime may be examined as a witness to provide firsthand information about the incident.

48. The State Government determines the language of courts subordinate to the High Court in a state, considering regional language and accessibility for legal proceedings.

49. A complaint for the restoration of an abducted female child can be presented to the District Magistrate, Sub Divisional Magistrate, or Magistrate First Class under Section 98 of the CrPC.

50. In a summons case, no formal charge is needed when the accused appears before the Magistrate. The summons serves as notice, and the accused can enter a plea based on the charges.

51. The Central Government notifies offences affecting the socio-economic condition of the country where plea bargaining is not applicable. These offences are typically serious violations impacting the socio-economic structure, and the government ensures uniformity by excluding them from plea bargaining.

52. The Chemical Examiner's report can be used as evidence in criminal trials, offering corroborative value. It supports other evidence but isn't sufficient by itself to establish guilt or innocence, requiring additional evidence for a fair trial.

53. The Sub Divisional Magistrate can initiate proceedings to remove obstructions, like a banner causing traffic issues. The Magistrate takes action under the Code of Criminal Procedure to maintain public safety and facilitate smooth traffic flow.

54. Section 304 of the Code of Criminal Procedure ensures that the State provides a pleader to an accused facing severe charges, like the death sentence or life imprisonment, when they can't afford legal representation.

55. In cases tried by the Court of Sessions or Chief Judicial Magistrate, the court or magistrate must forward the verdict and sentence to the District Magistrate. This allows the District Magistrate to oversee administrative and legal actions in their jurisdiction.

56. Under Section 164 of the Code of Criminal Procedure, a Judicial or Metropolitan Magistrate records a statement for investigation. The statement provides a legally admissible account of facts, ensuring its compliance with legal standards during criminal investigations.

57. The High Court has the authority to acquit an accused when reviewing a death sentence, even without an appeal. While confirming the sentence, it can reassess the evidence and grant acquittal if deemed appropriate.

58. An "unlawful assembly" is defined as five or more persons with a common objective of committing a crime. It is considered unlawful when the group's intent is to perform an illegal act or disrupt public order.

59. The police officer committed criminal breach of trust by misappropriating traffic fine money, using it for personal gain instead of depositing it with the State Treasury. This violates their duty to manage the funds properly.

60. Trespassing on a place for funeral rites with knowledge of likely offense to others' feelings violates Section 297 of the Indian Penal Code. The Section protects the sanctity of such places, penalizing actions that insult or hurt public sentiment.

61. Under Section 326-A of the Indian Penal Code, a person convicted faces at least ten years' imprisonment, potentially life, plus a fine. The fine compensates the victim's medical expenses due to injuries caused by the offense.

62. A police officer detaining a person after a bail order is guilty of wrongful confinement under the Indian Penal Code. This act unlawfully prevents the individual from being released, violating

their rights.

63. Under Section 277 of the Indian Penal Code, the hotel manager is guilty of fouling a public reservoir by discharging polluted water into it. This act of contamination endangers public health and violates environmental laws.

64. The term "he" in the Indian Penal Code is gender-neutral, encompassing any person, regardless of sex. This ensures the law applies equally to all individuals, without gender discrimination, maintaining fairness in legal proceedings.

65. In Ram Parkash vs. State, the Supreme Court clarified that the benefit of probation is not automatic and depends on the court's discretion. The court considers the offender's character and the case's specifics before granting probation.

66. Section 64-A of the Narcotic Drugs and Psychotropic Substances Act grants immunity from prosecution for addicts who voluntarily seek de-addiction treatment. This emphasizes rehabilitation over punishment for those attempting recovery from addiction.

67. An officer of a company is not liable under the Information Technology Act, 2000 if they prove the contravention was without their knowledge or despite their due diligence to prevent it. This promotes accountability while recognizing responsible actions.

68. Mr. 'X' can be charged under Section 509 of the Indian Penal Code and Section 66-A of the Information Technology Act for sending offensive messages. Both Section s protect against insults to modesty and offensive electronic communications.

69. All offenses under the Negotiable Instruments Act, 1881, are compoundable. Section 147 allows for settlement through compromise, where the complainant may withdraw the case, facilitating resolution without prolonged legal proceedings.

70. Under Section 138 of the Negotiable Instruments Act, mens rea (guilty mind) is not necessary to establish liability. The offense focuses on the dishonor of a cheque due to insufficient funds, regardless of the drawer's intent.

71. इसमें हिंदी भाषा की लिपि का उत्तर दिया गया है "देवनागरी" (विकल्प 3)। देवनागरी

लिपि हिंदी भाषा की मुख्य लिपि है जो भारतीय भाषाओं को लिखने के लिए प्रयुक्त होती है। इसमें स्वर और व्यंजनों को वर्ण रूप में दर्शाने के लिए विशेष अक्षरों का उपयोग किया जाता है। यह लिपि व्यापक रूप से भारतीय भाषाओं, जैसे हिंदी, संस्कृत, मराठी, नेपाली, और बंगला आदि, के लिए उपयोगी है। इसलिए, विकल्प 3 "देवनागरी" उत्तर सही है।

72. अनुप्रास अलंकार का उदाहरण दिया गया है "चारू चन्द्र की चंचल किरणें, खेल रहीं हैं जल थल में"। अनुप्रास अलंकार में, शब्दों में एक ही ध्वनि या वर्ण का बार-बार प्रयोग किया जाता है ताकि वह सुंदर और रसभरा लगे। इस उदाहरण में "च" ध्वनि का बार-बार प्रयोग किया गया है, जिससे शब्दों में लहराती हुई और रसभरी ध्वनि की प्राप्ति होती है। इसलिए, विकल्प 2 "चारू चन्द्र की चंचल किरणें, खेल रहीं हैं जल थल में" उदाहरण अनुप्रास अलंकार का सही उदाहरण है।

73. "अनुराग" का विलोम शब्द दिया गया है "विराग" (विकल्प 2)। अनुराग और विराग दोनों शब्द हिंदी में भाव प्रदर्शित करने के लिए प्रयुक्त होते हैं। अनुराग भाव को प्यार, प्रेम और आकर्षण की भावना से जोड़ा जाता है, जबकि विराग भाव उससे अलग होता है और अन्यों की ओर से निराशा, त्याग और अप्रेम की भावना को दर्शाता है। इसलिए, विकल्प 2 "विराग" विलोम शब्द के रूप में सही है।

74. "घर" का पर्यायवाची शब्द दिया गया है "सदन" (विकल्प 3)। "घर" और "सदन" दोनों शब्द हिंदी में निवास स्थान की भावना को व्यक्त करने के लिए प्रयुक्त होते हैं। इन दोनों शब्दों में विशेष रूप से अंतर नहीं होता है और दोनों शब्दों का उपयोग उसी अर्थ में होता है। इसलिए, विकल्प 3 "सदन" पर्यायवाची शब्द के रूप में सही है।

75. "उच्चारण" का संधि विच्छेद दिया गया है "उत् + चारण" (विकल्प 2)। "उच्चारण" शब्द में "उत्" और "चारण" दोनों ध्वनियों का संधि विच्छेद है। "उत्" ध्वनि का उपयोग उच्चारण के अर्थ को दर्शाने के लिए किया जाता है, जबकि "चारण" ध्वनि संधि विच्छेद के बाद के ध्वनि को दर्शाता है। इसलिए, विकल्प 2 "उत् + चारण" संधि विच्छेद के रूप में सही है।

76. विकल्प 2: सज्जन। यह संधि "सत्" और "जन" का जोड़ है। "सत्" शब्द का अर्थ होता है अच्छा या सच्चा, और "जन" शब्द का अर्थ होता है लोग। इसलिए, "सज्जन" शब्द का अर्थ होता है एक अच्छा या सच्चा व्यक्ति। यह शब्द एक गुणकारी विशेषण है जिसे भलाई, नेकी, ईमानदारी, और सदाचार के संकेत के रूप में प्रयोग किया जाता है।

77. विकल्प 4: सर्वनाम। यह शब्द "यह", "वह", "तुम" और "आप" को संज्ञा की जगह प्रयोग होने वाले सर्वनाम को दर्शाता है। सर्वनाम संज्ञाओं की जगह लेते हैं और व्यक्ति, स्थान, समय आदि की पहचान करने के लिए प्रयुक्त होते हैं। इन चारों शब्दों को सर्वनाम के रूप में विशेषण की जगह प्रयोग किया जाता है,

जहां उन्हें वाक्य में किसी व्यक्ति की जगह प्रतिस्थापित किया जाता है।

78. विकल्प 3: आशीर्वाद। यह शब्द सही रूप से लिखा गया है। अन्य विकल्पों में शब्दों की गलत वर्तनी या त्रुटियाँ हैं। "आशीर्वाद" शब्द का अर्थ होता है आशीर्वाद करना या आशीर्वाद प्राप्त करना। यह शब्द आमतौर पर किसी के लिए शुभकामनाएं या आशीर्वाद देने के लिए प्रयोग होता है।

79. विकल्प 3: जिज्ञासु। यह शब्द "जानने की इच्छा रखने वाला" को दर्शाता है। "जिज्ञासु" शब्द में "ज्ञान" का अर्थ होता है और यह एक प्रश्न करने या जानने की इच्छा रखने वाले व्यक्ति को विशेषित करता है। यह शब्द जिज्ञासा, अध्ययन, और ज्ञान की प्रेरणा को दर्शाने के लिए प्रयुक्त होता है।

80. विकल्प 3: आँख दिखाना। यह मुहावरा "गुस्से से देखना" को दर्शाता है। जब किसी व्यक्ति को गुस्सा आता है और वह अपनी आँखों से क्रोध या रोष प्रदर्शित करता है, तो उसे "आँख दिखाना" कहा जाता है। यह मुहावरा एक भावनात्मक स्थिति को व्यक्त करने के लिए प्रयोग होता है, जब व्यक्ति का गुस्सा या क्रोध उसकी आँखों में दिखता है।

81. विकल्प 2 "मुँह में राम, बगल में छुरी" एक लोकोक्ति है जो भीतर से शत्रुता और ऊपर से मीठी बात करने के भाव को व्यक्त करती है। इस वाक्य में "मुँह में राम" शत्रुता को दर्शाता है, जबकि "बगल में छुरी" मीठी बात करने के भाव को दर्शाता है। यह लोकोक्ति मानसिक स्थितियों को संकेतित करने के लिए प्रयुक्त होती है।

82. विकल्प 2 "अपना स्थान ग्रहण करने की कृपा करें" एक शुद्ध वाक्य है। इस वाक्य में स्थानापन्न को "कृपा" के स्थान पर "करें" कर दिया गया है, जो वाक्य को अशुद्ध बना देता है। विकल्प 2 ने इस त्रुटि को सुधारा है और यह सही है।

83. विकल्प 3 "किसान, भूमि" में कर्ता और अधिकरण का सही विभाजन किया गया है। "किसान" कार्य करने वाला है और "भूमि" उसका कार्यस्थल है। अन्य विकल्पों में कर्ता और अधिकरण का विभाजन गलत है।

84. विकल्प 2 "तदर्थ" एक उचित शब्द है जो "अन्तरिम कालीन" के लिए प्रयुक्त होता है। "तदर्थ" का अर्थ होता है "उसके अर्थ में" या "उसके अनुसार"। यह शब्द अवकाशित या अस्थायी स्थिति को दर्शाने के लिए प्रयुक्त होता है।

85. विकल्प 4 "गुणवाचक" शब्द "मीठे" का विशेषण है। "गुणवाचक" विशेषण किसी वस्तु, व्यक्ति या स्थिति को घृणा या अपमान का अनुभव कराने वाला होता है। इस वाक्य में "मीठे" शब्द से बताया जा रहा है कि सन्तरे गुणास्पद या नापसंदीग्रस्त हैं। यह शब्द उनकी गुणों की आलोचना करने के लिए प्रयुक्त होता है।

86. The correct answer is 3. "He has not yet recovered from his illness." The preposition "from" shows the source or origin of something. Here, it indicates that the person is still recovering from the illness.

87. The correct answer is 2. "It has been raining since yesterday." "Since" points to the starting time or event of an ongoing action. The rain started yesterday and continues until now.

88. The correct answer is 1. "This is a matter of little importance." "Of little importance" describes the significance of the matter, with "of" showing possession or association.

89. The correct answer is 1. "There is a cow in the field." The preposition "in" indicates location, meaning the cow is within the field.

90. The correct answer is 2. "He keeps in touch with his friends through the internet." "In touch with" means maintaining communication, showing that the internet is the means of contact.

91. The correct answer is 4. "I shall do it with pleasure." "With" expresses the manner in which something will be done, indicating enjoyment while performing the task.

92. The correct answer is 4. "The Chief Guest will give away the prizes." "Give away" means to distribute. The Chief Guest will hand out the prizes.

93. The correct answer is 4. "She has worked out all the sums." The present perfect tense, using "has," shows an action that was completed before now but has relevance to the present.

94. The correct answer is 3. "I am reading a book." The present continuous tense shows an action currently happening. It implies reading is taking place right now.

95. The correct answer is 3. "A miss is as good as a mile" means failing, regardless of how close one is to success, results in failure. The proverb highlights that failing is failure, no matter how near one is.

96. The correct answer is 1. "Strike while the iron is hot" means to act promptly when an opportunity arises. It emphasizes seizing the moment for success, as timing is crucial.

97. The correct answer is 1. "Books are sold in this shop." This is the passive voice of "This shop sells books," where the action is focused on books being sold in the shop.

98. The correct answer is 3. "The dinner has been cooked by mother" is the passive voice of "Mother has cooked the dinner." The object (dinner) becomes the subject in passive voice.

99. The correct answer is 3. The opposite of "extrovert" is "introvert." Extroverts are sociable and outgoing, while introverts are reserved and prefer solitude.

100. The correct answer is 2. The opposite of "urban" is "rural." Urban refers to city life, while rural relates to the countryside, emphasizing nature and agriculture.

R.J.S. Preliminary Examination 2015

1. The correct answer is option 3: Prescribed Authority. A bank can recover dues from an agriculturist, heir, or guarantor by applying to the Prescribed Authority under the Rajasthan Agricultural Credit Operations (Removal of Difficulties) Act, 1974.

2. The correct answer is option 2: Computed on the market value of the plaintiff's share. Court fees for a partition suit are based on the market value of the plaintiff's share in the property, as per Section 35 of the Rajasthan Court Fees and Suits Valuation Act, 1961.

3. The correct answer is option 2: The person drawing, making, or executing the release-dee[D] Under the Rajasthan Stamp Act, 1998, the expense of providing the proper stamp for a release-deed is borne by the person who draws, makes, or executes it.

4. The correct answer is option 2: "Shall not be called in question at any stage..." In case an unstamped instrument is admitted in evidence, its admission cannot be questioned during the same suit, except under Section 71 of the Rajasthan Stamp Act, 1998.

5. The correct answer is option 3: Both (1) and (2). A will can be presented for registration during the testator's lifetime or, after their death, by an executor or any person claiming under the will, as per the Registration Act, 1908.

6. The correct answer is option 2:

Voi[D] A contract is void if parties realize the law they based it on is not in force in Indi[A] It has no legal effect, as it lacks the intended legal framework.

7. The correct answer is option 1: Is of no effect. Acknowledgment made after the prescribed limitation period under the Indian Limitation Act, 1963, for a suit or application has no legal effect.

8. The correct answer is option 1: Within 240 days from the notice service. The Rajasthan Rent Control Act, 2001, sets a 240-day limit for disposing of petitions filed under Section 9 after serving notice to the tenant.

9. The correct answer is option 4: All the above. A firm may dissolve upon the expiration of its term, completion of an undertaking, or the death of a partner, as per the Indian Partnership Act, 1932.

10. The correct answer is option 4: None of the above. A finder of lost goods does not fall under bailor, surety, or bailee according to the Indian Contract Act, 1872, but has temporary custodial duties until the rightful owner is found.

11. The correct answer is option 3: Any matter under Right to Information Act, 2005. The Rajasthan Right to Hearing Act, 2012, allows filing complaints regarding grievances under the Right to Information Act, 2005, but not related to service matters or court matters.

12. The correct answer is option 3: National Legal Services Authority vs. Union of India (2014) 5 SCC 438. This judgment recognized transgender individuals as a "third gender" and safeguarded their constitutional rights.

13. The correct answer is option 1: The Constitution (Eighty-sixth Amendment) Act, 2002. This amendment inserted Article 21-A, making education a fundamental right for children aged 6 to 14 years.

14. The correct answer is option 4: All the above are correct. Under Section 20 of the CPC, a suit may be instituted in the court of the lowest grade, or within the jurisdiction where the defendant resides or where the cause of action arises.

15. The correct answer is option 3: Salem Advocate Bar Association vs. UOI. The Supreme Court upheld the constitutional validity of the 1999 and 2002 amendments to the Code of Civil Procedure, which aimed to streamline civil litigation.

16. The correct answer is option 2: Rule-9 of Order XXII. Under Order XLIII, an appeal lies from an order refusing to set aside the abatement or dismissal of a suit, as per Rule-9 of Order XXII.

17. The correct answer is option 3: Both statements are correct. A right to easement for light and air can be acquired through continuous enjoyment for twenty years. However, rights to light or air for an open space cannot be acquired by prescription.

18. The correct answer is option 3: The court cannot grant a refund of earnest money unless specifically claime[D] In a specific performance suit, the court can grant partition or possession or refund earnest money if claimed.

19. The correct answer is option 2: Wills for immovable property do not need to be compulsorily registered, though registration is recommended to avoid disputes. Other related instruments must be registered per the Registration Act, 1908.

20. The correct answer is option 3: Usufructuary mortgage. In an usufructuary mortgage, possession of the mortgaged property is transferred to the mortgagee, who receives income or profits from it during the mortgage period.

21. The correct answer is option 4: Both statements are incorrect. A transfer made to defeat creditors or without consideration is voidable, not void, at the option of the creditor or subsequent transferee.

22. The correct answer is option 2: A party may seek the appointment of a receiver even after an arbitral award has been made. This is allowed under Section 9 of the Arbitration and Conciliation Act, 1996 for interim measures.

23. The correct answer is option 3: Application. Under Article 137 of the Limitation Act, 1963, the three-year period applies to applications where no other period is specified.

24. The correct answer is option 2: Statement 'B' is correct. In computing limitation for appeals, the day of the judgment and time for obtaining a copy

of the decree are exclude[D] Statement 'A' is incorrect as the starting day is excluded.

25. The correct answer is option 2: Permanent Lok Adalat cannot handle non-compoundable offenses. According to Section 22-C of the Legal Services Authority Act, 1987, it does not have jurisdiction over such matters.

26. Option 1 is correct as the parties are within the degrees of prohibited relationship. Section 11 of the Hindu Marriage Act, 1955 outlines the grounds for declaring a marriage void, including being within prohibited relationships. Option 4 is incorrect as it overgeneralizes the conditions listed in the other options.

27. Option 3 is correct because the Hindu Succession (Amendment) Act, 2005 grants daughters equal rights to become coparceners by birth in a joint Hindu family under Mitakshara law. This amendment ensures that daughters have the same inheritance rights as sons.

28. The incorrect statement is that the husband is the natural guardian of a Hindu married girl. According to the Hindu Minority and Guardianship Act, 1956, a married Hindu woman's natural guardianship remains with her father and mother, not her husband.

29. Option 3 is correct as a Hindu wife can claim maintenance from her father-in-law under Section 19 of the Hindu Adoptions and Maintenance Act, 1956 after her husband's death. Other Section s of the Hindu Marriage Act and Succession Act address alimony and property distribution.

30. Option 1 is correct, defining a respondent under the Protection of Women from Domestic Violence Act, 2005 as anyone in a domestic relationship with the aggrieved person against whom relief is sought. Options 2 and 3 are incorrect because they specify gender or a specific action not mentioned in the definition.

31. Option 4 is correct as Section 3 of the Rajasthan Rent Control Act, 2001 exempts government company premises from rent control laws. Options 1, 2, and 3 do not pertain to this exemption.

32. Option 2 is correct because Section 242 of the Rajasthan Tenancy Act, 1955 allows civil courts to frame tenancy issues for revenue courts, but they may choose to accept or reject the revenue court's findings.

33. Option 1 is correct as Section 23 of the Rajasthan Land Revenue Act, 1956 does not mention regularizing unauthorized occupation. It covers issues like grazing rights, boundary disputes, and succession-related mutations.

34. Option 1 is correct as the Rajasthan High Court frames the General Rules (Civil) under Article 227 of the Constitution, which governs civil cases in Rajasthan.

35. Option 4 is correct as a written deed is not a requirement for a valid gift under Mohammedan law. The essential elements are the declaration, acceptance, and delivery of possession.

36. Option 2 is correct as under Sections 82 and 83 of the Code of Criminal Procedure, the court can attach property after publishing a proclamation under Section 82 for the accused to appear.

37. Option 3 is correct as a Magistrate not empowered by law to take cognizance of an offense under Section 190(1)(c) results in invalid proceedings.

38. Option 2 is correct as irregularities under Sections 190(1)(a) and (b) do not invalidate the proceedings. These clauses allow a Magistrate to take cognizance based on police reports or third-party information.

39. Option 2 is correct as an attempt to murder under Section 307 IPC is non-bailable, cognizable, and non-compoundable, making it a serious offense compared to other related offenses.

40. Option 4 is correct as Section 299 of the Indian Penal Code defines culpable homicide, while Section 300 further elaborates on its categories, such as murder and manslaughter.

41. Option 2 is correct as Section 313 of the Code of Criminal Procedure provides for the accused's statement on oath to explain circumstances arising from the evidence against them during the trial.

42. Option 4 is correct as all the statements about witnesses in legal proceedings, such as an accomplice being competent and leading questions dur-

ing cross-examination, are accurate under Indian law.

43. Option 3 is correct as Section 101 of the Indian Evidence Act allows the burden of proof to shift, particularly if the accused provides plausible evidence that creates doubt about their guilt.

44. Option 2 is correct as a Police Officer initiates proceedings under Section 145 of the Code of Criminal Procedure when there is a land possession dispute likely to cause a breach of peace.

45. Option 2 is correct as Dashrath Rupsingh Rathod vs. State of Maharashtra clarified that only the court within the drawee bank's territorial jurisdiction can try cases under Section 138 of the Negotiable Instruments Act.

46. Option 4 is correct as Sections 138 and 142 of the Negotiable Instruments Act set time limits for presenting a cheque, serving a notice, and filing a complaint, which must all be followed.

47. Option 3 is correct as Section 142 of the Negotiable Instruments Act allows a court to condone delays in filing complaints under Section 138 if sufficient cause is shown.

48. Option 1 is correct as Shreya Singhal v. Union of India struck down Section 66-A of the Information Technology Act, upholding free speech and digital rights.

49. Option 2 is correct as Section 25 of the Protection of Children from Sexual Offences Act, 2012 ensures that the child's statement is recorded without the presence of the accused's advocate to protect the child's privacy.

50. Option 4 is correct as probation officers are responsible for supervising probationers and assisting them in rehabilitation, but they are not typically tasked with arranging lodging and boarding.

51. The correct answer is 4: All the above. According to the Protection of Children from Sexual Offences Act, 2012, statements of children must be recorded in a safe, child-friendly environment. A woman police officer, preferably not in uniform, should record the statement at a location chosen by the child, ensuring no contact with the accuse[D] These provisions aim to create a supportive atmosphere for the child.

52. The correct answer is 1: Key pair. In asymmetric cryptography, a private key and its related public key form a key pair. The private key is kept secret and used for digital signatures, while the public key verifies signatures, ensuring secure communication and encryption.

53. The correct answer is 2: Originator. The originator is the person responsible for sending, generating, storing, or transmitting an electronic message. This role involves creating or initiating the message, such as emails or text messages, in the context of electronic communication.

54. The correct answer is 2: Not less than 6 months but which may extend to 5 years and also a fine not less than ten thousand rupees. Section 136 of the Electricity Act, 2003, penalizes individuals committing theft of electric lines and materials, with imprisonment between 6 months to 5 years, plus a fine of at least ten thousand rupees.

55. The correct answer is 2: Inspector. Under Section 78 of the Information Technology Act, 2000, the officer investigating cybercrimes must be at least of the rank of Inspector. This ensures the officer has the expertise necessary to handle complex cybercrime investigations involving digital evidence.

56. The correct answer is 4: Suresh Kumar Kaushal vs. Naz Foundation (India) Trust - (2014) 1 SCC 1. This judgment upheld the constitutional validity of Section 377 of the Indian Penal Code, which criminalized consensual homosexual acts, but was later overruled in 2018 in Navtej Singh Johar v. Union of India.

57. The correct answer is 4: All the above. Section 3(1) of the Scheduled Castes and Scheduled Tribes (Prevention of Atrocities) Act, 1989, lists acts like forcing inedible substances, insulting or intimidating with intent to humiliate, and forcing votes as atrocities, punishable offenses to protect these communities.

58. The correct answer is 2: He is under 18 years of age or is convicted for an offense punishable under Section 26 or 27 of the Narcotic Drugs and Psychotropic Substances Act, 1985. Probation can be granted to juveniles or

those convicted under specific Section s of the Act, aiming to rehabilitate offenders rather than imposing imprisonment.

59. The correct answer is 1: A juvenile who is alleged to have committed an offense and has not completed eighteen years of age on the date of the offense. The Juvenile Justice (Care and Protection of Children) Act, 2000 defines a juvenile as someone under 18 years old when the offense was committed, recognizing their need for special care and protection.

60. The correct answer is 3: The order passed by the Juvenile Justice Board in the absence of any member is invali[D] According to the Juvenile Justice (Care and Protection of Children) Act, 2000, the Board must have a complete composition, including a Judicial Magistrate and two social workers, for its order to be valid.

61. The correct answer is 3: If it relates to the cause of his own death. Under Section 32 of the Indian Evidence Act, 1872, statements made by a deceased person are relevant if they concern the cause of their death. Such statements help ascertain the circumstances surrounding the person's demise.

62. The correct answer is 3: He has undergone detention for one-half period of imprisonment specified for the offense. Section 436-A of the Code of Criminal Procedure, 1973 allows the release of an accused on bail if they have served half the imprisonment term of the offense, preventing prolonged pre-trial detention.

63. The correct answer is 2: They are relevant. Facts connected with a fact in issue, forming part of the same transaction, are relevant, even if they occurred at different times or places. These facts provide context and help in understanding the complete narrative of the case.

64. The correct answer is 1: Facts inconsistent with any fact in issue are not relevant. According to the Indian Evidence Act, 1872, facts contradicting the fact in issue are inadmissible. Only evidence supporting the fact in issue is relevant for determining the matter at hand.

65. The correct answer is 4: Selvi and others vs. State of Karnataka - (2010) 7 SCC 263. In this case, the Supreme Court ruled that narcoanalysis, poly-

graph, and BEAP tests conducted against a person's will violate their constitutional rights, including the right against self-incrimination and right to privacy.

66. The correct answer is 1: Both statements are correct. Rule 102 requires the court of sessions to submit proceedings to the High Court within four days after passing a death sentence. Rule 104 mandates the court to check if a female prisoner is pregnant before passing a death sentence.

67. The correct answer is 1: Six. Section 53 of the Indian Penal Code lists six types of punishments: death, life imprisonment, rigorous imprisonment, simple imprisonment, forfeiture of property, and fine, prescribed according to the seriousness of the offense.

68. The correct answer is 2: For a period not exceeding three months, if the term of imprisonment exceeds six months but does not exceed one year. According to Sections 73 and 74 of the Indian Penal Code, solitary confinement may be applied under certain limits, but the duration mentioned in option 2 is incorrect.

69. The correct answer is 3: A would be guilty of Section 302 IPC, and B would be guilty of no offense. A induces B to shoot at a bush, causing Z's death. A's intention to kill Z makes them guilty of murder, but B's unintentional action doesn't constitute an offense.

70. The correct answer is 4: A has committed no offense. A drops a child from a house-top during a fire, intending to save them. Although A knew the fall could harm the child, they acted in good faith, and their actions do not constitute an offense under IPC.

71. वे शब्द जो किसी संस्कृत या प्राकृत मूल से निकले हुए नहीं जान पड़ते और जिनकी व्युत्पत्ति का पता नहीं लगता, कहलाते है "देशज"। ये शब्द ऐसे शब्द है जिनकी उत्पत्ति और मूल भाषा से जुड़ना असंभव है या जिनकी व्युत्पत्ति के बारे में जानकारी नहीं होती है। इन शब्दों का प्रयोग विशेषतः काव्य और साहित्यिक रचनाओं में होता है।

72. स्वर, व्यंजन, विसर्ग - ये संस्कृत भाषा के विभिन्न ध्वनियों को दर्शाने वाले तत्त्व है। स्वर ध्वनि संयुक्त वर्ण और एकाक्षरिक वर्ण होते है, व्यंजन ध्वनि संयुक्त वर्ण होते है और विसर्ग ध्वनि स्वर या व्यंजन के बाद आने वाला ध्वनि होता है। इन तत्त्वों का ज्ञान भाषा विज्ञान में महत्वपूर्ण होता है क्योंकि इन्हें सही रूप से

उच्चारित करना भाषा के समझ में मदद करता है।

73. जिस सर्वनाम से वक्ता के पास अथवा दूर की किसी वस्तु का बोध होता हो, को कहते हैं "निश्चयवाचक सर्वनाम"। यह सर्वनाम उपयोग होता है जब व्यक्ति किसी विशिष्ट वस्तु को संकेतित करना चाहता हो जो वक्ता के पास हो या दूर हो। उदाहरण के रूप में, "यहां वह है" या "उसके पास यह है" जैसे वाक्यों में इस सर्वनाम का प्रयोग होता है।

74. संज्ञा के सर्वनाम का क्रिया के साथ संबंध निर्धारित करने वाले तत्व कहलाते हैं "कारक"। कारक शब्द क्रिया के साथ संबंधित होता है और क्रिया का कारक के रूप में उपयोग होता है। कारक विभिन्न प्रकार के होते हैं जैसे कर्ता, कर्म, करण, संबंध, अपादान, अधिकरण, साधन आदि। ये कारक क्रिया के विविध पहलुओं को समझने और संबंधित शब्दों को पहचानने में मदद करते हैं।

75. दो या अधिक शब्दों के परस्पर संबंध बताने वाले शब्दों अथवा प्रत्ययों का लोप होने पर, दो या अधिक शब्द में से जो एक स्वतंत्र शब्द बनता है, कहलाता है "समास"। समास एक शब्द या शब्दों के संयोजन से बना होता है जिससे उनका अर्थ पूर्ण होता है। इससे वाक्यों को संक्षेप में लिखने और समझने में मदद मिलती है। विभिन्न प्रकार के समास होते हैं जैसे तत्पुरुष, कर्मधारय, द्वंद्व, द्विगु आदि।

76. उत्तर: विस्मयादिबोधक (4) वाक्य "हाय! अब मैं क्या करूं।" में "हाय" शब्द विस्मयादिबोधक अव्यय है। यह अव्यय वाक्य में विस्मय, आश्चर्य, चिंता, या अनिर्णीत भावनाओं को व्यक्त करने के लिए प्रयुक्त होता है। यह अव्यय वाक्य के अर्थ और भाव को संदर्भित करता है और उसमें व्यक्त किए गए भाव की प्रतिष्ठा करता है। "हाय" शब्द यहां व्यक्त करने वाले व्यक्ति के आंतरिक दुख, चिंता, या अस्थिरता का प्रतिबिम्बित करता है।

77. उत्तर: काल (3) वाक्य "क्रिया के उस रूपान्तरण को, जिससे क्रिया के व्यापार का समय तथा उसकी पूर्ण अथवा अपूर्ण अवस्था का बोध होता है, को कहते हैं।" में जब क्रिया अपने व्यापार का समय, पूर्ण अवस्था, या अपूर्ण अवस्था का बोध कराती है, तो उसे "काल" कहते हैं। काल क्रिया के व्यापार के समय, अवस्था, या अवधि की प्रकटीकरण करता है और वाक्य में समय का प्रतिपादन करता है।

78. उत्तर: आशिर्वाद (4) शब्द "चांदनी" का समानार्थी शब्द "कालत्र" नहीं है। "चांदनी" का अर्थ होता है "चंद्रिका, प्रकाश, या रोशनी" जबकि "कालत्र" का अर्थ होता है "काल या मृत्यु"। इसलिए "चांदनी" का समानार्थी शब्द "कालत्र" नहीं होता है।

79. उत्तर: निष्काम-सकाम (1) विज्लोभ-युग्म के सही समानार्थी हैं "निष्काम-सकाम"। यह शब्दांतर कार्य के द्वारा दो शब्दों का एकीकरण है, जहां "विज्लोभ" का अर्थ होता है "निर्थकता" और "युग्म" का अर्थ होता है "युग्मन" यानी "साथ होना"। इस प्रकार, "निष्काम-सकाम" का अर्थ होता है "जो निर्थकता के साथ होता है या जिसमें कोई लालच नहीं होती है"।

80. उत्तर: पृष्ठांकन (1) मूल पत्र की प्रतिलिपि जब किसी विभाग को प्रेषित की जाती है, तो उसे "पृष्ठांकन" कहा जाता है। पृष्ठांकन के माध्यम से, मूल पत्र की यथासंभव विशेषताओं, निर्देशों, या सूचनाओं को विभाग के लिए स्पष्ट कर दिया जाता है। इस प्रक्रिया में, मूल पत्र की प्रतिलिपि एक स्थापित प्रोटोकॉल के अनुसार विभाग तक पहुंचाई जाती है, ताकि उसे विभाग के कार्यकारी अधिकारी द्वारा विचार किया जा सके।

81. घर की मुर्गी दाल बराबर' कहावत का अर्थ है कि अपने आदमी को कम महत्व देना यानी किसी को अपने करीबी या अपने संबंधित व्यक्ति को अधिक महत्वपूर्ण या महत्वहीन समझना। इस कहावत के माध्यम से यह बताया जाता है कि हमें अक्सर अपने आस-पास के लोगों को ध्यान देने और महत्व देने की आवश्यकता होती है।

82. "साध्वाचरण" शब्द का संधि विच्छेद साधु+आचरण है। यह शब्द धार्मिक और नैतिक आचरण को संकेत करता है जो ईमानदारी, सदाचार, और उच्च मानसिकता के साथ संबंधित होता है।

83. 'नीलोत्पलभ' में समास है "कर्मधारय"। कर्मधारय समास में दो शब्दों का संयोजन होता है जहां प्रथम शब्द अपेक्षित विशेषण का कार्य करता है और दूसरा शब्द उसका पूरक होता है। इस समास में "नील" शब्द का "उत्पल" शब्द को संयोजक बनाने के लिए प्रयोग हुआ है।

84. निम्नलिखित में से 'विध्युत' का पर्यायवाची शब्द नहीं है "कोदंट"। 'तडित', 'चपला', और 'चंचला' सभी इस शब्द के पर्यायवाची शब्द हैं जो बिजली के संबंध में उपयोग होते हैं।

85. 'जिन ढूँढा तिन पाइयाँ गहरे पाभी पैठ' लोकोक्ति का अर्थ होता है कि परिश्रम का फल अवश्य मिलता है। इस उपमहाकाव्य के माध्यम से यह संकेतित किया जाता है कि कठिनाइयों और संघर्ष के बाद सफलता प्राप्त होती है। इसे एक बच्चे के पहेली के रूप में भी देखा जा सकता है जहां जिन ढूंढने के बाद उसे जीत की प्राप्ति होती है।

86. The correct answer is option 3: Present Continuous Tense. "I am pleading for the preservation of trees" is in the Present Continuous Tense, which indicates an ongoing action happening at the time of speaking.

87. The correct answer is option 1: Was walking. "My sister saw a snake while she ___ in the garden" requires the past continuous tense "was walking,"

indicating an ongoing action when the snake was seen.

88. The correct answer is option 2: Obstinate. "Obstinate" is a synonym for "stubborn," meaning unwilling to change or compromise, while other options do not convey the same meaning.

89. The opposite of "arbitrary" is "methodical," meaning systematic or organized, in contrast to "arbitrary," which is based on random choices or personal whim.

90. The correct answer is option 3: A man of importance. "A man of weight" refers to someone of importance or influence, not physical weight.

91. The correct answer is option 2: A state of happiness for foolish reasons. "A fool's paradise" refers to a false or misguided sense of happiness based on unrealistic expectations.

92. The correct answer is option 3: The Policeman inquired where we were going. In indirect speech, "said" changes to "inquired," and the question is transformed into a statement.

93. The correct answer is option 2: The Judge commanded them to call the first witness. "Said" becomes "commanded" in indirect speech to reflect the judge's instruction.

94. The correct answer is option 4: She told me that she would play then. In indirect speech, "shall" changes to "would," and "now" becomes "then."

95. The correct answer is option 2: A bulldog was given to her by someone. In passive voice, "someone" becomes the agent and "her" becomes the subject.

96. The correct answer is option 3: A letter was being written by Mona to her father. The past continuous tense "was writing" becomes "was being written" in the passive voice.

97. The correct answer is option 4: The, the. The definite article "the" is used to refer to specific groups, making the statement about the rich and poor clear.

98. The correct answer is option 1: [A] "A pupil should obey his teacher" uses "a" to refer to any pupil, not a specific one.

99. The correct answer is option 3: The. "Kalidas is the Shakespeare of India" uses "the" before "Shakespeare" to specify the renowned figure being compared.

100. The correct answer is option 3: "Actus curiae neminem gravabit" means an act of the court shall not prejudice any individual, emphasizing fairness and impartiality in the legal system.

R.J.S. Preliminary Examination 2016

1. An arbitration agreement specifying four arbitrators is deemed to involve a sole arbitrator under the Arbitration & Conciliation Act, 1996. The agreement is assumed to appoint a sole arbitrator when the specified number is even.

2. Specific performance is ordered when monetary compensation is inadequate. It compels the breaching party to fulfill obligations, especially when the subject matter is unique or money isn't sufficient.

3. A partnership firm and its partners are not separate legal entities. The firm's rights and liabilities belong to the partners themselves, who jointly own the firm.

4. Section 105 of the Transfer of Property Act, 1882, defines a lease as the transfer of a right to enjoy property for consideration, which could include money, service, or crops.

5. Article 141 of the Constitution declares that the law declared by the Supreme Court is binding on all courts in India.

6. Leases exceeding one year must be executed by a registered instrument to be enforceable under the Registration Act.

7. Section 5 of the Limitation Act, 1963, extends the prescribed period for filing appeals but doesn't apply to suits or execution of decrees.

8. A suit can be dismissed due to the non-joinder of a necessary party, which is essential for a fair and complete resolution.

9. Acceptance is complete once it is transmitted and no longer within the acceptor's control, making it binding on the proposer.

10. A Commissioner under the Code of Civil Procedure can record evidence but cannot decide objections raised during the process.

11. Under the Rajasthan Rent Control Act, 2001, 'premises' excludes hostel accommodation, which isn't covered by the Act's scope.

12. 'Dominant heritage' under the Easements Act refers to the land benefiting from the easement, such as a right of way.

13. Lok Adalats, formed under the Legal Services Authorities Act, 1987, provide an alternative forum for quick, cost-effective dispute resolution through conciliation.

14. The Indian Evidence Act, 1872, applies to all judicial proceedings except certain courts-martial and arbitrations, but not to affidavits.

15. The Hindu Marriage Act, 1955 doesn't apply to Scheduled Tribe members who follow separate personal laws.

16. Section 163-A of the Motor Vehicles Act, 1988, offers compensation on a structured formula basis for accidents resulting in death or permanent disability.

17. The Negotiable Instruments Act, 1881 presumes that a lost negotiable instrument was duly stamped unless proven otherwise.

18. A registered document operates from the date it would have without registration, not from the time of its registration, as per Section 47 of the Registration Act, 1908.

19. Under the Rajasthan Tenancy Act, 1955, a sale, gift, or bequest of Khatedari interests by a Scheduled Caste member to a non-Scheduled Caste person is void.

20. Appeals from original decrees under the Rajasthan Tenancy Act, 1955, are provided for under Section 223, outlining the appeal process and authority.

21. When an instrument falls under multiple descriptions with different duties, the highest applicable duty is charged under the Rajasthan Stamp Act, 1998.

22. An instrument under the Rajasthan Stamp Act, 1998, cannot be admitted in evidence unless it is properly stamped.

23. The Rajasthan Agricultural Credit Operations Act, 1974 allows the prescribed authority to make orders against the tenant of an agriculturist for credit-related issues.

24. In partition suits in Rajasthan, if the plaintiff's share exceeds Rs.10,000, a fixed court fee of Rs.200 is payable.

25. Section 65-B of the Rajasthan Court Fees and Suits Valuation Act, 1961, mandates a refund of court fees if a suit is settled via alternative dispute resolution methods under Section 89 of the CPC.

26. Under the Hindu Succession Act, 1956, if a female inherits property from her father or mother and has no surviving children or their descendants, the property passes to the heirs of her father. This is outlined in Section 15(1), which directs the succession in such cases.

27. The Supreme Court ruled in Hafeeza Bibi vs. Shaikh Farid (2011) that Muslim Law does not require compulsory registration for a valid gift of immovable property if it meets the necessary conditions: declaration, acceptance, and delivery of possession.

28. Part IX-B, dealing with cooperative societies, was inserted into the Constitution by the Constitution (97th Amendment) Act, 2011. This amendment gives constitutional status to cooperatives and allows state governments to regulate them.

29. Once a valid adoption occurs under the Hindu Adoption & Maintenance Act, 1956, it cannot be canceled by the adoptive parent or anyone else. The adoption is legally permanent, ensuring a stable parent-child relationship.

30. Section 81 of the Rajasthan Land Revenue Act, 1956, grants the appellate authority the power to stay the execution of lower court orders in land revenue matters, allowing for a pause in enforcement during appeals.

31. Civil courts do not have jurisdiction over electoral registration issues under the Rajasthan Panchayati Raj Act, 1994. Electoral matters fall under the purview of the Election Commission and its appointed authorities.

32. Section 304 of the Rajasthan Municipalities Act, 2009, addresses suits against municipalities or their officers. It outlines the procedure, jurisdiction, and limitations for filing such suits.

33. The General Rules (Civil), 1986 regulate the taxation of legal fees as costs under a court decree. These rules ensure that legal fees are reasonable and proportionate to the complexity of the case.

34. Under the Rajasthan Rent Control Act, 2001, if a tenant dies, their surviving spouse, children, and parents inherit the tenancy rights, continuing the lease under the same terms.

35. Under the Rajasthan Tenancy Act, 1955, disputes over tree ownership and removal rights are adjudicated by the Tehsildar, a revenue officer at the tehsil level, who resolves such land-related matters.

36. The statement claiming that all participants in a criminal act are liable regardless of intent is incorrect. Criminal liability depends on both the act (actus reus) and the mental state (mens rea), meaning participants are liable based on their individual intentions.

37. In this case, 'A', a public servant, intentionally makes a false translation with the intent to harm 'B'. As the offense is non-compoundable, it cannot be settled out of court, and the prosecution proceeds with legal action.

38. The offense committed by 'A', who induces 'B' to pay an advance and later denies the agreement, falls under Section 420 of the Indian Penal Code for cheating and dishonestly inducing delivery of property.

39. The offense committed by 'A' for monitoring 'B's mobile phone and email without consent is considered stalking, as it involves repeated, unwanted surveillance that infringes on 'B's privacy.

40. The case Subramanian Swamy vs. Union of India upheld the constitutionality of Sections 499 and 500 of the Indian Penal Code, which deal with defamation, while recognizing some limitations to protect freedom of speech.

41. If the prosecution withdraws its case after evidence begins, the accused is acquitte[D] This means they are cleared of charges, and the court stops further proceedings.

42. Bail granted under Section 167(2) of the Code of Criminal Procedure is similar to bail under Chapter XXXIII. Both involve similar rights, obligations, and conditions for the accused.

43. A court can take cognizance of an offense even after the expiration of the limitation period if it is necessary in the interest of justice, considering the facts and circumstances of the case.

44. Under Section 95 of the Code of Criminal Procedure, an application to set aside the forfeiture of a book must be filed with the High Court, which reviews such declarations made by the State Government.

45. A person arrested without a warrant must be presented before a Magistrate without unnecessary delay, as per the Code of Criminal Procedure, to ensure timely judicial review of the arrest.

46. An error in the charge is considered material when it misleads the accused, affecting their ability to prepare a defense. The charge must provide accurate details to avoid confusion or prejudice.

47. Under Section 428 of the Code of Criminal Procedure, any period of detention during investigation and trial is subtracted from the final sentence, ensuring that time spent in custody is accounted for in the sentencing.

48. The recovery of the weapon of offense, based on a statement made during the investigation of another case, may be admissible in court if it leads to relevant facts for the current case.

49. The presence of relatives during a dying declaration does not necessarily affect its relevance. In fact, it may support its credibility, as long as the circumstances and the declarant's condition are appropriate.

50. A medical report detailing the victim's injuries is relevant and admissible in evidence, helping establish the nature and extent of the harm and supporting the prosecution's case.

51. The correct option is 2: When the matter in question is sufficiently prove[D] Leading questions may be permitted during examination-in-chief when the facts are already established, or to expedite proceedings or clarify evidence. Normally, leading questions

are not allowed, as they should be neutral. The court has discretion over their allowance.

52. The correct option is 1: Statement [A] Section 113-A presumption of abetment of suicide is not applicable if the marriage occurred more than seven years before the woman's suicide, even if cruelty is establishe[D] The presumption applies only if the marriage is within seven years prior to the suicide.

53. The correct option is 3: Section 154. In cases under Section 325 of IPC, leading questions may be asked during examination-in-chief if a witness provides adverse evidence. Section 154 allows this when the witness gives unfavorable testimony, allowing the prosecution to clarify or counter the evidence.

54. The correct option is 2: Statement B is correct. Communication through an electronic record does not invalidate a contract. Electronic records can form a valid contract, provided other legal requirements, such as meeting of minds and intention, are met. Electronic records are legally recognized in contract formation.

55. The correct option is 1: The offence of theft of electricity is committed if the meter is dishonestly tampered with. Tampering with the meter, such as bypassing or altering it, to gain unauthorized electricity constitutes theft. The act of moving or storing the meter without consent can be part of the offense.

56. The correct option is 2: Voi[D] A material alteration in a negotiable instrument, without the endorser's consent, renders the instrument voi[D] Changes to essential terms like amount or parties, made without proper authorization, affect the instrument's validity, making it legally ineffective.

57. The correct option is 4: Statements D & [A] Statement A is correct; the court may sentence the offender for the original offense or impose a fine up to fifty rupees for the first bond violation under the Probation of Offenders Act. Statement D is also correct, as compensation under Section 5 can be recovered as a fine.

58. The correct option is 1: State Government with the approval of the Central Government. Under Section 17 of the Probation of Offenders Act, 1958, the State Government frames rules with the Central Government's approval.

This ensures the proper implementation of the Act within the state jurisdiction.

59. The correct option is 2: The Controller. Under Section 84 of the Information Technology Act, 2000, the Controller is protected from prosecution if acting in good faith. This extends to subscribers and originators, but the statement specifically refers to the Controller's protection while performing duties under the Act.

60. The correct option is 1: State of Jammu & Kashmir. The Protection of Women from Domestic Violence Act, 2005 does not apply to Jammu & Kashmir. The state has separate laws related to domestic violence, but it may choose to adopt similar provisions or create distinct legislation for such issues.

61. The correct option is 2: Within a period not exceeding two months. Under Section 14 of the Protection of Women from Domestic Violence Act, 2005, the Magistrate must set a hearing date within two months when referring a case for counseling. This ensures timely action for the aggrieved party's support.

62. The correct option is 1: Within a period of ninety days. An appeal against a special court's judgment under the Scheduled Castes and Scheduled Tribes (Prevention of Atrocities) Act, 1989 must be filed within ninety days. This time limit ensures efficiency in legal proceedings and maintains judicial timeliness.

63. The correct option is 2: That accused was aware of the victim's caste. In cases of insulting a member of the Scheduled Caste, the court presumes the accused's awareness of the victim's caste if they had a close relationship and were neighbors for an extended period.

64. The correct option is 4: Exhibit Article A-1. A blood-stained shirt marked as evidence will be referred to as "Exhibit Article A-1." The labeling system ensures clear identification and documentation of evidence during trials for proper reference and transparency.

65. The correct option is 1: On expiration of fifty years, reckoned from 31st December next ensuing after the order disposing of the case. Papers related to stolen property identification can be

destroyed after fifty years from the order date. This ensures records are kept for sufficient time before disposal.

66. The correct option is 3: Half yearly. The Chief Judicial Magistrate must inspect the Court of a subordinate Judicial Magistrate every six months. These inspections help maintain judicial standards, assess performance, and ensure the proper functioning of the court system.

67. The correct option is 2: 18 years of age. Under the Juvenile Justice (Care and Protection of Children) Act, 2015, a "child" is defined as a person under 18 years of age. The law offers special provisions for the care, protection, and rehabilitation of juveniles in conflict with the law.

68. The correct option is 1: Chief Judicial Magistrate. The Chief Judicial Magistrate is responsible for reviewing the pendency of cases in the Juvenile Justice Boar[D] Regular reviews help ensure timely disposal of juvenile cases and the effective application of the Juvenile Justice Act.

69. The correct option is 2: A & [C] Statement A is correct: A Judicial Magistrate First Class can authorize detention in custody of a person accused under The Narcotic Drugs and Psychotropic Substances Act for up to fifteen days. This provision allows judicial control over the detention of the accused.

70. The correct option is 3: Woman police officer not below the rank of Sub-Inspector. Under the POCSO Act, 2012, only a woman police officer not below the rank of Sub-Inspector is authorized to record a child's statement. This ensures a sensitive and appropriate environment for the child during the process.

71. The correct option is 4: taking. The sentence uses the present continuous tense, "is taking," indicating an action occurring at the moment. Therefore, "taking" is the appropriate verb form in the context.

72. The correct option is 2: stolen. The sentence is in the present perfect tense, "has stolen," indicating an action completed in the past with present consequences. The books have been taken, and their absence is still relevant.

73. The correct option is 3: wins. "Slow and steady wins the race" is a proverb emphasizing the value of persistence. The verb "wins" correctly conveys the message that slow and steady effort leads to success.

74. The correct option is 2: The mirror was broken by the chil[D] The passive voice of the active sentence "The child broke the mirror" is formed by rearranging the sentence and introducing "was" and the past participle "broken."

75. The correct option is 3: Let these letters be sent by Registered Post. The passive voice of "Send these letters by Registered Post" is "Let these letters be sent by Registered Post." This polite construction indicates that the action should be performed.

76. The definite article "the" refers to specific shopkeepers facing difficulties, indicating that the sentence talks about particular known shopkeepers.

77. The word "little" expresses a small or negligible amount of knowledge about the drug's side effects, highlighting the lack of available information.

78. "Can" suggests that despite his age, the person still has the ability to read without glasses, indicating his current capability.

79. "Must" conveys a strong obligation to pay income tax, indicating a necessary action that cannot be avoided.

80. "Readable" is the opposite of "illegible," meaning the text is clear and can be easily understood.

81. In financial terms, "assets" are the opposite of "liabilities," representing resources or properties of value that can settle obligations.

82. "Bone of contention" refers to an issue or subject causing conflict or disagreement, something that people argue about.

83. The negative form of the sentence is created by adding "not" before "hiding," which means the accused was not concealing important evidence.

84. "Unless" introduces the condition that tigers will only attack if they are hungry, indicating the attack happens only under this condition.

85. "And" connects two ideas, showing that trusting in God and doing the right thing are linked and should happen together.

86. 'उत्+हार' संधि का अर्थ होता है 'उद्धार', जिसका वाचकार्थ होता है 'रक्षा' या 'मुक्ति'। इस प्रकार, उत्तेजित करने वाला शब्द 'उत्' और हार का अर्थ 'हार' संधिवाचक होता है। उद्धार शब्द इस संधि का उदाहरण है जो किसी व्यक्ति या वस्त्र को बचाने या छुड़ाने की क्रिया को दर्शाता है। इसलिए, उत्तर विकल्प 3, 'उद्धार', सही उत्तर है।

87. 'कामचोर' शब्द में अपादान तत्पुरुष समास है। इस समास में प्रथम पद 'काम' जो कार्य करने वाले को बताता है और द्वितीय पद 'चोर' जो चोरी करने वाले को दर्शाता है, प्रधान होता है। इस प्रकार, 'कामचोर' शब्द का अर्थ होता है 'चोरी करने वाला व्यक्ति'। इसलिए, उत्तर विकल्प 1, 'अपादान तत्पुरुष', सही उत्तर है।

88. निम्नलिखित में से 'पत्री' शब्द का पर्यायवाची नहीं है 'अबला'। 'पत्री' शब्द का अर्थ होता है 'पत्र की पत्री यानी 'पत्र की बेटी'। अबला शब्द का अर्थ होता है 'कमजोर' या 'दुबल'। इस प्रकार, उत्तर विकल्प 4, 'अबला', सही उत्तर है।

89. 'सृजन' शब्द का विलोम है 'संहार'। 'सृजन' का अर्थ होता है 'सृष्टि' या 'निर्माण' जबकि 'संहार' का अर्थ होता है 'नष्ट' या 'समाप्ति'। यदि हम इन दोनों शब्दों के अर्थ को विरोधाभासी रूप से देखें, तो विलोम शब्द बनता है। इसलिए, उत्तर विकल्प 2, 'संहार', सही उत्तर है।

90. निम्नलिखित में से शुद्ध शब्द है 'कवयित्री'। 'कवयित्री' शब्द का अर्थ होता है 'कविता लिखने वाली महिला'। इसलिए, उत्तर विकल्प 1, 'कवयित्री', सही उत्तर है।

91. विद्यार्थी कक्षा में उपस्थित नहीं था। यह वाक्य एक निषेधवाचक वाक्य है क्योंकि इसमें किसी कार्य की अनुपस्थिति का निषेध किया गया है। यह वाक्य बता रहा है कि विद्यार्थी कक्षा में उपस्थित नहीं था, अर्थात् उसने कक्षा में नहीं जाया था।

92. तुलसीदास ने रामचरितमानस का प्रणयन किया। यह वाक्य शुद्ध है क्योंकि यह स्पष्ट रूप से बता रहा है कि तुलसीदास ने 'रामचरितमानस' का प्रणयन किया है, अर्थात् उसने इसे रचनात्मक दृष्टिकोण से बनाया है।

93. शीला अपने पति से अपनी इच्छा के अनुसार काम करवाती है। यह वाक्य विशिष्ट व्यक्ति या संगठन के कार्य के संबंध में इच्छा की प्राथमिकता और उसे पूरा करने का बोध करवाता है। यह महावरा व्यक्ति की आत्म-स्वतंत्रता, स्वाधीनता और स्वावलम्बन का प्रतीक है।

94. रिश्वत देना। यह महावरा रिश्वत देने का बोध कराता है। 'मुट्ठी गरम करना' का अर्थ है कि किसी व्यक्ति या संगठन ने रिश्वत देने की प्रक्रिया शुरू कर दी है या रिश्वत के लिए तैयार हो गया है।

95. हर्ष-विस्मय यह युग्म विलोमता नहीं है क्योंकि यह एक विलोमता युग्म है जहां "हर्ष" और "विस्मय" एक दूसरे के विपरीतार्थक है।

विलोमता युग्म में दो शब्द एक दूसरे के पूरक होते है, जबकि यहां दोनों शब्द अपने अपने अर्थ में एक दूसरे के विपरीत है।

96. वर्तनी दोषपूर्ण होने के लिए उत्तर विकल्प 2, 'संग्रहीत', है। 'संग्रहीत' शब्द की सही वर्तनी 'संग्रहित' होती है। यह शब्द 'संग्रह किया गया' या 'इकट्ठा किया गया' का अर्थ होता है। वर्तनी दोष के कारण, 'संग्रहीत' शब्द को 'संग्रहित' रूप में लिखना चाहिए।

97. 'सत्+जन' संधि का उच्चारण 'सज्जन' होता है। 'सत्' का अर्थ होता है 'सच्चा' या 'निष्पक्ष' जबकि 'जन' का अर्थ होता है 'लोग'। इस प्रकार, 'सज्जन' शब्द का अर्थ होता है 'सच्चे और निष्पक्ष लोग'। इसलिए, उत्तर विकल्प 2, 'सज्जन', सही उत्तर है।

98. 'जानने की इच्छा रखने वाला' के लिए उपयुक्त शब्द है 'जिज्ञासु'। 'जिज्ञासु' शब्द का अर्थ होता है 'ज्ञान के प्रतीक्षारत' या 'जानने की आवश्यकता रखने वाला'। इसलिए, उत्तर विकल्प 3, 'जिज्ञासु', सही उत्तर है।

99. भीतर से शत्रुता और ऊपर से मीठी बात करने के भाव को व्यक्त करने वाली लोकोक्ति है 'मुंह में राम, बगल में छुरी'। यह वाक्यक्रम यह दर्शाता है कि व्यक्ति के मुख में वह शब्द कहता है जो सुखद और प्रिय होता है, लेकिन उसकी पृष्ठभूमि में कुछ खतरनाक और अप्रिय हो सकता है। इसलिए, उत्तर विकल्प 2, 'मुंह में राम, बगल में छुरी', सही उत्तर है।

100. 'जिन ढूँढा तिन पाइयाँ गहरे पानी पैठ' लोकोक्ति का अर्थ होता है 'जो प्रत्याशी या ढूँढने वाला मेहनत करता है, वह साधन या स्थान प्राप्त करता है।' इस लोकोक्ति में, ढूँढने वाले की प्रयासों और यत्नों का परिणाम बताया गया है। इसलिए, उत्तर विकल्प 3, 'जो प्रत्याशी या ढूँढने वाला मेहनत करता है, वह साधन या स्थान प्राप्त करता है।', सही उत्तर है।

R.J.S. Preliminary Examination

2017-18

1. The correct option is 2: A minor son. A minor son cannot be granted probate under the Indian Succession Act, 1925, as he is legally incapable of handling such matters. Probate can be granted to others like married daughters or illegitimate children, but not to a minor son.

2. The correct option is 2: Already adopted chil[D] Under the Hindu Adoptions and Maintenance Act, 1956, an already adopted child cannot be adopted again. Once adopted, the child is considered the legitimate child of the adoptive parents.

3. The correct option is 4: Banking Services. Banking services are not considered "Public Utility Services" under the

Legal Services Authority Act, 1987. These services primarily serve private individuals and businesses, unlike essential services such as transport or communication.

4. The correct option is 1: On the date the suit was institute[D] When a party is added during a suit, the suit is still deemed to have been instituted on the original date, not the date of substitution or addition.

5. The correct option is 2: 1/3. Under Section 163A of the Motor Vehicles Act, 1988, the compensation for third-party fatal accidents is reduced by 1/3, taking into account the victim's potential expenses.

6. The correct option is 1: Registration is compulsory. Under the Registration Act, 1908, registration is mandatory for the gift of immovable property to ensure its legal validity and provide evidence of ownership transfer.

7. The correct option is 1: Lessee. In a lease with no specified termination option, the lessee (tenant) has the right to terminate the lease before its expiration.

8. The correct option is 1: An act of the Court shall prejudice no man. This legal maxim means that the actions of the court should not cause harm to any party, emphasizing fairness and impartiality.

9. The correct option is 3: Marginal Notes appended to a Section . Marginal notes, which summarize Section s of statutes, are not considered binding in interpreting the law. They serve as references, but internal aids like the preamble are more authoritative.

10. The correct option is 1: Three menstrual courses after the date of divorce. A divorced woman must observe an iddat period of three menstrual courses before remarrying, according to Islamic law.

11. The correct option is 3: Bee farming and collecting honey. Under the Rajasthan Relief of Agricultural Indebtedness Act, 1957, bee farming and honey collection are not classified as agriculture, and thus do not fall under the Act's relief provisions.

12. The correct option is 2: Chief Controlling Revenue Authority. Any person aggrieved by an order from the Collector (Stamps) can apply for revision before the Chief Controlling Revenue Authority under Section 65 of the Rajasthan Stamp Act, 1998.

13. The correct option is 2: Article 142 of the Constitution of Indi[A] The Supreme Court can make necessary orders to ensure complete justice, as per Article 142, even if they go beyond existing laws or procedural rules.

14. The correct option is 4: Justice K.S. Puttaswamy & Anr. vs. Union of India & Ors. This landmark case recognized the right to privacy as a fundamental right under Article 21 of the Constitution of India.

15. The correct option is 2: Act of Go[D] An Act of God is a defense in tort law when an event, like a natural disaster, occurs beyond human control, exempting a defendant from liability.

16. The correct option is 4: After the expiry of the time for appealing, without any appeal having been presente[D] A divorced person can remarry after the appeal period expires, provided no appeal was filed.

17. The correct option is 3: Section 115. Promissory estoppel, based on Section 115 of the Indian Evidence Act, prevents a party from going back on a promise if it causes unfair detriment to the other party.

18. The correct option is 4: None of the above. The Hindu Succession (Amendment) Act, 2005, granted equal inheritance rights to all daughters, including married ones, removing gender-based discrimination in inheritance laws.

19. The correct option is 1: Section 91 of the Act. Section 91 of the Rajasthan Land Revenue Act, 1956, allows local authorities to evict unauthorized occupants of land that is under their disposal.

20. The correct option is 4: Any order of dismissal for default. An order of dismissal for default is not considered a decree under the Code of Civil Procedure, 1908, as it does not determine the rights of the parties.

21. The correct option is 3: Order XLII Rule 1-A CP[C] A party can appeal a decree based on a compromise recorded in court under Order XLII Rule 1-A of the CPC, challenging its validity.

22. The correct option is 4: Any premises situated in the municipal area of Jaipur City, let out for residential purposes, for a monthly rent of Rs. 8,000/-. The Rajasthan Rent Control Act, 2001 applies to these premises for regulating rent and eviction procedures.

23. The correct option is 3: Within six months next after the accrual of cause of action. A suit against a municipality must be filed within six months after the cause of action arises, excluding cases related to immovable property or title declarations.

24. The correct option is 4: The Indian Easements Act, 1882. The grant and transfer of licenses is governed by the Indian Easements Act, 1882, which regulates easements and licenses in India.

25. The correct option is 3: Before the hearing of the suit as contemplated by Order XVIII CP[C] Questions related to court fees and suit valuation must be decided before the hearing of the case, according to the Rajasthan Court Fees and Suits Valuation Act, 1961.

26. The correct option is 2: A contract that is inherently determinable cannot be specifically enforce[D] These contracts include provisions for termination upon certain conditions or events, making them unsuitable for specific performance, as the court cannot compel performance of such contracts due to their terminable nature.

27. The correct option is 3: Section 229. Section 229 of the Rajasthan Tenancy Act, 1955 grants the Board of Revenue and other revenue courts the power to review their own decisions, allowing them to correct errors and ensure fairness by revisiting previous judgments.

28. The correct option is 2: Fixed Deposit Receipt. A fixed deposit receipt is not negotiable because it cannot be transferred to another party to claim ownership or benefits. Unlike negotiable instruments like promissory notes, it simply represents a deposit with a fixed interest rate.

29. The correct option is 1: Hindi. In Rajasthan, the General Rules (Civil), 1986 mandate that all pleadings, applications, and petitions in civil judicial proceedings must be written in Hindi. This ensures uniformity and accessibility in the state's judicial process.

30. The correct option is 3: The High Court. In international commercial arbitration, the Arbitration and Conciliation Act, 1996 designates the High Court as the "Court" responsible for handling matters like arbitrator appointments, interim measures, and awards.

31. The correct option is 3: Section 37 of the Act. Section 37 of the Arbitration and Conciliation Act, 1996 allows an appeal against an order refusing to refer parties to arbitration under Section 8. This provision grants the right to challenge such decisions in court.

32. The correct option is 2: Section 38 of the Act. Section 38 of the Rajasthan Panchayati Raj Act, 1994 outlines the grounds and procedures for removing or suspending members or Chairpersons of Panchayati Raj Institutions, ensuring fairness in governance.

33. The correct option is 2: To indemnify the firm for any loss caused to it by his fraud in the conduct of the business of the firm. Partners must indemnify the firm for losses caused by fraud in the business. This ensures partners act in good faith and are accountable for fraudulent actions.

34. The correct option is 3: Money. The Sale of Goods Act, 1930 excludes money from the definition of movable goods. Money is considered separate from goods and is not included in the scope of transactions covered by the Act.

35. The correct option is 3: Principal officer of the corporation. When a corporation is a party to a lawsuit, the summons must be served on its principal officer, such as the CEO or managing director. This ensures the corporation is properly notified in legal matters.

36. The correct option is 1: Cognizable. Offenses under Sections 66B, 66C, 66D, and 66E of the Information and Technology Act, 2000 are cognizable. These serious offenses allow police to arrest the accused without a warrant and start an investigation.

37. The correct option is 4: Application for grant of leave to appeal in the High Court. In a case involving a complaint and judgment of acquittal, the complainant can challenge the acquittal by filing an application for leave to appeal in the High Court.

38. The correct option is 4: None of the above. An accused's statement under Section 27 of the Evidence Act does not require specific conditions such as the presence of a magistrate or independent witnesses. It can be recorded as long as it leads to the discovery of relevant facts.

39. The correct option is 3: (i) Birth Certificate issued from the school/matriculation certificate. (ii) Date of birth certificate issued by the Municipality. (iii) Ossification test report. The age of a person under the Juvenile Justice Act is determined by considering documents in a specified order of preference.

40. The correct option is 3: Sentence the child to imprisonment till he attains 18 years of age. The Juvenile Justice Board focuses on rehabilitation and does not have the authority to sentence a child to imprisonment until they turn 18. Alternative measures like education or community service are preferred.

41. The correct option is 2: Hold inquiry of the child as a Juvenile Justice Boar[D] The Children Court cannot conduct an inquiry of the chil[D] Only the Juvenile Justice Board is authorized to carry out inquiries regarding a child in conflict with the law.

42. The correct option is 4: Transfer the case to the Children Court for trial of the child as an adult. If a child above 16 commits a heinous offense, the Juvenile Justice Board may transfer the case to the Children Court for trial as an adult under the Juvenile Justice Act.

43. The correct option is 4: All of the above. Officers such as a Head Constable, Sub-Inspector, or Deputy Superintendent of Police can search a vehicle suspected of carrying psychotropic drugs, provided there are reasonable grounds for suspicion.

44. The correct option is 4: None of the above. Officers are not required to inform a suspect about the right to a search in the presence of a magistrate or other specified authorities before conducting a search for narcotic drugs.

45. The correct option is 3: If the owner proves that the vehicle was used in the commission of the offense without his knowledge or connivance. A vehicle used in an offense under the NDPS Act is not liable for confiscation if the owner proves they had no knowledge or involvement.

46. The correct option is 3: C (the subsequent purchaser). The subsequent purchaser (C) is the aggrieved party. Even if A failed to disclose a previous transaction, C should have conducted due diligence to verify the title and ownership of the property before purchasing.

47. The correct option is 4: An appeal. A bail application rejected by the Special Judge under the SC/ST (Prevention of Atrocities) Act can be challenged in the High Court through an appeal, which reviews the decision and allows reconsideration of the application.

48. The correct option is 3: 326 IPC and 3(2)(V) of SC/ST (Prevention of Atrocities) Act. X, who inflicts grievous injury on Y, a member of the Scheduled Caste, is guilty of offenses under both Section 326 IPC (grievous hurt) and Section 3(2)(V) of the SC/ST Act.

49. The correct option is 4: The place where such woman and her son reside. A police officer may record the statements of a woman and her son, witnesses to a murder, at their place of residence, ensuring comfort and efficiency during the investigation.

50. The correct option is 3: Warrant cases instituted upon a complaint. In warrant cases initiated by complaint, the court must record evidence before framing charges, ensuring sufficient material is available to proceed with the trial and protect the rights of the accused.

51. A protection order under the Protection of Women from Domestic Violence Act is essential for safety. Non-compliance with it is considered an offense, as it undermines the law's purpose and the victim's safety.

52. A statement made by a rape victim under Section 164 Cr.P.[C] is inadmissible if she dies before it's recorded at trial. The statement cannot be tested for truth or cross-examined, violating justice principles.

53. Section 12 of the Probation of Offenders Act doesn't allow directing that a conviction will not affect the offender's service. The Section deals with probation release, not service-related consequences.

54. Under Section 106 of the Evidence

Act, B must explain the murder circumstances, as they are the person with exclusive knowledge of the locked room where the murder occurred.

55. The proceedings under Section 406 IPC are not barred by limitation as the offense is not continuous. The case was within the three-year limitation, allowing the court to proceed.

56. A would be guilty under Section 354-C IPC for voyeurism. Watching B subject C to intercourse without consent violates privacy, even though B's role would need further legal assessment.

57. The accused can be convicted for injuries caused to individual members of the complainant party. The case involves individual injuries, and Sections 34 and 149 IPC may not apply.

58. Call details alone are not sufficient evidence in a conspiracy case under the Narcotic Drugs Act. Recorded conversations, if proven, may be used to establish the involvement of the accused.

59. An accused becomes entitled to bail on the 61st day of arrest if the prosecution fails to comply with Section 167(2) Cr.P.C., which mandates a limit on detention during investigation.

60. The Patwari's actions in falsifying land records don't fall under offenses like document forgery or criminal breach of trust. Specific laws on misconduct or record falsification would apply here.

61. The Supreme Court ruled that police must register an FIR for cognizable offenses regardless of jurisdiction, ensuring victims can file complaints at any police station.

62. In Meters and Instruments Pvt. Lt[D] vs. Kanchan Mehta, the Supreme Court allowed the closure of proceedings under the Negotiable Instruments Act if the complainant is compensated, even without consent from both parties.

63. The Supreme Court in Sakiri Vasu vs. State of U.P. empowered magistrates to ensure proper investigation by directing police to conduct thorough and fair investigations in criminal cases.

64. In Shafi Moh[D] vs. State of Himachal Pradesh, the Court ruled that secondary electronic evidence could be admitted without the certificate under Section 65-B, if the conditions for its admissibility are met.

65. The Supreme Court ruled in Amrutbhai Shambhubhai Patel that once the Magistrate has taken cognizance of a case, only a Special Judge can order further investigation under Section 173(8) Cr.P.C.

66. Under the Electricity Act, 2003, an offense is actionable upon a written complaint from a licensee or generating company, initiating legal proceedings in electricity-related cases.

67. Under the POCSO Act, the identity of a sexually assaulted child can only be disclosed with the permission of a competent Special Court in certain exceptional circumstances for justice or safety reasons.

68. When a police officer receives a reasonable complaint, they can issue a notice for the accused to appear at a designated place, allowing cooperation in the investigation without immediate arrest.

69. A Magistrate can examine court records at their private residence without permission, as they are responsible for handling and maintaining the integrity of these records for official purposes.

70. A Magistrate can take charge of court records without permission if they need to examine them at their private residence. As the custodian of the records, the Magistrate has the authority to access and handle them for official purposes.

71. उत्तर: 1. यण संधि। शब्द 'अभ्यन्तर' में 'अभि' और 'अंतर' दो उपसर्ग हैं। जब दो उपसर्ग एक साथ आते हैं और उनमें से पहले उपसर्ग का अर्थ पिछले उपसर्ग के अर्थ में सम्मिलित हो जाता है, तो उसे 'यण संधि' कहा जाता है। इस संधि के कारण 'अभ्यन्तर' का अर्थ होता है 'भीतर' या 'आंतरिक'। इसलिए, उत्तर 1 है।

72. उत्तर: 2. द्विगु समास। द्विगु समास एक संज्ञात्मक समास है जहाँ प्रथम पद संख्यावाचक अर्थात गणनाबोधक होता है और दूसरा पद प्रधान होता है। यह समास उपयोग में आता है जब दो पदों के अर्थ का गणनाबोध होना हो, और दूसरा पद पहले पद के प्रधानार्थ को सूचित करती हो। इसलिए, उत्तर 2 है।

73. उत्तर: 1. निर्विरोध। 'निर्विरोध' शब्द में 'नि' और 'विरोध' दो उपसर्ग हैं। 'नि' उपसर्ग का अर्थ होता है 'विपरीत' या 'विरोध', इसलिए उत्तर 1 है क्योंकि यहा सिर्फ़ एक उपसर्ग है। उत्तर 2, 3 और 4 में दो या दो से अधिक उपसर्ग होते हैं।

74. उत्तर: 3. वर्त्य। 'वर्त्य' शब्द पर्वत का सही पर्याय नहीं है। 'वर्त्य' का सही पर्याय होता है 'गिरि' या 'पर्वतीय'। 'वर्त्य' का अर्थ होता है 'वृत्ति करने वाला' या 'चक्कर में रखने वाला' जबकि 'गिरि' या 'पर्वतीय' का अर्थ होता है 'पर्वत सम्बंधी'। इसलिए, उत्तर 3 है।

75. उत्तर: 4. नैसर्गिक-कृत्रिम। 'नैसर्गिक-कृत्रिम' शब्द-युग्म में 'नैसर्गिक' और 'कृत्रिम' एक दूसरे के विलोम हैं। 'नैसर्गिक' का अर्थ होता है 'प्राकृतिक' या 'स्वाभाविक' जबकि 'कृत्रिम' का अर्थ होता है 'कृत्रिम' या 'नकली'। इसलिए, उत्तर 4 है। उत्तर 1, 2 और 3 में दिए गए शब्द-युग्मों में विलोम शब्द नहीं हैं।

76. जिजीविषा शब्द का अर्थ प्रकट करने वाला वाक्यांश है: 4. जिंदा रहने की इच्छा। शब्द 'जिजीविषा' से संबंधित भाव को दर्शाने वाला यह वाक्यांश व्यक्त करता है कि व्यक्ति में जीवित रहने की इच्छा है यानी उन्हें जीने की आग्रह है। यह वाक्यांश उस व्यक्ति के भाव को प्रकट करता है जो अपने जीवन को नष्ट करने या किसी अनुचित क्रिया के द्वारा अपनी हत्या करने की इच्छा नहीं रखता है।

77. निम्नलिखित में से शुद्ध शब्द है: 2. द्वारका। शब्द 'द्वारका' सही है और इसका अर्थ होता है "भगवान कृष्ण की प्राचीन राजधानी द्वारका"।

78. निम्न शब्द-समूहों में वचन की दृष्टि से कौनसा विकल्प सही नहीं है? 3. क्षमा - क्षमाएं। यह विकल्प सही नहीं है क्योंकि शब्द "क्षमा" का बहुवचन "क्षमाएँ" होता है और ऐसे ही शब्दों का बहुवचन उदाहरण रूप में "लता - लताएँ" और "गाथा - गाथाएँ" होता है।

79. आपके प्रश्न का समाधान मेरे पास है। यह वाक्य शुद्ध है क्योंकि इसमें कर्ता, कर्म और कर्मक के बीच सही संबंध है। "आपके प्रश्न" (कर्ता) का "समाधान" (कर्म) "मेरे पास" (कर्मक) है। वाक्य में संधि, वचन, और समास के कानूनों का भी सही प्रयोग किया गया है।

80. LICENCE शब्द का सही हिंदी रूपांतरण है: 2. अनुज्ञप्ति। शब्द "लाइसेंस" का सही हिंदी रूपांतरण "अनुमति पत्र" होता है। यह शब्द उस पत्र या दस्तावेज़ को संकेत करता है जिसके माध्यम से एक व्यक्ति को किसी कार्य की अनुमति दी जाती है, जैसे की किसी व्यापार की अनुमति पत्र (Business License) या ड्राइविंग लाइसेंस (Driving License)।

81. उत्तर: 1. HONORARIUM — मानदेय। 'HONORARIUM' शब्द का सही हिंदी अनुवाद 'मानदेय' होता है। 'HONORARIUM' शब्द का अर्थ होता है एक व्यक्ति को किसी विशेष कार्य के लिए दिया जाने वाला सम्मानार्थक भुगतान या प्रतिपूर्ति। 'मानदेय' शब्द भी इसी अर्थ को प्रकट करता है। इसलिए, उत्तर 1 है।

82. उत्तर: 2. ताकि। 'खूब मन लगाकर पढ़ो ताकि परीक्षा में प्रथम आओ' वाक्य में प्रयुक्त अव्यय 'ताकि' है। 'ताकि' शब्द एक

प्रयोजक अव्यय होता है और इसका अर्थ होता है 'इसलिए' या 'ताकि'। यह वाक्यांश पढ़ाई करने के उद्देश्य या मकसद को व्यक्त करता है, अर्थात् पढ़ाई करने का कारण या प्रयोजन बताता है। इसलिए, उत्तर 2 है।

83. उत्तर: 4. हंसपद चिह्न। लिखते हुए किसी शब्द के छूट जाने पर हम उसे लिखने के लिए 'हंसपद चिह्न' का प्रयोग करते हैं। यह चिह्न शब्द के आखिरी अक्षर के बाद लगाया जाता है और इसका अर्थ होता है कि उस शब्द के आगे और बाकी हिस्से को दुबारा लिखने की आवश्यकता नहीं है। इसलिए, उत्तर 4 है।

84. उत्तर: 1. चालाक ही चालाक की बात समझ सकता है। 'खग जाने खग ही की भाषा' वाक्य का अभिप्राय होता है कि चालाक व्यक्ति ही दूसरों की चालाकी की बात समझ सकता है। यह वाक्य एक मुहावरे की रूपरेखा है और उसका अर्थ होता है कि चालाक व्यक्ति दूसरों के चाल-धंधों को आसानी से समझ लेती है। इसलिए, उत्तर 1 है।

85. उत्तर: 3. कृतघ्न। 'किये हुए उपकार को न मानने वाला' का अर्थ होता है 'कृतघ्न'। 'कृतघ्न' शब्द का अर्थ होता है एक ऐसा व्यक्ति जी किए गए उपकार को न मानता है और उसके प्रति कृतज्ञता नहीं दिखाता। यह शब्द इसी अर्थ को प्रकट करता है। इसलिए, उत्तर 3 है।

86. The correct option is 4: She will have completed her assignment by midnight. This uses the future perfect tense, indicating that the action of completing the assignment will be finished before midnight.

87. The correct option is 3: Flung. "Flung" is the correct past participle of "fling," which indicates a recent action in the present perfect tense.

88. The correct option is 1: X. The sentence uses "X" to mean no article is needed before "man," referring to humans in a general sense.

89. The correct option is 4: Any. "Hardly any" emphasizes the very little or almost no money the person has.

90. The correct option is 3: Come nearer. "Close in" means to approach or get closer, describing the enemy's movement.

91. The correct option is 3: He is no longer in danger or difficulty. "Out of the woods" means the person is no longer in a tough or risky situation.

92. The correct option is 4: The poor must not be looked down on by us. The sentence is converted to the passive voice, with the poor as the subject.

93. The correct option is 2: Being a student, you must work har[D] This is in the active voice, with "you" as the subject.

94. The correct option is 1: So. "So" shows a cause-and-effect relationship, meaning the speaker did well because of studying.

95. The correct option is 2: Until. "Until" indicates that playing outside is allowed only before the father comes home.

96. The correct option is 3: She wished me a Merry Christmas. This is indirect speech reporting her greeting.

97. The correct option is 1: "Would that had made contact with him before his departure." This expresses regret about not having contacted him earlier.

98. The correct option is 2: "Shall I close the door?" This is a suggestion, offering to take action.

99. The correct option is 1: Strong. "Robust" means strong or vigorous, and "strong" is the closest synonym.

100. The correct option is 3: Mendacity. "Mendacity" is the opposite of "veracity," meaning dishonesty or lying.

R.J.S. Preliminary Examination 2

018-2019

1. The incorrect statement is 2: A prior intimation of at least three days to the tenant is not required under the Rajasthan Rent Control Act, 2001. The landlord can inspect the premises without specific intimation, making option 2 incorrect.

2. The correct combination is 2: (A) & (C). A public nuisance suit can be filed by the Advocate General and two or more persons with the court's permission, even without special damage, making options (B) and (D) incorrect.

3. Kishore's status is 1: Tenant holding over. When a tenant continues occupying the property after the lease term ends, paying rent to the original landlord, they are considered a tenant holding over.

4. The executive power of the State is vested in 4: The Governor. The executive power lies with the Governor, while the Chief Minister, Chief Secretary, and CEO play administrative roles but do not hold ultimate power.

5. Option 4 is correct. A decree for money cannot be executed by arresting a woman. Legal provisions safeguard women's personal liberty and dignity, offering alternative enforcement methods like attaching property instead.

6. The principle of not splitting claims is based on 3: Order II Rule 2 of the Code of Civil Procedure, 1908. It prevents plaintiffs from suing separately for parts of a single cause of action.

7. Rejection of a plaint under Order VII Rule 11 does not bar a fresh plaint, as stated in 2. A fresh plaint can be filed on the same cause of action unless specific grounds like res judicata apply.

8. The "Rule in Heydon's case" is known as 1: Purposive construction. It requires interpreting statutes in light of their intended purpose, considering the mischief the law aimed to remedy.

9. The Indian Evidence Act, 1872 applies to 3: Judicial proceedings before courts. It governs the admissibility and evaluation of evidence in court, not in arbitration or departmental proceedings.

10. The person who cannot be appointed as Advocate General is 3: An advocate with 7 years of practice. The requirement is at least ten years of practice for eligibility.

11. The incorrect statement is 1: An agreement made without consideration is not always voi[D] Certain agreements, like those based on natural love and affection or time-barred debts, can be valid without consideration.

12. A pauper suit is instituted 2: When the application for leave to sue as a pauper is made. This is the starting point for the suit's institution under the Limitation Act, 1963.

13. All listed contract types can be enforced, with compensation, determinability, or continuous duty involve[D] The enforceability may vary based on specific circumstances and applicable laws.

14. Section 43 of the Transfer of Property Act, 1882, deals with 2: Estoppel by deed, preventing someone from denying the validity of a transfer they made without authorization after acquiring an interest in it.

15. The provision barring review of a decree or order passed on a review is

3: Order XLVI Rule 9, which prohibits entertaining subsequent review applications for the same matter.

16. The provision dealing with permission for limited period tenancy under the Rajasthan Rent Control Act is 3: Section 8, which outlines the conditions for granting possession and tenancy.

17. The remedy against a final Rent Tribunal order is 3: Appeal under Section 19(6) of the Rajasthan Rent Control Act, 2001. It allows an appeal to the Appellate Authority.

18. The order of performance in the contract is 1: A's promise to build the house must be performed before B's payment, as construction contracts typically require work completion before payment.

19. The rule of construction "Noscitur a sociis" means 1: The meaning of a word is judged by the company it keeps. It suggests interpreting words based on their context and surrounding terms in a statute.

20. The correct option is 4. Acts in Schedule IX of the Indian Constitution are immune from judicial review, ensuring their validity even if they violate fundamental rights.

21. Section 65-B of the Indian Evidence Act, 1872, deals with 3: Electronic records, ensuring their admissibility in court with required certification to confirm authenticity.

22. A mutual mistake in an instrument can be rectified by 3: Instituting a suit under Section 26 of the Specific Relief Act, 1963, to amend the instrument reflecting the parties' true intention.

23. The power to amend or frame additional issues before decree is vested in 2: Order XIV Rule 5 of the Code of Civil Procedure, allowing the court to address new matters during the trial.

24. A High Court judge resigns by addressing 4: The President of India, as the President is the appointing authority for High Court judges.

25. In case of repugnancy between laws, 3: Article 254 of the Indian Constitution dictates that Parliament's law prevails, unless the President assents to the state law.

26. Article 17 of the Indian Constitution abolished untouchability and forbids its practice in any form. This provision promotes equality and dignity for all, aiming to eliminate caste-based discrimination and ensure equal rights for every citizen.

27. A court cannot issue a commission to collect evidence. The responsibility of collecting evidence lies with the parties in the case, while the court can issue a commission to facilitate witness examination or conduct investigations.

28. Section 21 of the Code of Civil Procedure mandates that objections regarding territorial or pecuniary jurisdiction must be raised at the earliest opportunity, typically in the first written statement, to avoid waiving such objections.

29. The Forty-Second Amendment of 1976 inserted the words "SOCIALIST SECULAR" into the Preamble of the Constitution, emphasizing the state's commitment to socialism and secularism to ensure social justice and religious freedom.

30. Article 215 of the Indian Constitution empowers High Courts to punish individuals for contempt of court, safeguarding the dignity and authority of the judiciary.

31. None of the provided options correctly represent the universally required facts to be proved in legal cases. The facts vary depending on the specific case.

32. Under the Limitation Act, 1963, the period to file a suit to set aside a transfer by a guardian is three years from the date of the ward's death.

33. Order XXI Rule 106 of the Code of Civil Procedure allows a party to apply for the restoration or setting aside of ex parte orders made under Order XXI if they failed to appear in court.

34. The Limitation Act, 1963 specifies a two-year period from the date the injured party first learns of the perversion of property use for filing a tort suit.

35. Section 56 of the Indian Contract Act, 1872 defines the doctrine of frustration, excusing contractual performance when an unforeseen event renders it impossible.

36. Section 443 of the Cr.P.[C] allows a court to issue a warrant of arrest and

require sureties from someone released on bail who fails to comply with bail conditions.

37. The Supreme Court in Shyam Pal vs. Dayawati Besoya (2016) held that sentences for multiple offenses under the Negotiable Instruments Act can run concurrently if they arise from a single transaction.

38. Section 53-A of the Indian Evidence Act ensures that evidence of a woman's prior sexual history is irrelevant in cases of rape or outraging her modesty, focusing solely on consent.

39. In summons cases, the court does not need to hear the accused formally but must state the offense's particulars, allowing a summary trial process.

40. Under Section 462 of the Indian Penal Code, Shayam committed mischief by causing damage to property entrusted to him.

41. The presumption of innocence for a child in conflict with the law applies in all situations unless specific circumstances, not provided in the options, indicate otherwise.

42. A police officer depositing a fine amount after the deadline commits criminal breach of trust under Section 409 of the Indian Penal Code.

43. Section 4 of the Probation of Offenders Act requires the court to seek a report from a Probation Officer when dealing with a convicted person who is not sentenced to death or life imprisonment.

44. If a cheque is dishonored after being filled in by the holder, they are entitled to file a complaint against the drawer under the Negotiable Instruments Act.

45. The Supreme Court case Vadivelu Thevar vs. State of Madras (1987) classified witnesses into three categories to assess their reliability and credibility during trials.

46. Under Section 18(3) of the Juvenile Justice Act, if a child becomes an adult during trial, the court may send them to a place of safety for care and protection.

47. Section 305 of the Cr.P.[C] requires a body corporate to appoint an authorized representative to handle inquiries or trials before a criminal court.

48. None of the provided options correctly describe the requirements for the presumption of abetment of suicide under Section 113-A of the Indian Evidence Act.

49. Bail cannot be denied solely because a child is accused of a heinous offense if they are declared an adult under Section 18(3) of the Juvenile Justice Act.

50. The judgment of conviction of Khema for stealing the car is irrelevant in the civil suit between Kalu and Ganesh, which focuses on the ownership of the car, not Khema's criminal actions.

51. The correct provision protecting against double jeopardy is Section 300 of Cr.P.[C] It ensures no person can be tried or convicted twice for the same offense. Once acquitted or convicted, individuals are protected from repeated prosecutions or punishments for the same crime.

52. The judgment that established a complaint for successive dishonors of a cheque is maintainable, even without a prior complaint, is (2013) 1 SCC 177, M.S.R. Leathors vs. S. Palaniappan. The Court ruled that each dishonor creates a fresh cause of action.

53. Section 395 of Cr.P.[C] allows a Sessions Court to refer questions regarding the validity of laws to the High Court. It empowers the Sessions Court to seek the High Court's opinion on necessary legal matters for case resolution.

54. Section 33 of the Indian Evidence Act permits the use of evidence recorded in a previous case if it involves the same parties and legal processes. It helps courts avoid unnecessary repetition by considering previously recorded evidence in later proceedings.

55. Section 73 of the Indian Evidence Act allows courts to order individuals to write words for comparison with disputed handwriting. It aids in verifying the authenticity of documents by comparing handwriting in the case.

56. Sections 217 and 311 of Cr.P.[C] grant courts the power to recall and re-examine witnesses. Section 217 allows recalling witnesses during a trial, while Section 311 allows recalling or summoning witnesses to ensure a fair trial.

57. In (2016) 2 SCC 75, Bridgestone India Pvt. Lt[D] vs. Inderpal Singh, the Supreme Court clarified territorial juris-

diction for complaints under the Negotiable Instruments Act. It established factors like the drawee bank's location to determine proper jurisdiction.

58. The right of private defense under Section 100 of IPC allows self-defense against grievous hurt on provocation, but does not extend to causing death or harm if the offense involves specific conditions listed in the law.

59. Section 364 of Cr.P.[C] allows the accused to request a translated copy of a judgment if it is in English and they do not understand the language. This ensures access to court decisions in a comprehensible form.

60. Section 366 of Cr.P.[C] requires a Sessions Court's death sentence to be confirmed by the High Court. This ensures thorough review to prevent errors or arbitrary imposition of the death penalty.

61. Section 461 of Cr.P.[C] lists irregularities that vitiate proceedings. Holding an inquest under Section 176 is not mentioned among those irregularities, meaning it does not affect the validity of proceedings.

62. Section 273(1) of Cr.P.[C] mandates the accused's presence during trial. If evidence is recorded in their absence, the judgment is vitiated, as it violates the accused's right to a fair trial and cross-examination.

63. Section 118 of the Indian Evidence Act makes all persons competent witnesses unless deemed incapable due to unsound min[D] This includes individuals with mental impairments, subject to the court's determination of their ability to understand questions and provide rational answers.

64. The Supreme Court in (2014) 3 SCC 712, Sarswathy vs. Babu, ruled that the Protection of Women from Domestic Violence Act applies retrospectively, covering acts of domestic violence that began before the Act's enactment but continued afterward.

65. Section 437-A of Cr.P.[C] requires an accused acquitted by the trial court to provide a bond for appearance in a higher court if the acquittal is appeale[D] This ensures their availability for future proceedings.

66. Certified copies of public documents cannot be admitted in evidence without formal proof. These copies are self-authenticating, meaning their authenticity is presumed, unlike other documents that require further proof.

67. No appeal can be filed against a Metropolitan Magistrate's sentence of three months imprisonment and a fine of Rs. 200, as per Section 260 of Cr.P.C., which limits appeals against such minor sentences.

68. If Public servant "A" knowingly issues a document with incorrect details that may harm another public servant "B," it doesn't constitute forgery or cheating. The situation does not fall under any of the listed criminal offenses.

69. Under Section 145(5) of Cr.P.C., a party can request an Executive Magistrate to drop proceedings if both parties submit a signed written agreement confirming amicable settlement, resolving the dispute without further litigation.

70. Section 358 of Cr.P.[C] allows a court to award compensation for a groundless arrest. If a person is wrongfully detained, they are entitled to compensation to address the harm caused by the unjustified arrest.

71. The active voice version of the sentence "It is said that the Government is spending too little money on roads" is "People are saying that the Government is spending too little money on roads." The subject performing the action in the active voice is "People," who are expressing an opinion.

72. "The last train leaves the station at 11.30 am." The simple present tense verb "leaves" indicates a habitual action, as the sentence is about a routine occurrence.

73. The correct verbs are "arrived" and "started." The sentence describes past events: the witness arriving and the judge starting the investigations, so the past tense forms are appropriate.

74. "Cite" is synonymous with "quote." It refers to referring to a source or using a quotation as evidence.

75. "Could" is the correct modal ver[B] It expresses past ability, indicating that the speaker could understand adults as a child but not now.

76. "Though" is the correct subordinating conjunction. It indicates a contrast between working hard and not winning, signifying an unexpected outcome.

77. "Counsel" is the synonym for "ad-

vise." It refers to providing guidance or recommendations, especially in professional contexts.

78. "To make a long story short" means to "come to the point." It is an idiomatic expression for summarizing and skipping unnecessary details.

79. "Calls for" is the correct phrasal ver[B] It means to require or demand something, in this case, great tact.

80. "May" is the correct modal ver[B] It expresses possibility, suggesting that laziness is possible but doesn't imply stupidity.

81. "Must" is the correct modal. It expresses strong probability, indicating the person likely escaped through the broken window.

82. "Have heard" is the correct form. It uses the past participle to indicate the speaker has received information about a verdict.

83. "Otherwise" is the correct subordinating conjunction. It introduces a condition: if the person doesn't act immediately, they'll be late.

84. "One, a" is correct. "One" refers to a single friend, and "a" is the indefinite article used before a singular noun.

85. The antonym of "Proclaim" is "suppress." "Proclaim" means to announce openly, while "suppress" means to restrain or prevent from being revealed.

86. उत्तर विकल्प 4, "अन्त्याक्षरी" है जो एक अशुद्ध शब्द है। "अन्त्याक्षरी" शब्द के स्थान पर सही रूप में "अन्त्येष्टी" शब्द का प्रयोग होना चाहिए। "अन्त्येष्टी" शब्द उत्तराखंडी भाषा में प्रयोग होता है और इसका अर्थ होता है "अंतिम संस्कार करने वाली महिला"। इसलिए, "अन्त्येष्टी" शब्द सही रूप है जो कवियत्री, रचियता और प्रमाणिक के साथ उपयोग हो सकता है। विकल्प 4 में दिया गया "अन्त्याक्षरी" शब्द गलत है और संज्ञा "अन्त्येष्टी" के स्थान पर पर्यायवाची नहीं है।

87. अवतरण चिह्न (।) का प्रयोग सामान्यतः वाक्य का अनुवाद करते हुए नहीं होता है, जो उत्तर विकल्प 4 है। अनुवाद के समय, वाक्यों को एकत्रित रखने के लिए अवतरण चिह्न की जरूरत नहीं होती है। अवतरण चिह्न सामान्यतः पूर्ण वाक्यों को अलग करने और पठनीयता को बढ़ाने के लिए प्रयोग किया जाता है। अतः, अनुवाद करते समय इसका प्रयोग सामान्यतः नहीं होता है।

88. शब्द "महैश्वर्य" का संधि-विच्छेद त्रुटिपूर्ण है, जो उत्तर विकल्प 4 है। संधि-विच्छेद शब्द के विभक्ति और प्रत्ययों के बीच में अलगाव करता है। "महैश्वर्य" का संधि-विच्छेद होना चाहिए "महा + ईश्वर्य", लेकिन यहा "ए" शब्द के स्थान पर "एे" शब्द का प्रयोग हुआ है, जिससे शब्द का संधि-विच्छेद त्रुटिपूर्ण है।

89. वचन संबंधी त्रुटि वाला वाक्य विकल्प 1 है, "महात्मा जी का दर्शन करके मैं धन्य हो गया।" इस वाक्य में एकता के बावजूद "महात्मा जी" शब्द का सिंगुलर वचन होना चाहिए था। इसलिए, यह एक वचन संबंधी त्रुटि है।

90. सभी शब्द पर्यायवाची विकल्प 2 है, "मधुकरी, भिक्षा, भीख"। पर्यायवाची शब्द वे शब्द होते हैं जो एक ही अर्थ या सामर्थ्य को व्यक्त करते हैं। यहां, उपलब्ध विकल्प में सभी शब्द पर्यायवाची हैं और "मधुकरी, भिक्षा, भीख" सभी "मधु" शब्द का पर्यायवाची हैं।

91. वाक्यांश "ताल कटना - संगीत में बाधा उपस्थित होना" का अभिप्राय गलत है। महावरा "ताल कटना" का अर्थ होता है कि संगीत में कोई बाधा उत्पन्न हो रही है जो गतिविधियों को बाधित कर रही है। इसे बड़े पूर्णतः उदाहरण के रूप में लिया गया है, जहा ताल की बाधा संगीत के नियमित चलन को रोक रही है। इसलिए, उचित उत्तर है विकल्प 4. "ताल कटना - संगीत में बाधा उपस्थित होना"।

92. निकटतम लोकोक्ति "घर के पीरों को तेल का मलीदा" अभिव्यक्ति के लिए सबसे उपयुक्त है। यह लोकोक्ति द्वारा कहा जाता है कि घर के अंदर की चीजों की अहमियत घर के बाहर वालों तक समझानी जरूरी नहीं होती है। इससे यह बताया जाता है कि लोग अपने घर या अपने परिवार की अहमियत को नजरअंदाज कर देते हैं। इसलिए, उचित उत्तर है विकल्प 2. "घर के पीरों को तेल का मलीदा"।

93. वाक्य में रेखांकित शब्द है "संज्ञा"। रेखांकित शब्द संज्ञा है जो एक व्यक्ति, स्थान, वस्तु या भाव को प्रदर्शित करता है। यहां "रगी" शब्द संज्ञा है, जो एक व्यक्ति को या एक गोदाम में रखी जा रही अनाज की प्रकृति को संदर्भित करता है। इसलिए, उचित उत्तर है विकल्प 1. "संज्ञा"।

94. वाक्य "वह आदमी आ रहा है" में "वह" शब्द की व्याकरणिक कोटि "विशेषण" है। "विशेषण" शब्द वह शब्द है जो एक संज्ञा या सर्वनाम की गुण, दशा, परिमाण या संख्या को संदर्भित करता है। यह शब्द एक व्यक्ति, वस्तु या स्थान को विशेष रूप से प्रकट करता है। इस वाक्य में "वह" शब्द एक आदमी को संदर्भित करता है, जिसे उपयोगकर्ता द्वारा विशेष रूप से बताया जा रहा है कि वह आदमी आ रहा है। इसलिए, उचित उत्तर है विकल्प 3. "विशेषण"।

95. वाक्य में क्रिया है "सकर्मक"। यह वाक्य दर्शाता है कि किसी नौकर ने चिट्ठी लाई है, जो एक क्रिया को प्रगट करती है। इसमें एक क्रिया के साथ कर्मक क्रिया-प्रवृत्ति शामिल होती है जो नौकर द्वारा की गई है। इसलिए, उचित उत्तर है विकल्प 2. "सकर्मक"।

96. उत्तर विकल्प 2, "तद्भव" है, 'कसौटी' शब्द

का उत्पत्ति या मूल स्थान हिंदी भाषा में है। यह शब्द अन्य शब्दों के तत्सम रूप को प्रकट करता है जो संस्कृत भाषा से उद्भूत होते हैं।

97. उत्तर विकल्प 3, "न्यून" है, जो 'नि' उपसर्ग से निर्मित शब्द है। उपसर्ग 'नि' का अर्थ होता है 'अभाव' या 'अव्यवहार्यता'। यह उपसर्ग शब्दों के अर्थ को उल्टा कर देता है और नया अर्थ प्रदान करता है। इस प्रकार, "न्यून" शब्द उपसर्ग 'नि' से निर्मित हुआ है और अर्थ में कमी या अभाव का संकेत करता है।

98. उत्तर विकल्प 1, "वह क्रोध में भरकर चिल्लाने लगा।" है, जो अशुद्ध वाक्य है। सही रूप से, वाक्य को "वह क्रोध में भरकर चिल्लाया।" के रूप में लिखा जाना चाहिए। वाक्य को वाच्यार्थी रूप में सुधारकर, अव्यवहित और सही रूप में लिखा जाना चाहिए।

99. उत्तर विकल्प 1, "भिज्ञ - अनभिज्ञ" एक सही विलोम वर्ग नहीं है। "भिज्ञ" का विलोम शब्द "अभिज्ञ" होना चाहिए जो ज्ञानी, विद्वान् या प्रबुद्ध का अर्थ देता है। "अनभिज्ञ" का अर्थ होता है अज्ञानी या निरभिज्ञ। इसलिए, विकल्प 1 एक अशुद्ध विलोम वर्ग है।

100. उत्तर विकल्प 3, "पष्टि - छह पष्ठी - साठ" एक त्रुटिपूर्ण शब्द-युग्म है। सही रूप से, "पष्ठी" का विलोम शब्द "छः" होना चाहिए, जिसका अर्थ होता है "छह"। "साठ" शब्द इस संदर्भ में सही विलोम नहीं है, क्योंकि इसका अर्थ होता है "साठ"। इसलिए, विकल्प 3 एक त्रुटिपूर्ण शब्द-युग्म है।

R.J.S. Preliminary Examination 2021

1. Option 3: The court may direct specific performance of the former part. If part of a contract can be specifically performed and stands separately from another part, the court may order performance of the former part. This is allowed under The Specific Relief Act, 1963, when conditions are met.

2. Option 3: Growing crops. Under the Transfer of Property Act, 1882, "attached to the earth" does not include growing crops. They are considered agricultural produce and can be severed from the land, not forming part of "attached to the earth."

3. Option 1: It is a contract of guarantee. A contract to discharge the liability of a third party in case of their default is a contract of guarantee under the Indian Contract Act, 1872. The guarantor ensures the obligations are fulfilled if the third party defaults.

4. Option 3: A caricature is not a document. Under Section 3 of the Indian Evidence Act, 1872, a "document" includes any matter expressed on a substance by letters, figures, or marks. A caricature qualifies as a document under this definition.

5. Option 3: If a state legislature member is absent for 60 days without permission, their seat may be declared vacant. This ensures legislative participation, emphasizing attendance, and replacing absent members to maintain an active legislature.

6. Option 4: Granting of a Permanent Injunction. Under the Code of Civil Procedure, 1908, granting a permanent injunction is not a supplemental proceeding. It is a final court order prohibiting or compelling a party to act permanently.

7. Option 1: The contract with a deceased party's lawyer continues until the pleader informs the court of their death. The lawyer must continue representing the deceased party until officially notifying the court, ensuring the legal process proceeds without delay.

8. Option 2: 5. According to Article 143 of the Constitution of India, at least five judges of the Supreme Court are needed to hear a reference from the President on important legal or factual questions.

9. Option 2: Where the principal does not disclose the name of the agent. If the principal does not reveal the agent's identity, no contract contrary to the agent's undisclosed status can be presumed under Section 230 of the Indian Contract Act, 1872.

10. Option 4: Invitation for proposal. An advertisement inviting tenders is an invitation for proposals, not an offer. It requests submissions from interested parties, and an actual proposal occurs when a response is made.

11. Option 3: The interpretation of a statute by the courts. Courts interpret statutes to resolve legal disputes, analyzing the language, purpose, and intent of the law. While Parliament enacts laws, it is the judiciary's role to apply them in specific cases.

12. Option 1: When the thing claimed is not held by the defendant as the agent or trustee. Under the Specific Relief Act, 1963, a person cannot be compelled to deliver property unless holding it as an agent or trustee for the plaintiff.

13. Option 4: Inspection in the pres-

ence of the tenant. The Rajasthan Rent Control Act, 2001 requires that inspections of rented premises be conducted only in the tenant's presence, ensuring tenant rights and awareness during inspections.

14. Option 3: 12 months. Under the Specific Relief Act, 1963, suits for specific relief must be disposed of within 12 months from the date of serving summons, ensuring timely resolution of disputes.

15. Option 4: Two years. The limitation period to enforce a right of pre-emption is two years. This period begins when the right to pre-emption arises and must be exercised within this timeframe to avoid forfeiture.

16. Option 2: Rule of reasonable construction. The Latin maxim Ut Res Magis Valeat Quam Pereat suggests that laws should be interpreted reasonably to fulfill their purpose. It emphasizes upholding statutes effectively rather than rendering them useless.

17. Option 4: Judgment. A signed judgment under the Code of Civil Procedure, 1908, is valid without requiring a stamp. The signature authenticates the judgment, while a stamp is not essential for its validity.

18. Option 1: This chapter applies to negotiable instruments. This is incorrect regarding Chapter VII of the Transfer of Property Act, 1882, which pertains to the transfer of actionable claims, not negotiable instruments governed by the Negotiable Instruments Act, 1881.

19. Option 1: Yes. Article 226 grants High Courts the power to issue writs for the enforcement of both fundamental and other rights. Its writ jurisdiction is broader than that of the Supreme Court, which is limited to fundamental rights under Article 32.

20. Option 2: Appeals. Section 15 of the Limitation Act, 1963, specifies that time exclusions for filing suits or applications do not apply to appeals. Limitation periods for appeals start from the decree or order being appealed.

21. Option 3: Noscitur a Sociis. The principle "Noscitur a Sociis" suggests that the meaning of an ambiguous term is derived from the context and associated words. This helps in interpreting words based on their usage in specific circumstances.

22. Option 3: 60 days. Under the Rajasthan Rent Control Act, 2001, applications under Section 23 concerning fair rent fixation must be disposed of within 60 days of submission, ensuring timely resolution of such disputes.

23. Option 4: Decree includes any adjudication from which an appeal lies. This is incorrect. In the Code of Civil Procedure, 1908, an adjudication that can be appealed is not considered a decree but is treated as an appeal from an order.

24. Option 4: None of the above option. The repeal of the Rajasthan Premises (Control of Rent and Eviction) Act, 1950, does not affect the options provide[D] Further analysis of the specific provisions is required to determine the impact of the repeal.

25. Option 2: Rs. 100/-. Under Section 22-E of The Rajasthan Rent Control Act, 2001, a court fee of Rs. 100/- is payable for applications seeking the release of rented premises due to non-residential use.

26. Option 3: Counterparts of documents as against the parties who execute them come under secondary evidence. Explanation: Counterparts of documents are primary evidence, not secondary evidence, as they are identical copies executed by different parties. Primary evidence refers to the original document, while secondary evidence includes copies or duplicates.

27. Option 1: Section 120 of the Indian Evidence Act, 1872. Explanation: Section 120 of the Indian Evidence Act allows spouses to be competent witnesses in civil suits, overriding the earlier rule that deemed spouses incompetent witnesses.

28. Option 4: Yes. Court cannot grant permission without following due procedure, being a representative suit. Explanation: In a representative suit, the court must inquire about the settlement's genuineness before approval, ensuring the rights of absent class members are protected.

29. Option 3: If the donee dies before acceptance, the gift is voi[D] Explanation: A gift under the Transfer of Property Act requires acceptance by the donee during the donor's lifetime. If the donee dies before acceptance, the gift is void.

30. Option 2: In Tenth Schedule. Explanation: The Anti-Defection Law is outlined in the Tenth Schedule of the Indian Constitution, which provides conditions for the disqualification of MPs and MLAs based on defection.

31. Option 2: Presumption as to books, maps, and charts. Explanation: Section 87 of the Indian Evidence Act presumes the authenticity of books, maps, or charts printed or published under the authority of a foreign government without needing proof of signature or authority.

32. Option 3: Cheque. Explanation: The Limitation Act, 1963 does not define the term "Cheque" under Section 2, though it is commonly understood as a written order directing a bank to pay money from a drawer's account.

33. Option 1: Knowledge of the correct facts of the case. Explanation: For valid ratification under the Indian Contract Act, 1872, the person ratifying must be aware of all the correct facts of the case before giving approval.

34. Option 1: 'Tort' means a civil wrong which is exclusively the breach of a contract or the breach of trust. Explanation: A tort is a civil wrong independent of contract or breach of trust, covering wrongful acts like negligence, defamation, or assault.

35. Option 4: Article 39-[A] Explanation: Article 39-A of the Constitution ensures free legal aid for those unable to afford it, promoting justice and equality for all citizens.

36. Option 1: two months. Explanation: Under Section 144 of the CrPC, an executive magistrate's order remains in force for a maximum of two months unless extended or withdrawn.

37. Option 3: In practice for not less than 7 years as an advocate. Explanation: Under Section 32 of the Protection of Children from Sexual Offences Act, 2012, a Special Public Prosecutor must have at least seven years of practice as an advocate.

38. Option 2: Penalty is prescribed for not discharging duty by the Protection Officer. Explanation: Under the Protection of Women from Domestic Violence Act, 2005, Protection Officers face penalties for failing to discharge their duties.

39. Option 2: Establishment of a proof that the property was derived from the commission of an offence. Explanation: Section 105-A of the CrPC does not include proving the origin of property in money laundering offenses but focuses on tracing and identifying the property.

40. Option 4: Punishment provided for the offence. Explanation: Under the Probation of Offenders Act, 1958, when considering probation, the specific punishment is not a deciding factor for releasing an offender.

41. Option 4: The consent given by a person who is under 12 years of age. Explanation: Section 90 of the IPC deems the consent of a person under 12 invalid, recognizing their incapacity to give meaningful consent.

42. Option 1: Making preparation to commit murder. Explanation: Preparation to commit murder is punishable under the IPC as part of criminal attempts to prevent the commission of the offense.

43. Option 1: The judgment against 'B' is irrelevant against 'C'. Explanation: A conviction for adultery against 'B' does not automatically prove 'C's marriage to 'A' in a separate prosecution for bigamy.

44. Option 1: Head Constable. Explanation: A Head Constable cannot be a Child Welfare Officer under the Juvenile Justice (Care and Protection of Children) Act, 2015, as they do not meet the required qualifications.

45. Option 3: Breach of protection order is a non-cognizable offence. Explanation: A breach of a protection order under the Protection of Women from Domestic Violence Act is a cognizable offense, not non-cognizable, allowing for immediate police intervention.

46. Option 4: State Government, with the approval of Central Government. Explanation: Under Section 17 of the Probation of Offenders Act, 1958, state governments can frame rules with the central government's approval to ensure uniformity.

47. Option 2: Forgery. Explanation: 'A' commits forgery by altering a will to deceive and make it appear that property was left to him and 'C', which is a criminal offense under the IPC.

48. Option 1: Prescribed for summons-

cases. Explanation: Evidence in Section 125 of the CrPC, which deals with maintenance, is recorded in the manner prescribed for summons-cases.

49. Option 3: 25 September 1987. Explanation: The Indecent Representation of Women (Prohibition) Act was published on 25 September 1987 to prevent the exploitation and indecent portrayal of women.

50. Option 3: Group of individuals. Explanation: Under Section 141 of the Negotiable Instruments Act, the term 'Company' does not include a group of individuals, but refers to bodies corporate, firms, and associations.

51. Option 3: Non-cognizable, bailable, and triable by any Magistrate. Offenses under the Juvenile Justice Act, 2015 punishable with less than three years of imprisonment are non-cognizable, meaning police cannot arrest without a warrant. These offenses are bailable and can be tried by any Magistrate.

52. Option 1: Cognizable, Non-Bailable, and triable by the court of Sessions. Offenses under Section 232 of the IPC are cognizable, allowing police to arrest without a warrant. They are non-bailable and triable by the Sessions Court.

53. Option 3: Medical examination or treatment is done with parental consent. Under the POCSO Act, a child's medical examination or treatment with parental consent is exempt from specific Section s related to offenses.

54. Option 4: Executive Magistrate. Under the CrPC, the Executive Magistrate can demand security for good behavior from individuals disseminating seditious material to prevent breaches of peace.

55. Option 1: Composition of an offense before charge discharges the accuse[D] Section 320 of the CrPC allows compounding offenses before charge, which discharges the accused from further liability.

56. Option 3: 16. Section 3 of the Juvenile Justice Act, 2015 lists 16 principles for the care and protection of children, emphasizing their rights and well-being in the juvenile justice system.

57. Option 1: Seven days. Solitary confinement exceeding three months cannot exceed seven days in any month, as per the IPC, to prevent prolonged isolation.

58. Option 3: Contravention of Section 23 provisions can lead to imprisonment of up to two years, a fine, or both, for publishing a child's identity in a sexual offense case.

59. Option 2: A second appeal lies before the High Court from a Court of Sessions order under Section 101(2) of the Juvenile Justice Act, 2015, not directly from the Juvenile Justice Board.

60. Option 3: A female under 18 years of age. Under Section 363-A of the IPC, a minor is defined as a female under 18 years old for specific offenses.

61. Option 2: Adaptation Order 1950. The definition of "Queen" under Section 13 of the IPC was repealed by the Adaptation Order 1950 to align with constitutional changes post-independence.

62. Option 3: One-half. The Internal Complaints Committee under the Sexual Harassment of Women at Workplace Act must have at least half of its members as women for gender-balanced representation.

63. Option 1: Act done by a person believing himself bound by law. A soldier acting under orders from a superior officer, in accordance with the law, is protected under this general exception in the IPC.

64. Option 3: Section 54-[A] The CrPC does not have a Section 54-A; Section 54 addresses the identification of arrested persons.

65. Option 1: Not exceed one-fourth of the maximum imprisonment term. Section 65 of the IPC limits imprisonment in lieu of fine to one-fourth of the maximum term for the offense.

66. Option 2: Who commits a cognizable offense in the presence of a police officer. Under Section 41 of the CrPC, a person committing a cognizable offense in front of a police officer can be arrested without a warrant.

67. Option 2: 6 February 2003. Sections 143 to 147 of the Negotiable Instruments Act, 1881, came into effect on 6th February 2003, relating to offenses involving negotiable instruments.

68. Option 3: Section 266 of the IP[C]

Possession of false weights or measures is punishable under Section 266 of the IPC, aimed at preventing fraudulent practices in trade.

69. Option 1: 'A' had the habit of shooting people to murder them. In a murder trial, this past habit of 'A' is irrelevant unless directly tied to the incident in question.

70. Option 4: Section 319 of the CrP[C] Section 319 allows the court to add a person as an accused during trial if evidence suggests their involvement in the offense, as per the Hardeep Singh case.

71. निम्न वाक्य की पूर्ति स्थानवाचक क्रियाविशेषण से कीजिये: "ये दिल्ली चला गया था।" यहा पूर्ति स्थानवाचक क्रियाविशेषण का चयन "दिल्ली" के अनुसार किया जाता है, क्योंकि वाक्य में बताया जा रहा है कि किस जगह चला गया था। इसलिए उचित उत्तर है विकल्प 3. "दिल्ली।"

72. "अपना अपना सामान उठाओ और चलते बनो" वाक्य में सर्वनाम है "अपना अपना"। यहा सर्वनाम का अर्थ होता है कि वाक्य में प्रत्येक व्यक्ति को अपने अपने सामान को उठाने के लिए कहा जा रहा है। इसलिए उचित उत्तर है विकल्प 1. "अपना अपना"।

73. "अध्यादेश" शब्द में उपसर्ग है "अधि"। यहा उपसर्ग का अर्थ होता है 'ऊपर' या 'अत्यंत'। शब्द "अध्यादेश" में "अधि" उपसर्ग के रूप में प्रयुक्त होता है, जिसका अर्थ होता है 'अत्यंत आदेश' या 'ऊपर की आदेश'। इसलिए उचित उत्तर है विकल्प 2. "अधि"।

74. शब्द "निषेध" का संधि विच्छेद विकल्प B के अनुसार होता है, जो निः और सेध के संयोजन से बना है। "निः" उपसर्ग है जो अप्रत्यय के रूप में काम करता है, और "सेध" शब्द में अर्थ को रोकने या निरस्त करने का बोध कराता है। इस प्रकार, "निषेध" शब्द एक ऐसा शब्द है जिसमें किसी चीज को रोकने या मना करने की क्रिया का अर्थ होता है।

75. शुद्ध वाक्य: "सीता की आँखों से आँसू बह रहे हैं।"। इस वाक्य में कोई भी वाक्यांश गलतियां नहीं है। वाक्य व्याकरणिक दृष्टिकोण से सही है और समझ में भी साफ है। इसलिए उचित उत्तर है विकल्प 4. "सीता की आँखों से आँसू बह रहे हैं।"

76. "कान में फूंक मारना" मुहावरे का अर्थ होता है 'ध्यान से सुनना'। इस मुहावरे में "कान में फूंक" शब्दांश का अर्थ होता है 'यह संकेत करना कि कोई ध्यान से सुने या सुनाया जाए।' जब हम किसी व्यक्ति को "कान में फूंक मारने" के लिए कहते हैं, तो हम उसे ध्यान से सुनने के लिए कह रहे होते हैं। इसलिए उचित उत्तर है विकल्प 1. 'प्रभावित करना'।

77. "'अकारण' शब्द का विलोमार्थी शब्द है 'सकारण'। शब्द "अकारण" का अर्थ होता है 'बिना कारण' या 'बेकार'। जबकि "सकारण" का अर्थ होता है 'कारण सहित' या 'कारणपूर्वक'। इसलिए उचित उत्तर है विकल्प 2. 'सकारण'।

78. निम्न में से अशुद्ध वाक्य है: "वह अनेकों भाषाएं जानता है।" इस वाक्य में त्रुटि है क्योंकि "भाषाएं" की जगह "भाषाएँ" होनी चाहिए। सही रूप में इस वाक्य का सुधार किया जाना चाहिए और यह उचित उत्तर है विकल्प 3. "वह अनेक भाषाएं जानता है।"

79. निम्न में से कर्मवाच्य का उदाहरण है: "रोगी को दवा दे दी गई है।" यहा वाक्य में क्रिया "दवा दे दी गई है" के माध्यम से व्यक्ति द्वारा किया जाने वाला कार्य बताया गया है। इसलिए उचित उत्तर है विकल्प 1. "रोगी को दवा दे दी यई है।"

80. निम्न में से सी एकवचन और बहवचन का मेल बताते हैं: "गुड़िया - गुड़ियां"। यहा "गुड़िया" एकवचन है और "गुड़ियां" बहवचन है। जब हम एक गुड़िया के बारे में बात करते हैं तो हम "गुड़िया" का उपयोग करते हैं, और जब हम एक से अधिक गुड़ियों के बारे में बात करते हैं तो हम "गुड़ियां" का उपयोग करते हैं। इसलिए उचित उत्तर है विकल्प 2. "गुड़ियां"।

81. अनुप्रास अलंकार का उदाहरण विकल्प 1, "निधियाँ न्यारी" है। अनुप्रास अलंकार एक ध्वनि अलंकार है जहां शब्दों के प्रथम अक्षरों की समानता या समान उच्चारण होता है। इस उदाहरण में, "निधियाँ न्यारी" में शब्दों के प्रथम अक्षर "न" की समानता है, जिससे अनुप्रास अलंकार प्रगट होता है।

82. बहवचन शब्द का उदाहरण विकल्प 4, "आसूं" है। यह शब्द बहवचन में है क्योंकि "आसूं" सिंगुलर शब्द "आंस" के बहवचन है। वही विकल्प 1, 2 और 3 एकवचन शब्द हैं।

83. 'ढक्कन' शब्द में प्रत्यय है विकल्प 1, "अन"। प्रत्यय शब्द के अंत में जुड़कर उसे पूर्ण शब्द बनाता है और उसका अर्थ निर्धारित करता है। यहा "ढक्कन" शब्द में "अन" प्रत्यय शामिल होने से इसका अर्थ "ढक्का करने वाला" होता है।

84. "अक्ल का पुतला" मुहावरे का अर्थ विकल्प 2, "बुद्धिमान" है। इस मुहावरे में "अक्ल" शब्द से संबंधित है जिसका अर्थ "बुद्धि" होता है और "पुतला" शब्द का अर्थ "तंग" होता है। इस प्रस्तावित अर्थ के अनुसार, "अक्ल का पुतला" मुहावरा "बुद्धिमान" या "बुद्धिहीन" के विपरीत अर्थ में उपयोग होती है, इसलिए विकल्प 2 सही उत्तर है।

85. निम्न में से शब्द और उसके संधि-विच्छेद का सही मेल बताते हैं: "गंगोदक - गंगा + उदक"। इसमें शब्द "गंगा" और "उदक" का संधि-विच्छेद किया जाता है। "गंगा" नदी को दर्शाने वाले शब्द है और "उदक" का अर्थ होता है 'पानी'। जब हम इन दोनों शब्दों को मिलाकर "गंगोदक" बनाते हैं, तो हमारे पास एक शब्द होता है जिसका अर्थ होता है 'गंगा का पानी'।

इसलिए उचित उत्तर है विकल्प 4. "गंगोदक"।

86. Option 1: "India will become a superpower shortly" needs the indefinite article "a" before "superpower" because it refers to a general superpower, making it countable and singular.

87. Option 3: "Extraneous" means irrelevant, so its opposite is "relevant," which refers to something directly related or pertinent to the context.

88. Option 3: "Lethargy" means lack of energy, and "listlessness" is a fitting synonym, also indicating a lack of interest or vigor.

89. Option 2: "Monotonous" is correctly spelled and refers to something repetitive, dull, or lacking variety.

90. Option 2: "Carried out" means to perform or conduct tasks or experiments, indicating that multiple experiments were done before launching the missile.

91. Option 4: "The needy shall be helped" is the passive voice of "Help the needy," shifting focus to the action being done to the subject.

92. Option 3: "Put up" means to stay temporarily, commonly used to refer to accommodation for a short period.

93. Option 4: "A water detection test on Mars was conducted successfully by scientists" is in passive voice, focusing on the action rather than the doer.

94. Option 2: "An" is used before "elephant" because "elephant" begins with a vowel sound.

95. Option 1: "Verbose" means overly wordy, and "talkative" is a synonym, referring to someone who speaks a lot.

96. Option 1: "Has left" is the correct verb form as the subject "The Chief Guest, with his wife" is singular.

97. Option 3: The indirect speech conversion of "He said he was writing an application" changes to "He said that he had been writing" for correct tense use.

98. Option 4: "Mother asked her son why he was leaving the house early" changes the question structure and verb tense to fit indirect speech.

99. Option 4: "Congenial" means friendly or agreeable, so its opposite is "unpleasant," meaning not agreeable or enjoyable.

100. Option 2: "When I woke up, he had already eaten breakfast" uses the past perfect tense to indicate an action completed before another past event.

R.J.S. Preliminary Examination 2024

1. 3: B can claim setoff because both sums are definite pecuniary demands, and the amounts are fixed—one for compensation in trespass and the other for the promissory note.

2. 3: It is unnecessary to state the name, description, and place of residence of all defendants unless they are the Central or State Governments, according to Section 80 of the CPC.

3. 3: Section 116 of the Transfer of Property Act applies when the lessee continues possession with the lessor's consent after the life tenant's death, as shown in this case.

4. 4: The Deputy Chairman cannot be removed except by the President, after an address by the Council of States supported by the majority of its members.

5. 2: Article 19 applies to arrears of rent, Article 52 is for specific performance, Article 63 covers foreclosure, and Article 54 relates to money lent.

6. 3: The court can order execution at the instance of a transferee of the decree under Section 39 of the CPC, but it does not have power to order attachment of a decree.

7. 2: Judicial review of judge appointments under Article 217 of the Constitution was ruled in Anna Mathews vs. Supreme Court of India.

8. 3: Communications related to a forged will are not protected under Section 126 of the Indian Evidence Act, as it involves illegal actions.

9. 4: The sale of immovable property must wait for one month from the proclamation date, as per Rule 68 of Order 21, CPC.

10. 2: The Civil Procedure Code is part of the Concurrent List, as it affects both central and state legislations.

11. 3: The surety is discharged when the principal debtor fails to repay and the creditor doesn't sue for a year after

the debt becomes payable.

12. 2: "B" cannot treat "C's" decree as a cross decree as the decrees are not in relation to the same matter.

13. 1: "Vigilantibus non dormientibus jura subveniunt" (The law assists the vigilant, not those who sleep on their rights) is the maxim behind statutes of limitation.

14. 2: Compensation cannot be awarded unless specifically claimed in the suit, as it's a separate cause of action under Section 21 of the Specific Relief Act.

15. 3: In simple mortgages, possession of the mortgaged property is not delivered, unlike in other types of mortgages.

16. 4: The Supreme Court declared the Right to Privacy as a fundamental right in the Justice K.S. Puttaswamy case.

17. 2: Attachment under a precept under Section 46 of CPC shall continue for a maximum of two months.

18. 3: The rule of interpreting specific words followed by general words, limiting the general words, is the Rule of Homogeneous Interpretation.

19. 1: In Supriyo @ Supriya Chakraborty and Anr. v. Union of India, the Supreme Court discussed same-sex marriage as not a fundamental right.

20. 1: In execution of a decree for restitution of conjugal rights, periodical payments may be ordered by the court.

21. 4: "The first hearing of the suit" refers to the framing of issues, which marks the first formal hearing.

22. 1: The correct matches are: (1) - (d), (2) - (a), (3) - (b), (4) - (c).

23. 2: The Doctrine of Estoppel applies based on conduct and cannot be applied against minors, contrary to what is stated in the question.

24. 2: The legal maxim "Ur Res Magis Valeat Onam Pareatis" is known as the Rule of Reasonable Construction.

25. 3: The agreement involving the attachment of life insurance is void ab initio, as such a condition is considered illegal.

26. 2. Ashutosh Samante (D) by LRs and others Vs. SM. Ranjan Bala Dasi and others: The Supreme Court held that the presumption under Section 90 of the Indian Evidence Act does not apply to wills, as they require strict proof of execution and validity.

27. 2. After making the reference, the court who made the reference can proceed in the case and may pass a decree contingent upon the decision of the High Court on the point referred.: The referring court can still proceed and may pass a decree contingent on the High Court's decision regarding the referred question under Order 46 Rule 1 of the CP[C]

28. 1. is lawful: The agreement to increase rent by 4% per annum is lawful under Section 7 of the Rajasthan Rent Control Act, 2001, provided it follows the Act's guidelines.

29. 2. The doctrine of imbibing essence: The doctrine of imbibing essence is applied when laws from different legislatures affect each other's scope harmoniously.

30. 1. An interest in property restricted in its enjoyment to the owner personally can be transferred by him.: Property with restricted enjoyment (like life interests) cannot generally be transferred unless allowed by the terms, making such a transfer impossible here.

31. 2. Compensation depriving landlord from the use of the premises: Mesne profit refers to compensation for deprivation of the landlord's use of the premises, not rent revision or agreed rent.

32. 3. Order 45: Order 45 of the CPC deals with appeals in matters of decree-related decisions from final orders.

33. 2. Equal Justice and free legal aid: Article 39A of the Indian Constitution mandates that the state provides equal justice and free legal aid for the disadvantage[D]

34. 1. To elucidating matters in controversy: Oral examination under Order 10 Rule 2 of the CPC aims to clarify the issues between the parties.

35. 2. An Order under Rule 17 of Order 6 of the Code of Civil Procedure, 1908: Orders made under Rule 17 of Order 6 are not appealable as they pertain to procedural changes, not substantive decisions.

36. 1. Mischief: Ramlal committed mischief by intentionally damaging the motorcycle with the aim of causing loss.

37. 4. Any member of the family of the employer: Domestic workers are de-

fined as employees but not including members of the employer's family under the Sexual Harassment Act.

38. 4. Censure passed in good faith by the person not having lawful authority over another: The defamation exception does not cover statements made in good faith without lawful authority.

39. 3. Vijay has committed the offence of murder of murder and Suresh has committed the offence of culpable homicide not amounting to murder.: Vijay's direct action resulted in murder, while Suresh's response, though provoked, resulted in culpable homicide.

40. 3. During and until the conclusion of trial: A Magistrate can remand the accused until the trial's conclusion as per the Code of Criminal Procedure.

41. 3. A single male is eligible to adopt a girl child.: The Juvenile Justice Act allows only married couples to adopt a girl child, not single males.

42. 2. A Magistrate: Only a Magistrate is authorized to conduct investigations and oversee legal processes under the law.

43. 2. a proceeding between the prosecutor and the accused: Under Section 33 of the Indian Evidence Act, criminal trials regarding evidence in later proceedings are considered between the prosecutor and accuse[D]

44. 2. shall, on proof of one fact, regard the other as proved, and shall not allow evidence to be given for the purpose of disproving it.: If one fact conclusively proves another, the court accepts it and prohibits evidence to disprove it.

45. 3. Such report is a confidential document, although, the court may, if it so thinks fit, communicate the substance thereof to the accused.: The Probation Officer's report is confidential, but the court may share its substance with the accused at its discretion.

46. 1. Ramswaroop can subsequently be charged with and tried for robbery on the same facts.: Ramswaroop can be charged with robbery based on the same facts under the law.

47. 3. Distribution by way of samples whether free or otherwise: Distribution of samples, whether free or paid, is considered distribution under the Indecent Representation of Women Act.

48. 3. Offence punishable under Section 414 of the Indian Penal Code, where the value of property concealed is Rs. 5000/-: Under the CPC, an offence under Section 414, with property value above Rs. 5000, is not triable summarily.

49. 4. Married daughter who has attained majority and by reason of any physical or mental abnormality or injury unable to maintain herself: A married daughter who cannot maintain herself due to physical or mental issues can claim maintenance under Section 125 of the CP[C]

50. 2. Vinay has committed the offence of attempt to theft.: Vinay's actions amount to an attempt to steal, even though he did not succeed in stealing anything.

51. 4: To commit cheating is not an offence that would make an assembly unlawful by itself. An unlawful assembly typically involves an objective to commit violence or cause fear; cheating is not inherently a violent act.

52. 2: Chetna has committed the offence of Dishonest Misappropriation of Property. By pledging a government promissory note, which belonged to Vijayta, without consent, Chetna misappropriated it dishonestly for her benefit, even though she intended to return it later.

53. 3: When such person commits a non-bailable and cognizable offence in his presence. A private person can arrest someone only for a cognizable offence that is non-bailable, and the offence must be committed in the presence of the person making the arrest.

54. 3: Charan Singh Vs. State of Uttarakhand clarified that the mere unnatural death in matrimonial home within 7 years is insufficient for conviction under Section 304-B and 498-A IPC unless cruelty or harassment is proven to have occurred soon before the death.

55. 3: Completed the age of 18 years but have not completed the age of 21 years. "Aftercare" refers to the provision of support for juveniles who have left institutional care but are still transitioning into adulthood between 18 and 21 years of age.

56. 4: Fear of causing injury is not an element of theft. The primary elements of theft include dishonest intention, movable property, and possession of the property by the owner, without the need for injury.

57. 2: Amount of fine shall be recov-

ered from his house. Upon Hariom's death, the fine can be recovered from his estate, specifically his house, as it remains part of his assets liable for debts.

58. 1: The evidence of the child shall be recorded within 30 days and trial shall be completed within one year. The Protection of Children from Sexual Offences Act, 2012 mandates that the child's evidence be recorded promptly, and the trial must be completed within one year to ensure swift justice.

59. 3: This is the question of the discretion of the court. Under the Protection of Women from Domestic Violence Act, 2005, whether proceedings are in camera is at the discretion of the court, based on the circumstances and necessity.

60. 4: Not permissible to ask about illicit relations with the ex-Sarpanch during cross-examination unless it directly relates to the case at han[D] This question is deemed irrelevant to the trial for rape.

61. 4: District Magistrate, Sub-Divisional Magistrate or Magistrate of first class only are empowered to issue search warrants under Section 94 of the CrPC, allowing law enforcement to seize documents or property.

62. 3: Cognizable and Non-Bailable is the nature of an offence under breach of a protection order under the Protection of Women from Domestic Violence Act, 2005. The breach involves immediate police intervention, making it cognizable.

63. 2: Till it is cancelled by the court which issued it or it is executed is the duration for which a non-bailable warrant remains in force. It is in effect until it is either executed or the court cancels it.

64. 2: Offence punishable with imprisonment of three years is the category under which Section 306 CrPC does not apply. The Section is relevant for offences that carry higher imprisonment sentences.

65. 1: Relevant is the fact about the guarded house and entry restrictions. The evidence establishes that only Suresh and Ramesh could have committed the murder, excluding external access.

66. 3: Rachit has committed the offence of culpable homicide not amounting to murder. Rachit acted in a state of sudden provocation and was not acting under self-defense when he shot Vikas, leading to culpable homicide.

67. 1: A partner in the firm is considered a "Director" under the Negotiable Instruments Act, 1881, since partners are typically responsible for the actions of the firm.

68. 4: Parents of the child or any other person in whom the child has trust or confidence must be present when the statement of the child is recorded under the Protection of Children from Sexual Offences Act, 2012, to ensure comfort and protection.

69. 3: Such trial and conviction can be quashed only in the condition when it appears that such error has in fact occasioned a failure of justice. The mistake of jurisdiction may not necessarily void the trial unless it affects the fairness of the trial.

70. 1: Vested in a civil court under the Code of Civil Procedure, 1908 when trying a suit. The internal committee for sexual harassment inquiries under the 2013 Act has powers similar to those vested in civil courts during the trial of a suit, ensuring the ability to summon witnesses.

71. अशुद्ध शब्द है - 1: "अभ्यार्थी" का सही रूप "आवेदक" है। यह शब्द संस्कृत से लिया गया है लेकिन आमतौर पर गलत माना जाता है।

72. पारिभाषिकता की दृष्टि से गमेलन नहीं है - 3: "विधिपण" शब्द "valid" का पर्याय नहीं है, बल्कि "validate" का गलत रूप है। "विधिपूर्वक" और "विधिमान्य" शब्द सही हैं।

73. अपने आप को स्वयं मारने वाला वाक्यांश हेतु उपयुक्त शब्द है - 4: "आत्मघाती" शब्द आत्महत्या या खुद को मारने के संदर्भ में उपयुक्त होता है। "आत्मघात" भी सही है, लेकिन "आत्महाया" और "आरबंधक" शब्द इस संदर्भ में सही नहीं हैं।

74. संज्ञा से बनने वाला क्रिया नहीं है - 2: "अपनाना" शब्द संज्ञा से नहीं, बल्कि क्रिया से बना है। "बतियाना", "हथियाना", और "स्वीकारना" सभी क्रिया शब्द हैं।

75. तत्सम शब्द नहीं है - 3: "चीता" एक विदेशी शब्द है, जबकि "छटा", "महार", और "कान" संस्कृत के तत्सम शब्द हैं।

76. बहुवचन में यथावत प्रयोग हेतु उपयुक्त शब्द है - 2: "प्राण" शब्द बहुवचन में भी यथावत प्रयोग होता है। "लड़की", "घोड़ा", और "बकरी" इन शब्दों का बहुवचन रूप अलग-अलग होता है।

77. उपर्युक्त विलोमता वाला विकल्प नहीं है - 3: "अभिज्ञ" का अर्थ है "ज्ञानी" और "भिज्ञ" का कोई अर्थ नहीं है। "असूया - अनुसूया", "अनिवार्य - निवार्य", और "आर्द्र - अनार्द्र" सही विलोम शब्द हैं।

78. किस विकल्प में सभी शब्द पुल्लिंग हैं? - 1: "गुलाब", "सेब", और "शरबत" सभी पुल्लिंग शब्द हैं, जबकि अन्य विकल्पों में स्त्रीलिंग शब्द शामिल हैं।

79. 'ईन' प्रत्यय से निर्मित शब्द नहीं है - 4: "प्रवीण" शब्द "ईन" प्रत्यय से नहीं बना है। अन्य शब्द जैसे "कुलीन", "ग्रामीण", और "शालीन" "ईन" प्रत्यय से बने हैं।

80. शुद्ध वाक्य है - 4: यह वाक्य शुद्ध है, क्योंकि इसमें सही व्याकरण का पालन किया गया है। अन्य वाक्य अशुद्ध हैं।

81. विस्मयादि बोधक चिह्न के अशुद्ध प्रयोग वाला विकल्प है - 3: यह वाक्य विस्मयादि बोधक चिह्न के गलत प्रयोग का उदाहरण है। सही प्रयोग "हे भगवान!" होना चाहिए।

82. अनु उपसर्ग से निर्मित शब्द नहीं है - 2: "अनुपस्थित" शब्द "अनु" उपसर्ग से नहीं बना है। अन्य शब्द जैसे "अन्वेषण", "अन्वय", और "अनुष्ठान" उपसर्ग "अनु" से बने हैं।

83. "दाल में कुछ गिर गया है।" वाक्य में 'कुछ' शब्द में सर्वनाम का प्रकार है - 1: "कुछ" शब्द अनिश्चयवाचक सर्वनाम है, क्योंकि यह किसी निश्चित मात्रा या व्यक्ति को संदर्भित नहीं करता।

84. व्यंजन संधि से निर्मित शब्द रूप नहीं है - 4: "समुद्रोर्मि" शब्द व्यंजन संधि से नहीं बना है। "वाड्मय", "शरच्चन्द्र", और "सुषुप्ति" शब्द व्यंजन संधि से बने हैं।

85. दमड़ी की सूरत, सवा मन मलीदा लोकोक्ति का निकटतम अर्थ है - 1: यह लोकोक्ति तब उपयोग की जाती है जब कोई व्यक्ति थोड़ा लाभ पाने के लिए अत्यधिक खर्च करता है।

86. 2 - "Our surroundings ought to be kept clean" is the correct passive form. In passive voice, the object becomes the subject, and the verb "ought to" remains unchanged.

87. 2 - "Will" is used to express a strong threat or future action. The sentence is indicating a threat about punishing someone if they don't behave.

88. 2 - "Object of a Transitive verb" is correct as "where you live" acts as the direct object of the verb "tell."

89. 2 - "Had stayed" is the correct past perfect tense indicating the action was completed before another past event (father's death).

90. 2 - "A" is the correct article before a singular countable noun that starts with a consonant sound.

91. 1 - "Flawless" means perfect, without any faults, which is a synonym of "impeccable."

92. 2 - "Some" is the best fit, indicating an unspecified quantity of the staff who can speak Japanese.

93. 3 - "The" is used before a specific noun, here referring to the unique and well-known beauty of Cleopatra.

94. 3 - "Retrospect" is the opposite of "prospect," as it refers to looking back rather than forward.

95. 2 - "Will have finished" is the correct future perfect tense, indicating completion of the action by a specific future time (Tuesday).

96. 3 - The indirect speech transformation changes the present perfect to past perfect ("had lost"), fitting the context of an exclamation.

97. 3 - "Fall behind" means to lag behind, but the sentence requires "fall through," meaning plans that fail or do not happen.

98. 4 - "Spent" is the correct simple past form, indicating the action was completed in the past.

99. 1 - "Runs down" means to criticize or belittle, which fits the context of rivalry.

100. 1 - "He has already been given a notice" is the correct passive transformation, with the action completed in the past, focusing on the recipient of the notice.